FROM
SANTA TO
SEXTING

FROM
SANTA TO
SEXTING

Helping Your Child Safely Navigate Middle School
and Shape the Choices that Last a Lifetime

Brenda Hunter, PhD
and **Kristen L. Blair**

LEAFWOOD
PUBLISHERS

FROM SANTA TO SEXTING

Helping Your Child Safely Navigate Middle School and Shape the Choices that Last a Lifetime

LEAFWOOD
PUBLISHERS

Copyright 2012 by Brenda Hunter, PhD, and Kristen L. Blair

ISBN 978-0-89112-130-5
LCCN 011045817

Printed in the United States of America

LIBRARY OF CONGRESS CATALOGING-IN-PUBLICATION DATA
Hunter, Brenda.
  From Santa to sexting : helping your child safely navigate middle school and shape the choices that last a lifetime / Brenda Hunter, Kristen L. Blair.
     p. cm.
  Includes bibliographical references (p. 249) and index.
  ISBN 978-0-89112-130-5 (alk. paper)
  1. Parenting. 2. Middle school students. I. Blair, Kristen. II. Title.
  HQ755.8.H887 2012
  649'.1--dc23
                                                              011045817

The Author is represented by and this book is published in association with the literary agency of WordServe Literary Group, Ltd., www.wordserveliterary.com.

Cover design by Thinkpen Design, Inc.
Interior text design by Sandy Armstrong

Leafwood Publishers is an imprint of
Abilene Christian University Press
1626 Campus Court
Abilene, Texas 79601

1-877-816-4455
www.leafwoodpublishers.com

12 13 14 15 16 17 / 7 6 5 4 3 2 1

To Austin and Katie.

Who else could it be?

Contents

Acknowledgments

We are fortunate women. Not only do we have husbands who are encouragers and cheerleaders, but they are friends who have given us great practical help. Both have happily picked up children after school, run errands, fixed meals, and given valuable editorial advice. What would we ever do without them? Thank you immensely, Greg and Don.

Additionally, we want to thank Holly, the other writer in our family, for her timely and invaluable help. Holly, who has her own marketing business, gave us our eye-popping title for the book, *From Santa to Sexting*. People have told us they love the title and believe it captures the world of the middle schooler today. Holly, our technology guru, also read the chapters on media and technology and provided strategic input. We have welcomed her suggestions and are grateful to have her in our corner. We have promised this daughter and sister a girl's outing when the book is done.

We also want to thank Austin and Katie who have lived through the book-writing process. They are glad it is finally done! Austin, who just graduated from eighth grade, has taught us a lot about the joys and stresses of middle school. Katie is waiting in the wings and will soon begin her own middle school journey. It is for these children that we have gone so deep into the middle school world. As mother and grandmother, we have a huge investment in the well-being of these children whom we love dearly.

We are also deeply grateful for the parents, middle schoolers, teachers, school administrators, counselors, psychologists, physicians, and youth directors who allowed us to interview them for this project. They added depth and breadth to this book and taught us so much in the process. We'd like to thank Pam Stroup and the parents of McLean Bible Church who shared their views on the "wild ride" of adolescence.

Without all of these voices, we would have a sterile, research-driven book.

We need to say that, in numerous instances, we have changed the names of parents and children to protect their identities if they requested we do so.

We also want to thank our friend and former editor, Carol Bartley, for taking a look at our first chapter during a weekend when she was swamped with her own work. She gave us timely and critical editorial feedback as a friend. Thanks, Carol. You helped us so much in our rewrite when we were truly lost in the weeds.

We want to thank Robyn Burwell, Managing Editor at Leafwood Publishers, for her invaluable input as we went through two versions of this book. We know we tried her patience as we pushed ourselves for accuracy and excellence. Thankfully, we all survived the process. And we are grateful to Gary Myers, Leafwood's sales director and head of acquisitions, for believing this book was needed in the culture. He told our literary agent, Greg Johnson, that because he had a thirteen-year-old daughter, he knew we had a message that needed to be heard.

We want to thank our literary agent, Greg Johnson, for believing in this book through a series of rejections over a period of a year. He never gave up on us. Greg shared our passion for the project and encouraged us to hang in there when we got discouraged. We did. He did. And now we have a book we are proud of and that we hope will be enormously helpful to parents around the world. Yes, we hope this book will travel the world because young adolescents live everywhere.

Finally, we want to thank God for his provision and for his plan for this book. He made it all come together.

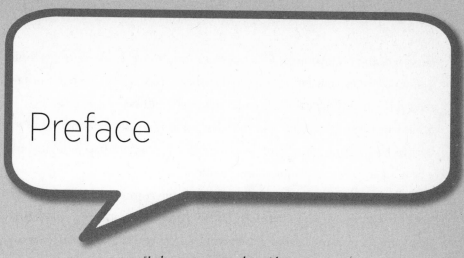

Preface

*"I always try not to be strident,
but I do try to be forceful about things that are right."*
The late **Bernadine Healy, MD**

Two years ago, we began reading research indicating that middle schoolers in this country were in deep trouble. That period of life—eleven to fourteen years of age—has always been problematic, right? It's that time in child development when the hormones kick in, when fitting in with peers is all-important, and when parents aren't so popular anymore. But what we were reading led us to believe that this age group is currently encountering pressures that are unprecedented—from the culture, school, media, and the Internet. The more we read, the more concerned we became.

The mother of a tween and a middle schooler, I, Kristen, have been writing in the education arena for years, noting the decline of academic performance and the lapses in the character development among American youth—something we write about in the following pages. And I, Brenda, a psychologist and practicing psychotherapist, had been witnessing the fallout of early sexual experiences in the lives of twenty-something clients who came into my office. We also became aware that many of the risky behaviors that have troubled high schoolers for years (sex, drugs, and alcohol) have filtered down to middle schoolers and even younger kids. As we became more involved in this topic, a view of modern parenting emerged. We heard repeatedly that parents have relinquished authority in their children's lives and that role reversal lives. In other words, parents want to be buddies rather than authority figures in the lives of their young adolescents—a trend that has serious psychological and emotional repercussions for young people.

The more we learned, the more we became committed to writing this book. When we went to parents and listened to their concerns, we realized they were deeply worried about their children, especially about how to handle technology, social media, and the Internet. Some said they felt alone. At sea. They spoke of longing for a sense of community with other parents—of actually being able to have a place where they could speak honestly about all that impinges on their kids' lives. Most were afraid. How could they counter the unremitting presence of media and kids' constant connectedness? How could they still raise moral kids in a culture that actively works to destroy innocence?

They felt they needed a road map as they parented their tweens and teens—but where to find it?

We decided to try to provide such a road map, and we set to work. Quickly, this book became exceedingly difficult to write, not because of the subject matter or interviews with experts, but because of what began to happen in our personal lives. Things started to fall apart.

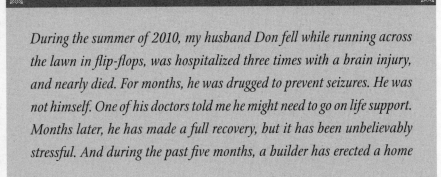

During the summer of 2010, my husband Don fell while running across the lawn in flip-flops, was hospitalized three times with a brain injury, and nearly died. For months, he was drugged to prevent seizures. He was not himself. One of his doctors told me he might need to go on life support. Months later, he has made a full recovery, but it has been unbelievably stressful. And during the past five months, a builder has erected a home

thirteen feet from my house, creating horrendous daily, even hourly, noise. Try being creative while listening to hammering, loud voices, and the sound of whirring saws. Exhausting!

—*Brenda*

During the same summer my dad was in the hospital, my husband Greg joined the ranks of the unemployed, and our family entered a period of heavy stress. We were already struggling financially, and the money pressures mounted even more. Then, as I worked on this book, my computer crashed. I borrowed a laptop to continue writing. That one also broke down. We purchased another. So it has taken three computers for me to write this book.

—*Kristen*

And then the heating and air conditioning systems failed in both our houses. Cars lived in repair shops, and a refrigerator died over a weekend. It has been a season of unprecedented mechanical breakdown.

Yet as our trials increased, we came to believe even more strongly that we were working on a timely and important project. We do not believe for a moment that these painful and difficult trials have happened during the writing of this book by coincidence. Rather, what has occurred has helped us identify with the millions of middle-class families in America who are struggling to make ends meet and rear secure children at a time of high personal stress. We, too, have been part of this stressed-out nation.

But we soldiered on. You see, we believe strongly that these middle school years are critical for the whole of life, and the choices your child makes will influence his development across the life-span. Much is at stake: his sexual identity, his academic success, his faith in an intimate, personal God, and his feelings of self-worth. As you learn more about the pressures that bombard your kids on a daily basis, you may agree that something is wrong in this culture, and we need to change it—for their sakes and for the future of society.

Hear these children in the pages ahead. Listen to their parents, their teachers, their principals, and their counselors. Work with us to protect your children's innocence and keep them younger longer. Let's band together to create strong families that produce strong children.

Brenda Hunter, PhD
Kristen Blair
Chapel Hill, North Carolina

Chapter One

FROM SANTA
TO SEXTING

"Middle school is a fork in the road. Kids can go either way."
—**Ellen**, mother of sixth grader, Sim,
in Palm Desert, California

It is a chilly Sunday morning in early February, and we are launching the first phase of our *From Santa to Sexting* book project: a focus group of parents at McLean Bible Church, a megachurch in northern Virginia. Pam Stroup, the head of family ministries at MBC, has done a masterful job assembling a diverse group of parents. Asian, black, white—these parents hail from a variety of backgrounds. They head up single-parent, two-parent, and blended families. Some have children who attend public school; others are paying for private education. Yet they share a powerful common denominator: All are parenting tweens and teens.

And all are worried about helping their children safely navigate middle school.

Eager to talk about their concerns, several said they felt overwhelmed.

"Control? We've lost it," said one father. "Control is impossible. It's an illusion."

"We're trying to find balance," said one forty-something mother. "I know technology is important, but how much?"

"Sex is much more pervasive than it used to be," said a single mother. "Oral sex and 'real sex.'"

The list of parental worries continued: angry kids, bullying and "extreme teasing" at school, pressures to fit in and be like everyone else, and the pain of lost friendships.

Parents were also weighed down by the need to prepare kids for engagement with modern life. Said one father, "The thing that keeps me up at night is making sure we're building character in our children. I'm worried about that. The world is closing in on our kids, and it's more so now."

Of media, he added, "You can't put up enough walls to prevent that stuff from getting in. Let the kids put up their own walls."

Have we just described you?

DRAMA, DRAMA, DRAMA

Your parental worries are justified. It's a rough, tough world out there for American middle schoolers growing up today. But even as parents and kids struggle with unprecedented cultural influences, middle school still offers the mainstream drama it always did—the anxiety over friends, crushes, and grades; the fashion dilemmas, the pimply ravages of puberty, and the unsightly trappings of orthodontia. Fitting in during that first foray into the school cafeteria, as a child scans the room frantically searching for a place to sit, is as fraught with peril as it ever was. Listen to Susan, a twelve-year-old cheerleader at her private Catholic school, who has just begun sixth grade:

> At my school it's really new for me. Kids who were mean to me are now my best friends. I kinda had to work my way to fit in. I feel lots of pressure academically. I have nice teachers, but some are really strict.

There's one teacher and I was on safety patrol and she put me on probation because I missed a couple of assignments. I will find out tomorrow if I get back on patrol.

Everyone will know.

My best friend is Annie. We used to talk to each other every single night and tell each other everything. Now we're growing away from each other. Annie and I got in a big fight. I called her and she said, "Susan, I don't have your homework. Bye." I talked to her and we're friends again, but we don't talk to each other every night and that's hard.

Friends are the most important part of my life. But boys also figure a lot in my life. There's a boy in my class who asked to take me to a movie, and I didn't know what to say. I said to Dad, "Tell me I can't go." He said I could go if I went with my girlfriends, so I called the boy and went to Julia's house and went in the hot tub. Then my girlfriends said they wouldn't go to the movies with us, so I decided not to go. The boy was crushed—really mad.

I'm not allowed to have a cell phone until eighth grade, and all my friends have a cell phone. They always talk about it. I always feel left out.

Don't you love Susan? Any parent can identify with her poignant account of the trials and tribulations of early middle school. We have all been through it. But in addition to the struggles middle schoolers have always faced, kids this age are under greater pressure than ever before—from the culture, from school, and from parental expectations. Many are growing up at warp speed. For them, the loss of innocence has been profound.

Not long ago these kids were in elementary school, and some believed in Santa Claus. They were fresh and free. They rode their bikes, brushed and braided their doll's hair, and stacked LEGOs. They doodled, consumed delicacies from their Easy-Bake Ovens, and memorized their math facts. Barely on the cusp of adolescence, they are now thrust into an adult world stripped bare of the parental protections afforded to previous generations. Marketers have coined the term "age compression" to describe the brevity of contemporary childhood. Sadly, for some, childhood ends at age nine.

IT'S A MEDIA-MAD WORLD

Middle schoolers are coming of age in the most digitized and technologically advanced period of our world's history. Are they ever wired! It's a media-mad world for the 20 million kids between the ages of ten and fourteen in America today.[1] Across the board, parents have told us they are struggling with managing the technology and media that infiltrate every area of their children's lives.

Kids are spending more time with media than ever before, averaging seven and a half hours per day with devices such as cell phones, iPods, computers, and television.[2] It isn't unusual for kids to check their cell phones during the school day and log on to social networking platforms and online video games the minute they return home from school. The explosion in mobile technology, experts say, is driving up kids' consumption.[3] Vicky Rideout, vice president of the Kaiser Foundation, a group which tracks kids' media use over time, says of modern childhood, "There is nothing that occupies more of young people's time than media. Not school. Not church. Not family."[4]

SEXTING AND CYBERBULLYING

Increasingly, kids are using their mobile phones to swap sexually explicit, even nude, images of themselves. This practice, called *sexting,* is causing some kids painful, unintended consequences, since some of the images get passed on or go viral. Kids may think the practice is harmless or even exciting, but it can be devastating to those who find that a private photo sent to a crush is suddenly on every cell phone in their middle school. Hope Whitsell, a thirteen-year-old, committed suicide after a nude image she sent to a boy she liked went viral and she was shunned by classmates. Moreover, kids who pass along nude images of other minors may face serious legal consequences themselves; in some states, sexting is a felony.

Mobile technology and the Internet amplify bullying, a familiar problem during middle school. Kids may send nasty texts, spread rumors or post hurtful comments on social networking sites, or even use a classmate's password to engage in cyber-impersonation. Of cyberbullying, Debra Scott, the principal of McDougle Middle School in Chapel Hill, North Carolina, says, "It's constant. It used to be that what happened in a bad neighborhood or a rough neighborhood on Saturday night, we'd deal with on Monday morning. Well, now we're dealing with what happened online."

ACADEMICS

Academics, which has always been important, is increasingly stressful for children in this age group. Course work is becoming more rigorous, even for "tweens" (those children in the eight to twelve age range). At the same time, parents work anxiously with their middle schoolers on resumé building— their sights set on admission to an acceptable college. It's no longer enough to achieve academically and volunteer in the community; a child needs to start his own nonprofit, build a business, or become an expert on a thrillingly obscure, yet culturally relevant, issue. Parents fear their children may not stay afloat in a competitive global marketplace—and with good reason—in an era when millions have lost their jobs.

DRUGS AND SEX

Other areas of concern are also keeping parents awake at night. Drug problems are affecting kids at younger ages, and middle school is a critical time of transition. Dr. Mark Piehl, a pediatric critical-care physician and medical director of WakeMed Children's Hospital in Raleigh, North Carolina, told us he has seen an uptick in high-risk behaviors in recent years. When asked about trends among nine- to fourteen-year-olds, he said, "Certainly we are seeing more experimentation with drugs. When kids arrive in the ER with significant complications from drug use, I'd say half are due to experimenta-tion and half to suicide attempts."

Piehl says he has seen an increase in kids trying to inhale substances to get high—hair spray, paints, and aerosols. "They're snorting psychiatric meds in the home—pain killers, antidepressants." One of Piehl's patients, a fifteen-year-old boy, was admitted to the hospital after he had collected all of the meds in his home, having crushed and snorted an antidepressant and tranquilizer. His system became so depressed he couldn't breathe and had to be put on a ventilator until the effects wore off. "He could have died," says Piehl.

Not only is prescription drug abuse on the rise among adolescents, but sex is a real issue as well. Just talk to parents of middle schoolers, and they will tell you that kids are making their sexual debut at earlier ages. Sexual activity is surprisingly common among younger adolescents, which of course places them at risk for a variety of sexually transmitted infections (STIs). "Within two years of initiating sex, half of the girls will have acquired an STI," says Piehl. Young girls are at the greatest risk of contracting STIs.

By eighth grade in particular, some kids are having sexual intercourse. Seventh grade teacher Amanda Klee, who has worked with middle schoolers for nine years in Ohio and North Carolina, says, "The majority of seventh grad-ers are not having sex." But, "in eighth grade, no way; most kids are having sex." Klee says parents accept this state of affairs, but "it's a sad sort of settling."

Counselors have told us oral sex in middle school is commonplace and fairly widespread, and that kids just don't view it as sex. "It's no big deal," many kids say.

WHAT ABOUT YOU?

Now it's time to take a breath and exhale slowly! This is a lot to take in, isn't it? We get it. Though you may be tempted to close the book, we would urge you to keep reading. We have heard from many good parents, just like you, who are worried about what they see happening to tweens and older middle schoolers in America.

But hang in there a little longer. There's good news coming. As you will see as you read on, you still have more influence in your child's life than anyone else. Your child carries you forever in his heart. At the same time, we believe you need to be informed and proactive—now more than ever. We've learned throughout our interviews that it's the child of the *unaware* parent who gets into trouble. Those adults who work with kids in middle schools every day have reinforced this theme: many parents don't know what their kids are up to; nor do they understand the immense pressures they face every day of their lives.

EXPERTS WEIGH IN

You've heard from concerned parents already. But what do teachers and school personnel have to say about the challenges of early adolescence?

Listen to Candace Odell, a schoolteacher at Carrington Middle School:

At 5:00 A.M. Candace Odell is in her car driving to Carrington Middle School in Durham, North Carolina, where she teaches band, and after the school day is over, functions as the school's athletic direc- tor. Candace, who has taught for twenty years, believes she was "destined to be a teacher." Her colleagues must agree. In 2009, the North Carolina Middle School Association voted Candace a regional "Teacher of the Year."

Odell has seen "tremendous changes" in middle schoolers over the span of her career. For one, kids in her class sometimes use alco- hol with parental approval. When she asked her seventh grade class this year how they spent New Year's Eve, some of the students said their parents let them "sip alcohol just for fun." Odell also says that kids know more about everything than they used to. "Technology allows them to connect with the world around them and this gives them access to porn. Some parents do a good job of monitoring the Internet. Others do not."

She believes that academics have gotten harder over the years, with "high school rigor trickling down to middle schoolers. Most parents want their kids to be in AIG (Academically or Intellectually Gifted), and this puts a lot of pressure on kids. Some breeze through it, some struggle. But all of these kids want to please their parents."

Odell says that some of her students get home hours after she does, at 9:00 or 9:30 at night. She says that after they're at school all day, they're hard at work, building their resumés for college through extracurricular activities: "These are busy children." Do they complain? "They're tired because they're up until 11:00 P.M. doing homework. How profitable is that?" she asks.

Odell is aware that middle schoolers just want to fit in. The way they dress—the saggy pants, the too-short skirts, and the holes in new jeans in inappropriate places—all scream, "Do not call attention to me, because I look like everybody else." She feels that if kids can blend in, they're less likely to cause their teachers trouble.

This "teacher of the year" is concerned about the lack of moral values in some of her students. In one class, fully half of the girls said they watch the MTV show *16 and Pregnant* almost daily. She asked the class, "If you watch this, why wouldn't you do it yourself?" She laments the culture's acceptance of early sexuality without consequences and the absence of healthy role models for her students.

Odell is only one of a number of worried middle school personnel we interviewed about what's happening to middle schoolers today.

As principal of Carrington Middle School, Holly Emanuel, Candace Odell's boss, presides over one of North Carolina's largest public middle schools. Every day, twelve hundred middle schoolers in sixth through eighth grades stream through Carrington's double doors. Linda Reyner, a seasoned counselor, has worked with hundreds of middle schoolers over the years. Both women are parents as well as professionals.

What are their greatest concerns about middle schoolers?

Our conversation turns quickly to technology, social networking, and media. Emanuel says, "Students are much more educated than their parents and us. We're at a loss about what they're doing. Although we try to monitor them, even as parents, there are just some things that we don't seem to be keeping up with." She continues, "We see a lot more cyberbullying than anything else." Emanuel adds, "The biggest problem is that parents don't know what's going on." There's that unaware theme again! She continues, "A lot of the bullying comes from kids who are from good homes and are good kids."

Reyner says of parents, "I think they're just ignorant about how bad the bullying can be online." According to Reyner, anonymity makes it easier for kids to say hurtful things. She says, "There's still the sense that they're behind the computer screen and they're not saying that directly [to another child]. It's amazing what kids say. I think parents are shocked that their child would actually do that."

Why do some parents have a hard time monitoring their children's behavior? According to Emanuel, who is herself a single mother, moms and dads are busier than ever. She adds, "You're either a single-parent or a two-parent household where everybody's working." Every day after the last afternoon bell rings, eighteen buses roll out of Carrington's parking lot. "Normally," says Emanuel, "those children go home to an empty house. And we have about one hundred who go to the public library." But these kids aren't doing homework. They're outside the library. Hanging out. Or, as Emanuel says, "They're on the side of the road." Reyner adds, "It's not a good situation. But the parents think, *what* could be wrong with the library?"

How are Carrington students faring emotionally? "I've never seen so many angry students," says Emanuel. "They're not always fighting, but they're just very aggressive—in their tone [of voice] with teachers, and even their tone with other students." Reyner agrees students exhibit a lot of anger. And she has witnessed a "huge increase in emotional issues" in Carrington's student population since she began working at the school in 2004. The kids she works with are struggling, and they're not doing their schoolwork. For many, home is a lonely or tough place to be.

Stress is pervasive. "I think we are all stressed. I think this is a nation of stressed-out people. Everything is moving so fast, and we're all trying to get to the next place," Emanuel says. She adds, "Ours is a culture of everybody wanting more. We take our kids to day care much earlier in the morning, and we work much later at night than we should. So our children are being raised by a lot of people other than parents."

The net result? Parental anxiety.

COSMIC UNEASE

Fueling parental anxiety is a sense of cosmic unease. As parents today, we know about *everything*. We're exposed to an unremitting Twitter feed of child abductions, murders, natural disasters, war, and terrorism. And it's all happening in real time. Because of Websites and cable news, one father of a middle schooler told us, "Parents aren't seeing a summed-up story. They're seeing live footage of a tsunami crashing into a Japanese city or an earthquake hitting the northeastern U.S."

This father also mentioned the seismic shift in our sense of national security and parental consciousness following the terrorist attacks of 9/11. U.S. Senator Dan Coats of Indiana, former head of the Senate Armed Services Committee, told us, "For most of our nation's history, we trusted our two oceans for our security. 9/11 shattered that illusion. Now we're just like everybody else."

As a result of what's happening globally and nationally, we have become obsessed with our children's safety.

For decades, we have purchased the right car seats, lead-free toys, and bike helmets. We vet administrators, teachers, and curricula with zeal. We want schools to conduct criminal background checks for other parent chaperones. By middle school, we provide our children with the modern-day equivalent of the parental tether: the cell phone. We want—we demand—constant access, 24/7. Nothing must impede our ability to reassure ourselves that our kids are safe—unharmed.

But in our quest to keep our children safe, have we settled for smoke and mirrors? Have we put our faith in *things*, not relationships? Have things, over the years, become a substitute for on-site parental supervision and presence? As parents, we plan for virtually every exigency:

- Antibacterial lotion? Check.
- Kids who know to stop, drop, and roll if they're on fire? Check.
- Kids who run from strangers? Check.
- Charged-up cell phone to receive our incessant texts? Check.

Many of our children have every gadget known to modern man—but do they have *us*? Do they own our hearts? Our time? In short, do they have warm, secure, stable connections with us?

WHY WE CARE

At this point, you may wonder why we have written this book about middle schoolers. As a mother-daughter team working in psychology and education, we have watched the studies pour in, chronicling the impact of cultural change and family strain on kids. What we have read, heard, and witnessed has made us sad. And mad. We deplore the loss of innocence and the sexualization of boys and girls in America today. So we wanted to do something about it—to push back against cultural influences that are wreaking havoc in kids' lives. We wanted to speak directly to you, parents who love your children, and encourage you to join us in saying, "Enough!"

Let us just add at this juncture: this is no idle academic exercise for us. We too have been affected by the changes to the American family. And we've certainly had our share of stress.

As a developmental psychologist and psychotherapist, I have watched the effects of cultural change play out in my office as I have worked with clients. I am deeply concerned about the self-destructive behaviors that I see drifting down from high school to middle school, since I have seen the toll that early involvement in sex and drugs has on young lives.

For those of you who are single parents, I want to tell you I have stood where you stand now. I was raised by a single mother after my father drowned when I was two. And I was a single parent myself to my two young girls for five years after my first marriage ended in divorce. I certainly understand family stress. I have lived through job loss, cancer, and years of financial struggle.

Most importantly, I believe the middle school years are pivotal for the rest of life. The decisions that your children make will influence their self-worth, their propensity for depression, their predilection for later substance abuse, and their ability to form lasting emotional bonds with the opposite sex. I want to help you help your children make good choices.

—Brenda

As a former policy analyst and now education writer and columnist, I have written for years about the effects of cultural shifts on kids during the K–12 years. Modern family? I've lived in one most of my life. As a child of divorce, I grew up navigating between two homes. Now I'm married to another adult child of divorce, and our children have eight grandparents and step-grandparents! My kids say to my husband Greg and me, "Mom and Dad, we know this divorce thing was hard for you growing up, but we sure don't mind! Our grandparents love us and they're really generous."

If you are trying to parent in the midst of financial stress or job loss, know that I understand. My husband was out of work as we were trying to sell this book to a publisher in 2010. I wondered if we would lose our home. We didn't: God was faithful and took good care of us, but it hasn't been easy.

As you read through these pages, know that I am in the trenches with you. I am the mother of a tween, ten-year-old Katie, and a teen, fourteen-year-old Austin, who finished his last months of middle school even as I was writing this book. Believe me, I know how hard it is to be the parent of a middle schooler in America today.

—Kristen

BROKEN-DOWN WALLS

As we have gathered data and talked to parents and professionals who work with middle schoolers, a recurring image has emerged: since the 1960s, the walls that protect the American family have been dismantled—by society, the media, marketers, and even, in some cases, by parents themselves. Consequently, anything can go in and out of the family.

We have been reminded of Nehemiah in the Old Testament, the Hebrew cupbearer to the Persian king following the Jewish exile, who felt compelled to return to Jerusalem and assess the damage himself after hearing that it lay in ruins. He found that the city's walls were broken down, and its gates were burning. Economic distress was rampant. The people were vulnerable—unprotected.

What he saw moved him to tears. But then he took action. With God's help, Nehemiah and the Jewish people rebuilt the walls of Jerusalem in just fifty-two days. Although they experienced fierce opposition, God gave them victory over their enemies.

How does this theme of broken-down walls apply to the American family? While we know there are homes where the walls are strong and sure, in many families the walls lie in ruins. The gates of Jerusalem are burning. But just like the ancient city of Jerusalem, the walls of the family can and *must* be rebuilt.

For those of you whose family walls are already in place, we want to show you how to make your family stronger yet. We do not believe, nor do we advocate, that the family home become a fortress. But if we exert little control over what goes in and out of our homes, we cannot parent effectively. And if we simply deny the impact of cultural forces, we remain in the dark and are unable to help our children.

The culture presses your child to grow up too soon, but he needs to grow up at his own pace. Joyfully. This book will show you how to keep your children younger longer.

And for those of you who feel your family walls are down? We want to encourage you and help you repair and buttress these walls to keep your children safe—to give them the space and freedom they need to be children. And yes, in middle school, they are still children.

Ours is a culture that long ago forgot that parental walls and fences make childhood possible.

SUMMING UP

Although you may feel unsupported as you attempt to raise a child with a strong moral compass, you can get the job done. Remember that decades of child-development research shows that you are your child's touchstone. Also, remember that these middle school years are fleeting. In the following pages, we will help you to make the most of this time. We will show you how to launch your child securely into high school and beyond.

Along the way we will share inspiring stories from awesome parents who are raising secure and competent children, like Nilda Melendez of Bethesda, Maryland, whose older son (one of nine) just graduated from the Naval Academy. When Francisco Javier first applied, he wrote an essay stating that his mom ran "a tight ship." In our interview, he even called her a "saint" for the way she parented him and his siblings, two of whom are currently in middle school.

In addition to moms and dads, we have also spoken with middle schoolers themselves and with a bevy of experts—those teachers, school counselors, psychologists, physicians, and principals who work with young adolescents. You might be surprised by what they have to say. Since we are not simply dispassionate researchers, we will share our own stories—some vulnerable, some funny, and some embarrassing—from the front lines.

Writing this book has changed our thinking and our lives. It has given us a sense of mission and passion.

We hope it will do the same for you.

Chapter Two

THE
WILD RIDE

*"When I was a boy of fourteen, my father was so ignorant
I could hardly stand to have the old man around.
But when I got to be twenty-one,
I was astonished at how much he had learned in seven years."*

—**Mark Twain**, "Old Times on the Mississippi,"
Atlantic Monthly, 1874

A thirty-something mother found that she was unprepared for the *behavioral changes she witnessed in her eighth grade daughter. She had always been close to this child, and she loved the daily conversations in which her daughter hung on her every word and acted like she enjoyed her mother's companionship. But one day when they were shopping in the mall, the girl started to speed walk. "Slow down," said the mother, breathless as she tried to catch up. The daughter sped away. When the mother finally reached her side, she asked, "What's going on?" "I don't want to be seen with you," the girl replied, and kept walking. "Stop!" said the mother in a commanding voice. "I will not walk behind you as a pariah. Either we walk together or we go home."*

They went home.

Logan, a sixth grader in Fairfax, Virginia, told us he's not interested in girls, though most of the girls in his class are "obsessed" with Justin Bieber and talk incessantly about him. His parents say that twelve-year-old Logan is a good kid, except that he sometimes has a short fuse on the tennis court. But they're working on that. Logan says his life "is really good right now." How would he grade his parents, who consider themselves competent disciplinarians? A true preadolescent, Logan says, "Sometimes I want to give them an F, but when I compare them to other kids' parents, I give them an A+."

One Sunday afternoon, two mothers of thirteen-year-old boys were talking as their sons played flag football nearby. The two attractive women in their early forties wondered how they could get water bottles to their teens without being noticed; their sons had suddenly developed an aversion to being seen with their mothers in public. One mother lamented, "All he wants from me now is a ride to and from his activities." The other mother chimed in, "Rides, yes. But they also want home-cooked meals, clean clothes, and a place to sleep. That's about it."

Ah, the stings and arrows of early adolescence. It can nearly break a parent's heart when the loving ten-year-old who adores his parents and is easy to live with becomes the surly, critical eleven-year-old. And as the sunny, cooperative twelve-year-old suddenly morphs into moody thirteen, parenting skills can become so taxed that parents find themselves longing for a return to those halcyon preteen days. Some even feel a sense of loss as their son or daughter begins to spread wings and leave childhood behind. The family feels different somehow, as if a new person has come to live in the house. And just when parents are finally adjusting to thirteen, along comes vital, energized fourteen who's critical of the way his parents dress and converse. In fact, fourteen-year-olds of both sexes are notorious for being embarrassed by their antiquated parents.

In the developmental classic *Your Ten- to Fourteen-Year-Old,* authors Louise Bates Ames, PhD, Frances Ilg, MD, and Sidney Baker, MD, of the Gesell Institute of Human Development, write: "It is almost as if, during the time when your typical thirteen-year-old was brooding in his room, both father and mother have aged and deteriorated in a horrible way. A wicked witch has been at work on these formerly lively and acceptable people."[1] These child-development experts say that the fourteen-year-old objects to the way his parents dress, to their boring stories about their youth, and to their opinions. They object to the people their parents are.[2]

ADOLESCENCE DEFINED

Before we get too deep into the topic of adolescence, we need to define what we mean. When does adolescence begin and when does it end? According to psychologist Laurence Steinberg, whose seminal book *Adolescence* is in its ninth edition, the word is derived from the Latin word *adolescere*, which means to grow into adulthood.[3] All societies, even primitive ones, feel there is a definitive period between childhood and adulthood that stands alone and is marked by transitions. Steinberg, who is a professor at Temple University, states that during this time of transitions (biological, psychological, social, and economic), youth become "wiser, more sophisticated, more self-aware, more independent, and more concerned about the future."[4] In mid-to-later adolescence, they also become more interested in sex. Adolescence, in its broadest definition, begins at age ten and ends in the early twenties. According to Steinberg, the boundaries of adolescence are divided thus: early adolescence (10–13 years), middle (14–17 years), and late (18–21 years of age).[5]

Steinberg describes adolescence as a complicated time for parents and their children, especially since children begin to question parental values and opinions.[6] Although you are no longer the adored parent of earlier years, you need to remember during the wild ride of adolescence that you are still the major authority in your child's life, even as he pushes for more independence. Steinberg writes that "adolescents care what you think and listen to what you say, even if they don't always admit it or agree on every point."[7]

It is during early adolescence and the beginning of middle adolescence that you, as middle school parents, witness such dramatic changes in your children. First, let's look at the physical transformation your son or daughter will experience during the years of middle school. These are years of rapid but irregular growth.

PHYSICAL CHANGES

Your girls will begin puberty about two years earlier than your boys. They may begin to develop breast buds as early as eight years old and will achieve full breast development sometime between twelve and eighteen years of age.[8] They will acquire pubic hair, underarm hair, and leg hair around nine or ten. But it will not look like an adult woman's until they are thirteen or fourteen.[9] The beginning of menstruation may occur as early as ten or as late as fifteen, but the average age is twelve and a half years of age. Also, there's a rapid growth in height that peaks around twelve years of age.[10]

Boys show a wide range of growth rates; some stand short among their peers, while others are quite tall. They develop pubic, leg, chest, facial, and underarm hair starting at age twelve and reaching adult patterns at fifteen and sixteen; their testicles and scrotum enlarge, the penis lengthens, and erections become more frequent. Boys also experience occasional wet dreams that typically occur between thirteen and seventeen years. They grow rapidly in height between ten and eleven years of age and then again between sixteen and eighteen.[11] They also begin to sweat more and may develop acne. This is the time to reacquaint yourself with the inescapable trappings of teen-dom: benzoyl peroxide and a bleached-out pillowcase!

While preadolescents may welcome some of the physical changes, they may also feel uncomfortable with their evolving adult bodies and compare themselves unfavorably to their peers. It is during these years that girls begin to worry about weight; some girls develop eating disorders. It is also a time when a male basketball player who is short may compare himself unfavorably to the budding Michael Jordan on his team.

Ellen, a divorced mom and freelance writer who lives in Palm Desert, California, is happy that her adopted Vietnamese daughter, Sim, is developing slowly. "Sim, who is twelve, wears a size 8," says Ellen, who complained about the "trashy clothing" now available for girls. "Aren't Asian women supposed to be small?" asks Ellen. Sim is an A student in her advanced classes, loves science, and has kept nearly all her friends from elementary school. Ellen feels that, for the moment, she has a pass on some of the worries about physical and behavioral changes because her daughter is a late bloomer.

EMOTIONAL AND PSYCHOLOGICAL CHANGES

In addition to all the physical changes, the middle school years are a time of noticeable psychological changes. For one thing, your child will develop a growing sense of independence from your family and home. She will someday leave home, and she gathers her strength by beginning to assert her growing individuality and by developing an emerging sense of self, starting around age eleven. As a parent, you may not be thinking along these lines until your sunny, devoted ten-year-old has seemingly allowed a difficult, often angry eleven-year-old to inhabit her body. "Who ate my daughter?" you may wonder. Rest assured: this is part of the process of growing up.

First, let's look at the eleven-year-old. She or he may be entering sixth grade, the first year of middle school. Eleven is described by Dr. Louise Bates Ames as "prickly, quarrelsome and objecting."[12] Do you recognize your child? Parents are no longer adored or seen as wise; rather, eleven-year-olds "argue about everything," starting early in the morning and setting a fractious tone for the day. One father we interviewed said he would greet his eleven-year-old son in the morning with a cheery, "How are you?" only to hear an indecipherable "Ahhhhhhhhhh," as he walked by. "OK, I'll take that as good," said the dad and smiled.

At this age and stage, eleven-year-olds still like to go on outings with their fathers and confide in their mothers, but in middle school they quarrel more with siblings than at any other time.[13] Prepare to put out some fires on the home front! This age has been described as either very good or very bad—difficult at home but charming in the outside world. However, the "belligerence, selfishness, unapproachableness—are expressions of a search for a self, a self that is trying to emerge."[14]

LET'S HEAR IT FOR TWELVE-YEAR-OLDS

Fortunately for you, twelve-year-olds appear to be from a more convivial planet and are sometimes described as "tolerant, sympathetic, and friendly."[15] Whereas eleven is described as "searching for self," by the time he is twelve, the child is beginning to find himself.[16] Enthusiastic and easier to get along with inside the family, the twelve-year-old is less dependent on teachers, needs to be with parents less often, and needs his friends more. This is the age when some boys become interested in girls, though many are oblivious at eleven and may still be so even at thirteen. At twelve, girls talk, talk, talk about boys. They value their chat time *about* boys with their girlfriends more than actually *doing anything with* boys.[17]

But not every twelve-year-old finds the physical and hormonal changes of preadolescence smooth sailing. Janet, who is in sixth grade, is—her mother is convinced—about to start menstruation. Julie says her daughter is either "100 percent happy or 100 percent pissed off." She adds, "All those hormones are a cocktail for butting heads. At times, life with Janet is traumatic, emotional, and full of testing. We used to argue a lot. Now I give her consequences. If she engages in an argument, she loses her privileges for twenty-four hours. If she continues to argue, she loses them for two days. So far we have only had one two-day period of lost privileges."

Julie, who works as a psychotherapist, describes her daughter as a "really smart and sensitive kid who thinks a lot. Her usual emotionality is heightened by hormones. Sometimes she's crazy, and my husband and I work to control the craziness. Consequences consistently doled out help greatly."

A mother-father duo said that their son used to be the sweetest kid. But he woke up bright-eyed on his twelfth birthday and said, "OK, I'm mad now." They added with a sigh, "At our house, we're seeing a lot of anger."

ALONG COMES THIRTEEN

Whether your twelve-year-old is sunny, angry, or overly emotional, along comes age thirteen. Just as Difficult Eleven took over Adoring Ten, now Agreeable Twelve gives way to Distancing and Hormonally Driven Thirteen. Dr. Ames states that the thirteen-year-old withdraws from his family both physically and emotionally. Some keep their doors closed or even locked. Ames says that it is almost as if the thirteen-year-old realizes he is not ready to go out into the world, so he withdraws, ruminates, and inwardly attempts to create a stronger sense of self.[18] Thirteen-year-olds are sensitive to criticism, are extremely conscious of how others view them, and don't want to be hugged or touched in public. They are not as eager to enter family games, preferring to read alone or go to another room. They often feel things deeply, like when they haven't been invited to a party. Then boys and girls cry and look most often to their mothers for consolation.

Ames writes: "Thirteens, though they may seem so callous at times, have a very sensitive core. Feelings are easily hurt. It's not only what people say to them but also disappointments and failures, as in schoolwork, that hurt their feelings. . . . Thirteens, increasingly, are aware of their feelings. Many show their feelings and don't care if others know how they feel. But many want to 'hide' and 'cover up' their feelings, or will let people know when they are happy but not when they are sad. Often they will let only their intimate friends and, on occasion, their mothers, know how they feel."[19]

Julie says her almost-thirteen-year-old daughter has "big feelings." "She was moody pre-hormones. Now she's moody on steroids. She can be snippy, mean, cranky, or dissolving into tears about anything."

Thirteen-year-olds are concerned about their body image, and their friendships tend to be group focused. Moreover, this is a time when self-esteem can be at a real low, and this makes them super sensitive to any criticism.

A GOOD KIND OF AGGRESSION

In addition to this new inward focus, thirteen-year-olds can also have an executive, bossy core. One mother said her eighth grade son strode through the house one morning, shouting, "Two more minutes. TWO MORE MINUTES until we have to leave for school." The mother got angry and asked, "When have you ever been tardy?" "Once," her son replied, still in his commanding voice. "Well, who drove you to school that day?" she asked. "Dad," he replied sheepishly. "See, you don't need to walk through the house, shouting at us, like you're herding cats," said her chagrined mother.

After the inwardness and moodiness of the thirteen-year-old, the fourteen-year-old is a welcome addition to family life. Energetic, full of enthusiasm and vigor, the fourteen-year-old has friends of both sexes, likes school, may become involved in the community, and generally gets along well with siblings. He is seriously interested in girls, and fourteen-year-old girls reciprocate the attention. He feels good about himself and is learning to master the world at large. What is the downside of this expansive kid? He has become the critic of mom and dad in the extreme. While it may seem that your child earlier objected to family rules, now he feels that you and your spouse have become pretty objectionable people. Ah, that hurts.

On the whole, fourteen is sunnier than thirteen, and these kids are more open about their feelings. They don't get disturbed by problems as much as they did at thirteen; they simply don't worry as much. This is, however, a time when girls get into arguments and fights with their mothers, especially around issues of dating and curfew.[20] Often fathers have to intervene, and this gets tricky. A dad can end up with all the women in his life mad at him. Maybe some of you fathers can relate.

IDENTITY

As you have already surmised, all the changes and upheaval of early adolescence are for a purpose. Your child is beginning to forge an identity that is uniquely his or her own. Psychologist James Marcia, whose foundational work on adolescence started in the 1960s and continues today through other child-development experts, believed that the adolescent's chief task is to explore and then commit to an identity in a variety of areas: vocational, religious, relational, and gender. Marcia suggests that when the adolescent is forging his sense of self, he goes through two distinct phases: *crisis* (a time when values and choices are being examined and reevaluated—a time of upheaval) and *commitment*. According to Marcia, identity involves the adoption of 1) a sexual orientation; 2) a set of values and ideals; and 3) a vocational direction.[21] Of course, all of this inner work is not completed until late adolescence. And when your child has established a firm sense of his own identity, he will have a set of values and beliefs that will differ from your own.

They are his and no one else's.

SEXUAL IDENTITY

One of the areas of identity that is part of the national conversation is sexual identity. Preadolescence can be a time of sex role confusion for some, depending on what's going on in the family. Erik Erikson, the famous psychoanalyst whose eight theories of psychosocial development strongly influenced James Marcia, felt that the resolution of a clear sexual identity was necessary in order to move on to the early adult stage of life: intimacy versus isolation. The development of a sexual identity occurs during the years of adolescence in the context of one's culture, and in America the "presumption of heterosexuality" exists. When boys and girls choose an identity based on heterosexuality, they do not have the conflicts that often trouble homosexual adolescents.[22] Currently in American culture, the homosexual youth is often bullied and stigmatized.[23] What helps young adolescents accept a heterosexual sex role identity? Psychiatrist David P. Ausubel, the author of *Theory and Problems of Adolescent Development*, writes that accepting a heterosexual sex role is aided by the following: 1) witnessing a happy marriage between parents; 2) having positive experiences with the opposite sex; and 3) possessing a strong, positive identification with the parent of the same sex.

In addition, Ausubel believes that parents exert a strong influence on their adolescent's adoption of a particular biological sex role. For example, if the parent of the opposite sex is negative about the sex role of his child, the child will find it difficult to identify with that role. Suppose a father, for example, puts his wife down and is negative about women. Then his impressionable young daughter will find it hard to embrace her femininity and identify with her own sex. The converse is true for boys.[24] According to Ausubel, the preadolescent, depending on the "psychological climate" of his home, may adopt one of three attitudes toward gender: 1) acceptance, leading to heterosexuality; 2) rejection, leading to homosexuality or asexuality (the renunciation of all sexual expression); and 3) ambivalence, resulting in bisexuality, perversion, or sexual delinquency.[25]

YOUR ADOLESCENT'S BRAIN

The important thing to keep in mind is that your child's brain is undergoing dramatic changes during adolescence. The adolescent brain is, according to David Walsh, PhD, author of *Why Do They Act That Way?* "not a finished product but a work in progress."[26] Walsh states that even though the teen brain does not change in shape and size, an amazing amount of growth is occurring during middle school and beyond.

Walsh writes:

The blossoming and pruning spurts in the brain were believed to finish by age ten and myelination by seven. . . . In fact, key brain areas undergo their blossoming and pruning periods only during adolescence. Further, the corpus callosum, which connects the right and left hemispheres, is still undergoing major construction from childhood into adolescence. The myelination process in certain parts of the teen brain actually *increases* by 100 percent from the beginning of adolescence to the end. One of the circuits involved in emotional regulation, for example, is still being myelinated during adolescence, a fact that accounts for the lightning-quick flashes of anger you see when you tell an adolescent she has to get off the computer so other people in the family can use it.[27]

The fact that the teen's brain is "under construction" explains the impulsivity of youth and the fact that the prefrontal cortex can't always distinguish a good decision from a bad one. Walsh adds, "At the same time that adolescents are having trouble stifling impulses, they are being barraged with an unprecedented onslaught of powerful urges, lightning-quick mood changes, and confusing new feelings."[28] And don't forget the hormones. One father of two daughters, ages twelve and fourteen (both of whom were menstruating), with a perimenopausal wife, sighed when he said, "In any given month there's never a good week."

Because of the dramatic brain changes, it is important for parents to help their middle schoolers control their impulses and make good decisions. We need to help them do what they are having a hard time doing. Walsh writes, "Adolescent brains get the gas before the brakes. Puberty gives adolescents a body that looks like an adult's, a brain that is prone to wild fluctuations and powerful surges. The brain's gas pedal is ready for a NASCAR-paced adulthood. But because the PFC (pre-frontal cortex or reasoning part of the brain) is not up to snuff, the brain's got the brakes of a Model T."[29]

How are you feeling now?

A TEACHER SPEAKS OUT

As your middle schooler grows and matures, you need to remember that sometimes middle school can be a tough experience, even if your child comes from a strong family or attends a school with a relatively benign atmosphere.

Eighth grade teacher Susan Hinebauch describes it thus:

Middle school is an exciting and grueling adventure, a time of great change and of great realization. There is a variable swing of emotions among middle-school children, from euphoric highs to dismal lows. It is a time when kids consciously begin to consider who they are as independent beings and shape that being into the person they become, often with the unwelcome assistance of their peers. They are vulnerable. In the course of being goofy and spontaneous, they begin to realize that unconditional acceptance by their peers is no longer a given and a more mature sense of global pain and suffering brings about a certain loss of innocence.[30]

REMEMBER THE FEELINGS, NOT JUST THE FACTS

Remember when you were in middle school? You didn't have to deal with all of the technology for sure, but you had boy or girl issues, problems with teachers, and difficulties with friendships. Maybe you had acne and wore braces like we did. You may have felt more distant or detached from parents, and the worst thing ever was standing out from the crowd. You wanted to be just like everyone else and fit into the middle school culture. Moreover, because of your brain's immaturity, a small problem became a tsunami.

Other people who work with kids agree. Zac Collins, the youth director at Stony Point Church outside Richmond, Virginia, told us, "The greatest challenge from an adult perspective is that we forget what it was like to be a middle schooler. *Everything* about what it's like to be a middle schooler. We expect them to be adults and to be mature and they can't be. It's impossible."

Susan Hinebauch remembers the time in middle school when one girl in her group spat on her gym bag. It did not immediately occur to her that the spitting was intentional until some time later when she realized she was being shunned. The girls accused her of thinking she was "cool," of walking into a room and becoming the center of attention. Stunned, she came to realize that she had become an outcast simply for being herself.

When she became a middle school teacher, Hinebauch said:

I found myself facing latter-day Susans, Harpers, Julies, and Pams, and, surprisingly, loving it. It was easier to be back in middle school as a teacher, yet I never forgot the pain and awkwardness of my own middle-school years, and, interestingly, I've found that I am not alone in my vivid memories of this period of schooling. Whenever I am engaged in conversation with another woman and the topic of profession is addressed, I am met with groans when I share that I teach eighth grade. "I *hated* middle school," is the almost universal cry.[31]

So whenever you are having a hard day with your middle schooler, try to remember your own middle school experience. Remember not just the facts, but also the feelings. And instead of telling your child to rise above it or ignore the ill treatment, you can say, "I know just how you feel. This is what happened to me. I have been there, too." You cannot imagine how relieved your child will feel—how understood.

STAY ENGAGED

Your child is growing up, and this may be hard—it requires different parental skills to handle an adolescent than it does a toddler. Sometimes it may feel like parenting isn't fun anymore, particularly in heated moments when you feel rubbed out and devalued. But don't ever give up or check out. Stay engaged.

One mother said that it sometimes felt like a tug-of-war with her fourteen-year-old daughter, but she knew if she let go of the rope, her daughter would fall and hurt herself. So she held on even when she didn't feel like it. Because she loved her daughter, she didn't walk away.

How should you parent your adolescent? Research shows that kids need a loving, affectionate parent who has high expectations and sets well-defined limits. Effective parents have rules and enforce them consistently. While they listen to their children and discuss reasons for boundaries and rules, when reasoning fails, these parents stand firm and assert their authority. What do psychologists call these parents? Authoritative. They are not permissive, anything-goes parents; nor are they rigid and authoritarian. Instead, they beautifully connect love and warmth with high demands.[32] Everybody wins.

WE HEAR FROM THE FRONT LINES

After all the theory about adolescent development, we found it heartwarming and enlightening to talk to the kids themselves. Listen to one girl who is about to leave middle school behind.

Carol, who is Susan's thirteen-year-old, eighth grade sister (Susan was quoted in Chapter One), told us that one of the girls at her school told the others that Carol stuffed her bra, but she decided not to make an issue of it. She says her "friends are always for me and they always have my back." A confident girl who is number seven in her family and is squarely in the middle of her twelve siblings, Carol has had her share of ribbing. At four feet eleven inches, she has often been called "short" by her peers, but she claims, "It is no big deal to me." Aware that this is her last year in middle school, she feels she has had a good experience, but says that the "drama" is the worst part of middle school. "If something is going on, everybody gets caught up in that, and the 'drama' goes on and on."

Sounding wise beyond her years, Carol says:

Because of my older siblings, I know what I'm headed for in high school with the drugs and the alcohol. I don't want to get in the same trouble that other people have that I have witnessed. These kids have no idea of what's ahead. What they think is important is probably the smallest thing in high school, and they have to understand that the step from eighth grade to freshman is probably the biggest step in your entire life.

IT'S ALL ABOUT PERSPECTIVE

As I sit in my home office, looking out the window as night falls in dead winter, I am so grateful to be the mother of two adult daughters whom I love, cherish, and admire. It's hard to believe Holly and Kristen were once obstreperous, mouthy middle schoolers. I do remember, however, that one threatened to write her own *Mommie Dearest* when she grew up. At that moment she and her sister were squabbling in the back seat as I drove them home from the mall. To stop their arguing, I said something I refuse to repeat. (It shouldn't be printed, so I'll leave you guessing.) That's when the squeal went up from the back seat of the car: "Mommie Dearest! Mommie Dearest!" They were referring, of course, to the exposé of actress Joan Crawford written by her daughter.

If middle school was frustrating, high school was even more challenging. The girls had access to a car, so they had FREEDOM. I used to say that one worked hard to make me anxious and keep me off balance during the high school years while the other, my more compliant daughter, waited until college. But throughout those eight years, my husband and I prayed. And prayed. And prayed. For their physical safety, for their souls, and for their morality. Our goal? To get them to adulthood without having them make major messes of their lives. Somehow we succeeded. Of course they made mistakes, but something amazing happened along the way. Over the years, these girls who wore braces and coke-bottle glasses became lovely women, generous to their core, compassionate toward the poor, well educated, and thoroughly responsible. Moreover, both have a terrific work ethic.

My advice to you? Take the long view, stand firm, pray. And in the words of a childhood song, "Hang on, Snoopy, hang on." (My daughter Kristen says this is "cheesy," but it is how I feel as I sit here on Valentine's Day, 2011.)

—Brenda

PARENT TIPS

First, become a student of your child. Because early adolescence brings so many maturational changes, learn all you can about your child from his teachers, pediatrician, youth director, and other parents.

Learn to truly listen to your child. Can you hear the *need* in the complaint? Can you hear the *truth* in your daughter's criticism of you? Don't presume on time. Now is the time to address whatever need your child brings up.

Insist on respect and show respect. Remember that love and respect fit together like hand and glove. Give it and insist that your kids speak to others politely as well. It may be tough going, as this age can be mouthy and naturally rude. But insist anyway.

Finally, remind yourself often that your children are a blessing.

Lon Solomon, senior pastor at McLean Bible Church in Vienna, Virginia, said in a Mother's Day sermon entitled "Mothering with No Regrets" that we need to see "our children as fine crystal rather than Tupperware." He acknowledges that they can so easily exasperate us or push us to the edge. And whenever that happened as he and his wife Brenda were raising their four children, one of whom is handicapped, he would pray, "Lord, crystal, not Tupperware!" Solomon continued, "These are the children that the Lord has graciously given me. God designed your child for you—a specific gift from Almighty God."[33]

Believe it. On good days and bad.

Chapter Three

FITTING IN:
FINDING FRIENDS

"We were best friends in middle school. I know, right?
It's so embarrassing."

—**Regina George**, in the movie *Mean Girls*

"[The popular kids] strut around and think they're the best.
It doesn't seem fair. They're no better than anyone else. They say
bad words and wear a lot of makeup and stuff."

—**Sim**, age twelve

Jenna, a bright-eyed, engaging eighth grader, is in the middle of a wrenching "breakup" with her best friend Nancy—the second girl ever to hold this vaunted role in her life. Filled with longing for the ease and closeness she and her ex–best friend once shared, Jenna laments, "We used to talk for hours and we never ran out of anything to talk about. Now sometimes it's like we don't know what to say to each other. We just don't talk to each other the same way." As she watches this once-cherished relationship fragment and drift away, Jenna feels the loss keenly.

US AGAINST THE WORLD

Oh, the pain and pathos of adolescent friendship. The middle school ties that bind are powerful indeed. And when they fray or, heaven forbid, break, they leave a cascade of sadness and hurt that is not soon forgotten.

Jenna's mother, Ann, has helped her daughter process her disappointment and reframe the growing distance in her friendship with Nancy.

Jenna's mom states:

I've tried to talk to her about it, saying, "Maybe Nancy isn't shopping for another best friend. Maybe she's just trying to have a few more friends. You guys were really exclusive for a while. It was the two of you against the world, and you weren't hanging out with other girls like you used to. Just because you're branching out doesn't mean you're no longer good friends."

Yet, says Ann, she knows this truth can't insulate Jenna from stabs of jealousy as her ex–best friend moves on. "Jenna is afraid that some other girl is going to be best friends with this girl and take her place."

THE BREAKUP

In some ways, Ann likens Jenna's pain to the feelings experienced after the loss of a romantic relationship.

Jenna's mom goes on to say:

Some of the things I hear her say about breaking up with this best friend are things you'd typically hear someone say about breaking up with a boy. And the jealousy is more like what you would expect if your boyfriend starts going out with another girl. The longer I'm watching them and looking at them, it's almost like a tryout for how they're going to behave in a boy-girl interaction.

The pain from shifting adolescent friendships is keen and acute. And it comes around again and again. Ann says, "Girls are fickle. They trade dance partners like it's a square dance. They'll say, 'I'm in love with this one, now these three.' One week, they'll say, 'Oh, I don't like her. *Nobody* likes her.' And then the next week, they'll insist, 'Oh, I *have* to go to her house.' They can be very superficial at this age."

BOYS AND BELONGING

What's it like for boys? It's different, but the longing to connect is every bit as powerful. Twelve-year-old Jacob sits rigidly by the phone, waiting and willing it to ring. Twenty minutes ago, his new friend Cole invited him to a basketball game. With promises to call right back, Cole hung up the phone to finalize transportation arrangements with his parents. But the minutes have ticked by since Cole said he would call.

Jacob looks anxiously at the clock yet again, biting his nails down to the quick. What if Cole never calls back? Or worse, what if he has decided to ask someone else instead? A new student, Jacob has found the process of finding friends to be emotionally trying. Those much-coveted invitations to out-of-school functions with new classmates have been few and far between.

Jacob's mother, Katherine, says:

> The kids at his school are friendly and welcoming on a superficial level. But few have reached out to Jacob. They have long-standing relationships with each other, and they don't think to make room for him. Jacob has struggled to find his place there and to transform school friendships into comfortable, easy, out-of-school friendships.

At last the phone rings, and Jacob hurtles forward to answer it. A smile lights up his face as he hears Cole lay out their plans. "See you in thirty minutes," Jacob says to Cole, relief flooding his voice as he signs off. He gives his mother Katherine a thumbs-up and races down the hall for the shower, flicking his towel happily as he goes. She sighs gratefully and heads downstairs in search of snack and soda money for Jacob, immensely thankful that—at least for today—he feels accepted.

CONQUERING THE CAFETERIA

Acceptance. Fitting in. Making friends. As kids blaze into the socially charged atmosphere of middle school relationships, is anything more important to them? As the parent of a middle schooler, you already know the answer. *Nothing* matters more to your child than fitting in and finding his place. Seventh grade teacher Tommy Jones says of middle schoolers, "Their challenges are just where they're at in their life—figuring out their bodies, their social skills, where their status is with the other kids." This social awareness, says Jones, manifests itself in terms of "who they sit with at lunch, and who they walk with in the hall, and when the teacher says you can pick your seats." Jones, a thoughtful teacher, adds, "I have to be very careful of the kid who no one wants to sit with, or who doesn't have the social skills to communicate."

Middle schoolers' desire to belong takes center stage on day one. Dr. Mark L'Esperance, an associate professor in middle grades education at East Carolina University, who has spent his academic career studying middle schoolers, says that the most important event occurs in sixth grade when a child gets his lunch on the first day of school and surveys the cafeteria, looking for a place to sit.

Which table do kids choose once they complete their all-important cafeteria reconnaissance mission? They gravitate towards an identity group. Such groups—the popular kids, the nerds, the jocks, the sensitive "emo" kids (more on these kids later), the loners, the wannabes—coalesce around the lunch table. As authors Charlene Giannetti and Margaret Sagarese state, "You can go into any lunchroom in any part of the country and see a social order. The middle schoolers know exactly at which table in what part of the room to set down their lunch tray."[1]

As all of us know, conquering the cafeteria is not a new hurdle for middle schoolers; rather, it's a task that has stood the test of time. High-stakes drama, the cafeteria's unique set of social dynamics can usher in a sense of belonging or feelings of abject humiliation.

How well I remember the middle school cafeteria. It was the site of my greatest rejection in middle childhood.

Seventh grade started out as a challenging year for me. I had a skinny body, unforgiving limp hair, and an enormous orthodontic appendage. The official nomenclature indicated it was a bionator—a top and bottom retainer all in one—but really, it should have had a far more nefarious name. All during seventh grade, I wore this cruel contraption around the clock. I talked with it, teeth clenched together. I slept with it.

So attired, I plunged into the seventh grade lunchroom at Sparta Junior High School in northern New Jersey. Fortunately, I had a small group of friends from elementary school who welcomed me to their lunch table. Sandy, an easygoing tomboy, and Kory, a petite girl with scoliosis who wore a back brace, occupied a table in the corner of the lunchroom with several other girls and me. But one day in late spring as I was eating my lunch, a slip of paper circulated around the table. I watched, puzzled, as several girls signed it. As it made its way to Sandy, the leader of our group, she opened it and informed me that the girls had conducted a vote. They had just decided, via their own brutal brand of adolescent democracy, that I was no longer welcome at the lunch table. I had been voted off. Effective immediately.

Momentarily frozen, I quickly gathered my things and left. I felt embarrassed, stricken, and deeply rejected. Mercifully, I had only a few lonely weeks of school to endure before seventh grade—and my interface with the lunchroom mean girls—ended. That summer, my family relocated to Vienna, Virginia, so I had the chance to start over in eighth grade at a new middle school, outfitted with normal braces and a fresh identity. I could reinvent myself. But even now, almost thirty years later, I can still recall the sting of my public humiliation in the middle school cafeteria.

—Kristen

A CRAVING FOR ACCEPTANCE

Few of us emerge unscathed from our middle school years. Let's face it. Kids can be cruel. And when it comes to dishing out the nasties, seventh grade girls take top prize. Don't just take it from us. One mother whose daughter is now enjoying the relative tranquility of eighth grade, says, "I think seventh grade is the hardest. There have been hard days, and there has been some hurt." Jessie, a petite tenth grader who hit rough waters in middle school, responded to us with a visceral reaction: "Seventh grade was the worst year of my life. It was bad. It was *awful*."

Fortunately, life gets better. So if you're reading this and you're the parent of a seventh grade girl, hang on. The truth is, while kids can be mean in middle school, they can also be kind. Most kids are on the receiving end of a little bit of both as they traverse their way along the middle school journey.

One thing is certain: during this stage of development, adolescents crave peer acceptance. They yearn for close connections as their world becomes ever more peer-focused.

THE FAMILY ANCHOR

But they also need you, the parent, as much or more as they ever did. In fact, your relationship with your middle schooler can be a powerful anchor during the social storms of adolescence. As children strike out into the world, making and establishing friendships and finding their way, they draw strength from parents who love them. When relationships sour or change, as they so often do in middle school, family can be the ultimate refuge—a sanctuary of safety from the strife and tension of friendship volatility.

Peer relationships, as one parent wisely told us, "are important, but so too is the family. So finding balance is essential." How do parents walk this fine line? By having regular family time that builds unity and cohesion. As a mother of two said, "They're getting their identity from their friends, but we still want them to have a family identity." We'll talk more in later chapters about ways to build family identity. But as your child looks for connections with peers, know this: your middle schooler needs regular touchpoints with *you*, his parent. These are the connections that will see your child safely and securely through the ups and downs of adolescent friendship.

DON'T LOOK AT ME, LOOK AT HIM

One thing you have undoubtedly noticed about your middle schooler is how self-conscious he or she is. Kids at this age are painfully aware of how they appear to others. That translates into agonizing choices in the clothes closet for girls, or a forced nonchalance about personal appearance for boys.

This high level of self-consciousness impacts how kids interact with each other all the time. How? Kids know they can't fit in if they attract too much attention to themselves. Says a mother of two young teens, "I'm sure my kids have been picked on. But they manage to fly under the radar." Kids deflect attention from themselves in the most obvious and time-honored way possible—by pointing to others.

Jaime Knox, a teacher at Shiloh Middle School in Hampstead, Maryland, told us the pressure to fit in plays out "all the time." She says:

> It's constant—the comments that other kids make. Just today a student came in with one of those Cheesehead hats because he was a Green Bay Packers fan. I said, "I don't care if you're wearing it in my class, but it can't be a distraction." The other guys were poking it—doing their eighth grade boy thing—so I took it away. And right away one of the kids said, "Ohhh dude, *your hair*!" And this boy immediately put his hood up. I looked at the boy who made the comment and asked, "Was it necessary? *Really*?" It's just so sad.

Cathy, a mother of two middle schoolers, says, "Kids are on assault all day long. They're called out for anything they say or do that's going to stand out." Cathy was ten minutes early to pick her seventh grade daughter Emily up from a party recently, and Emily told her later how grateful she was. Why? She was very tired and didn't want the other kids to see her yawning. She knew that if she yawned, she would attract attention, and the kids would make fun of her for being a baby. Cathy shakes her head, incredulity in her voice, "Kids pick on each other about *every* little thing. Emily is worried about *yawning*!"

POPULARITY AND PEER GROUPS

Where do kids look for the peer acceptance and relationship connections they crave? Most gravitate to a group, or clique, that gives them a sense of identity and belonging. Parents need to be aware of the social stratifications of school and help kids understand that genuine friendship, rather than popularity, is most important.

Rebecca told us her seventh grade daughter Olivia's growing awareness of the social pecking order at school has been eye-opening and difficult. She says, "It seemed to be harder at the beginning of this year for her than it has been in years past. She's learning there are all these different groups—the self-proclaimed popular group, the bookworms, the loners." But Rebecca says Olivia is grateful for her friendships, even if they don't offer admission to the "in" crowd. "Olivia has her group of friends, and she's coming to the realization that whatever group she is in, that's fine. She doesn't have to be in the most popular group or the one that everyone wants to be a part of."

This is a good message for kids to internalize. In fact, research shows those kids who are members of smaller groups based on shared interests—called "friendship circles"—are the most content and have higher self-esteem than kids in other groups.[2] As authors Giannetti and Sagarese indicate, these kids are "able to count on loyalty from their friends," and they don't live "with so much anxiety about losing their position in the hierarchy." The popular kids, on the other hand, "tend to wear anxiety along with the latest fashions."[3]

What makes kids popular? In some ways, it hasn't changed all that much. Here's what one middle school teacher told us:

Typically, it seems like it's the same thing it has been for a while. Are you attractive? Do you dress right? Are you in sports? Here [at this teacher's high-achieving school], if your grades are good that helps. A lot of the students are really pretty good students for the most part. So that one doesn't become a cool factor. And in some schools that backfires—they're like, "Oh, you're too nerdy. Oh, you do your work." It does seem to be the same things. It seems like sports for some reason still works—for boys definitely.

FITTING IN AND FINDING A GROUP

How hard is it to fit in and find friends? It all depends. For some kids, it's smooth sailing. For others, the journey is rough and turbulent. As a concerned and weary parent of a struggling child can attest, no Dramamine will help ride those waves! In fact, the powerful urge to fit in starts years before middle school.

Todd and Anna Patrick, parents to two girls, say they have seen the social drama play out both ways. One daughter has been on the outside gazing in; the other has been thick as thieves with her girl "posse."

Todd and Anna's oldest daughter, Janine, now in high school, struggled terribly as she made the transition from fourth to fifth grade as a new student in her Virginia public school. Janine found the girl groups impenetrable to outsiders. Anna, who spoke to us from the kitchen of her home with Janine nearby, said:

> We moved here right when she went into fifth grade. And it was . . . she's just here whispering, going "horrible." She was the new kid, and her class moved up from fourth grade to fifth grade, so they all knew each other. It was really tough, and she was one of only two kids who were put in that group. It was very difficult, because boys are more accepting in situations like that.

Adds Todd:

> Sixth grade was a little bit better because she started to begin to make some friends and begin to get connected. And when she got to middle

school [which wasn't until seventh grade in her public school], that's when she really took off relationally. She really started to have close friends and her little circle that she could hang with, and they do stuff together in and outside of school. So she had a great middle school experience.

Todd and Anna's younger daughter, Kelsey, now in sixth grade, had a much easier time fitting in since she has been in the same school since first grade. But Todd says being an insider can have a downside, too. "I think we've started seeing some of the not-so-pleasant aspects of relations where the girls get together and they have a lot of cattiness—who's wearing the coolest clothes, making jokes with each other, but mean jokes, even a little bit of bullying with other children who are not in the group—the posse."

THE CLIQUE

What about these posses or cliques? After all, no chapter on adolescent friendships would be complete without addressing the power of cliques; they're out in full force in the preteen and teen years. How do experts define a clique? In her bestselling guide to the "girl world," *Queen Bees and Wannabes*, author Rosalind Wiseman describes them this way:

> The common definition of a clique is an exclusive group of girls who are close friends, but I see it a little differently. I see them as a platoon of soldiers who have banded together to survive adolescence. There's a chain of command, and they operate as one to the outside world, even if there may be dissatisfaction within the ranks. Group cohesion is based on unquestioned loyalty to the leaders and an "us-versus-the-world" mentality.[4]

The siren song of the group platoon is particularly alluring in middle school. Said one parent, "When my daughter started middle school, she was pretty insecure. She really liked one-on-one friendships, and didn't really like big groups. Now she's very different. She likes the big groups. Self-esteem doesn't seem to be a problem anymore. In fact, she's quite full of herself!"

THE QUEEN BEE AND HER DRONES

According to Wiseman, the players in any clique break down into fairly typical roles. The Queen Bee, "a combination of the Queen of Hearts in Alice in Wonderland and Barbie," is "the epitome of teen girl perfection."[5] Remember the 2004 movie *Mean Girls*? Regina, the Queen Bee, is described by the character Damian this way: "She's the queen bee—the star. Those other two are just her little workers."

In fact, Wiseman says the Queen Bee does have a Sidekick, "the lieutenant or second-in-command, the girl who's closest to the Queen Bee and will back her no matter what because her power depends on the confidence she gets from the Queen Bee."[6] Other members of the clique take on various roles. Unfortunately, cliques usually have a Target—a girl the clique seeks to exclude or humiliate, and this girl may or may not be a member of the clique herself, says Wiseman.[7]

But cliques also have a Champion, says Wiseman. This is the girl we all want our daughters to be—she is self-confident and isn't tied to just one group; she possesses the requisite courage to face down the infernal Queen Bee and put her in her place.[8] If you have a Champion on your hands, you've raised a girl who is strong enough to stand alone.

ALPHA MALES AND BOY CLIQUES

What about boys? Are they immune to the social power structures and cliques we so often associate with girls? Not at all. Boys have their own hierarchical group structure, centered on the "alpha male." Clinical psychologist Michael Thompson describes the alpha male as the "dominant, physically adept, and socially powerful" boy in a group.[9]

While the alpha male rules the roost, he is surrounded by a group of other boys who joust for position. Writes Thompson:

Once the alpha boy is in place, the other boys in his group don't usually challenge him unless they see a sign of weakness. But they turn around and fight with one another over second place, third place, and so on, quickly creating a dominance hierarchy. . . . Boys manage their lives in these groups by recognizing their place in the group and maintaining it.[10]

Go-to girl authority Wiseman acknowledges that boys do have cliques—she prefers the term *groups*—but she says boys' rules regarding outside friendships are less oppressive than girls' dictates. Boy groups, she writes, usually "have more flexibility than girls do to have different friends."[11]

BOYS' PRESSURE TO CONFORM

But for some boys, the pressure to conform by relinquishing relationships can be every bit as powerful as it is for girls. Andrea, whose fourteen-year-old son, Drew, is in eighth grade, says this "kind of behavior was very surprising. I always anticipated that would be how it would be with girls, but not so much for boys." Her son Drew experienced a lot of pressure from the "popular" kids to set aside other friendships.

Andrea says, "Kids were telling [Drew], 'If you want to be popular and be in the "in" group, then you need to hang out with us and be friends with us.'" One of Drew's classmates, a boy power broker in the clique—which, incidentally, included *both* boys and girls—told him, "I can talk to these girls and they'll listen to me and you can be in."

But Drew was troubled by the clique's directive that he would need to give up current satisfying friendships in order to be accepted. He countered their attempts to control him and exclude others by saying, "I have a lot of friends that I play sports with, and they're my friends too." His parents helped him stand firm. Says Andrea, "We had a lot of talks with Drew about how you make friends and how you can't be someone you're not just to be liked."

GOSSIP AND GUILE

Pssst. You know what we're talking about. Among young adolescents, gossip is a potent force, wreaking havoc and ruining reputations. Girls do it, of course. But so do boys. Why do kids talk smack about each other? According to Duke psychology professor Dr. Martha Putallaz, gossip is "a way kids vent and establish solidarity."[12] It's the sticky stuff that binds cliques together. Putallaz's research shows that most kids' gossip isn't intended to cause pain: good friends gossip with the desire to hurt someone just 7 percent of the time.[13]

But even if gossip isn't borne from spiteful intent, it can hurt. And it causes wear and tear on kids. One twelve-year-old girl told us she found gossiping to be one of the "stressful" parts of friendship. Kids, she said, spread rumors about who likes whom, even when these crushes aren't real. She said of rumors in her sixth grade, "It's stupid 'cause everybody knows they're not true. But then everybody like keeps on telling other people about it."

Who gossips? Or should we say, who doesn't? Among girls, author Wiseman says, "99.99 percent of girls gossip, including your daughter . . . the worse gossip you are, the worse your daughter will be (and you thought she didn't listen to you!)."[14] In the gossip realm, parents lead by example.

At one time or another, most kids, especially those who are more popular, will get drawn into gossip. Sociologist Donna Eder, who studied middle schoolers' conversations, found that kids responded favorably to an initial "gossip gambit" 80 percent of the time.[15]

Eder found that objecting to gossip early on was the best way to end it. She says, "What I learned from this study is if you are in a group, and someone is being evaluated and you disagree, say it right away. I do this all the time in faculty meetings—I know it will be easier to disagree with one person than to disagree with the whole group."[16]

For those beleaguered parents who think the middle school rumor mill will never sputter and slow down, take heart. Research shows the practice of using gossip and "relational aggression" to get ahead socially drops off in high school.[17]

And *that* is a balm for ears singed too many times by unkind words.

PARENT-DRIVEN POPULARITY

Who propels kids to seek popularity? Mom and dad. Ask yourself how important it is to *you* if your child is popular. Guess what? Your son or daughter already knows and is using this information to filter his or her experiences in the middle school social realm. In their book, *Cliques: 8 Steps to Help Your Child Survive the Social Jungle*, Charlene Giannetti and Margaret Sagarese say that the value we parents place on popularity makes an enormous difference in how our children interpret their position in the social hierarchy.

They state:

> Do you offer suggestions on how your child can lose weight or dress a certain way to qualify for a more popular group? Popularity primers like that tend to single out a child's shortcomings.... Your role should not be to spearhead a popularity campaign. Instead, you need to balance your young adolescent's desire for social approval. Evaluate how important prestige and status symbols are in your life right now.[18]

Such self-evaluations indicate what we value. Do you place a premium on relationships that help you climb the social ladder, or do you invest time in your friends simply because you enjoy them and they make you a better person?

In order to flourish and feel at ease with themselves, your children need to be freed up from your expectations about school popularity. If you can let this go, you can help lay the groundwork for your children to establish genuine, fulfilling friendships.

THE BENEFITS OF FRIENDSHIP

Psychologist Dr. Kathryn Wentzel and her colleagues have found that friendship can be a buffer against the stresses and strains of middle school. Their research indicates that those students who start out sixth grade with good friends do better in school and experience less emotional distress than children without warm, reciprocal friendships.[19] The power of friendship endures across the span of middle childhood. Two years later, students who were rich in friends as sixth graders were better-adjusted eighth graders than those without friends.[20]

Conversely, friendless students were more likely to show signs of emotional distress. Says Wentzel:

> Friends and friendships are especially important at this age. During early adolescence, students begin to form a sense of self based in part on their interactions with their peers. They also tend to look to each other for help and support as they make other important physical, cognitive, and school-related transitions.[21]

We asked two middle schoolers, a girl and a boy who felt good about their friendships, what they liked best about their friends.

Todd and Anna Patrick's sixth grade daughter, Kelsey, says, "My best friends are Patty, Holly, and Katrina. I can go and talk to my friend Patty about anything. Holly is funny, and she's nice. And I can really relate to Katrina." Friends, says Kelsey, are one of the best parts of sixth grade.

What makes John, an eighth grader, happy at school? "Laughing with my friends about stuff. I have stuff in common with them—stuff we like to do—sports and Xbox. They accept me for who I am. When I am with them, I feel relaxed. I can be myself."

FRIENDSHIP AND PARENTAL DIVORCE

Often kids must manage social relationships at a time when their primary adult relationships are fractured, tenuous, or difficult. For example, the stresses of parental divorce make forging healthy peer bonds more difficult. Christine Evans, who has been divorced for several years, says her greatest concern for her fourteen-year-old daughter Leah is "definitely the social area—getting friends, keeping friends, being able to go out with other girls her age, being able to have close relationships." Now an eighth grader, Leah does have some friends, but has "no one she can confide in."

That worries her mother greatly, particularly since Leah is on the cusp of high school. Christine says:

> When [Leah] goes to high school next year, oh, that's huge. For her, the fact that she doesn't have close friends means that she's going to be hungry for friends. I hope that she has discernment as to what a good friend is. She's heavily involved in her church, but a major concern for me is who her friends are going to end up being. She lacks self-confidence and has low self-esteem. So if any boy pays her attention, I'm afraid she's going to fall hook, line, and sinker.

Leah is struggling with her stepmother right now, and Christine says these interactions are coloring her friendships at school. But Christine hopes Leah's hobbies and interests will strengthen her self-confidence. Leah is a stage manager in a theater group, and Christine says she has "forced her to stay after school, to get involved in clubs, and find something she loves to do."

Christine has started writing Leah a letter to give her on her first day of ninth grade, saying, "I'm so proud of you. Here are my hopes for you. . . . I hope you will find these great friends." Christine tells us, "I want to tell her she will be bombarded by sex, gangs, the desire to belong, by peer pressure. There will be mean girls, because that's the way high school is." As a sensitive parent, Christine hopes to help Leah grow stronger during the summer before ninth grade to prepare her for what's ahead.

ALONE OR LONELY?

What if your child is alone a lot? What can you do to help? Start by taking a close look at what's going on in his or her inner life. Is your child depressed because he has lost friendships or been rejected, or is he a strong introvert who needs time alone? There is, says author and psychologist Dr. Lawrence

Cohen, a big difference between kids who are loners and those who are just plain lonely.[22]

Children who are more introverted by temperament, Cohen says, are "developing a very important life skill: to be able to entertain themselves and to be self-sufficient."[23] Some famous childhood loners, such as Beatrix Potter, Rudyard Kipling, and Michelangelo, clearly employed their times of solitude to enliven their minds and fuel creativity.[24]

But those who are alone because they have struck out with peers need parental help. As Cohen says, "These children aren't loners out of preference. They are lonely because of social awkwardness or social exclusion. Sometimes it is so painful that they cry themselves to sleep night after night—and they often keep their loneliness hidden, so that parents may not notice."[25] If these words describe your child, he needs you—and other adults in his immediate orbit, such as teachers or a school counselor—to step in and help.

According to Cohen, concerned parents should ask their child four questions:

1. Do you spend time alone because you feel rejected or excluded by your classmates?
2. Is anyone at school teasing you, or making cruel comments about you?
3. Do you feel lonely or sad most of the time?
4. Do you wish your life was any different than it is?[26]

An affirmative answer to any of these questions means it's time for action. Kids might need to talk to a counselor about their feelings. Parents should take a close look at what's going on in the family; they may also want to consider family therapy.

HOME: THE HUB

Parents can also help facilitate friendships by setting aside time for kids to be with their peers and by prioritizing friendship opportunities. What does this look like practically? Let your home be the social hub. Writer Susan Yates, a mother of five (now grown) children, converted her family garage into a recreation room furnished with old sofas and a ping-pong table when her kids were teenagers.

When your house is party central, you also get a bird's-eye view of what kids are doing. Nilda Melendez says, "I would rather have a hundred kids here than have one of my kids somewhere else." She says to her children, "You can invite your friends, and we will have a party. The whole family will cook together and clean up." She observes, "The other kids must like it because they keep coming to our house."

What if your child's self-confidence is so tenuous, she doesn't even feel comfortable extending an invitation? You can help. Invite her new friend's family over for dinner. Arrange for your child to carpool with the family of a classmate he or she likes, and take turns driving yourself. Set up low-key, low-stress opportunities for your child to be around other kids she enjoys *as much as possible*. Your child may need help shoring up the courage to reach out if he or she has been rejected and has flagging self-confidence.

WHEN CHANGE IS NEEDED

What if your child is completely miserable at school for a protracted period of time? Consider changing schools. This may sound drastic, but such timely intervention may be necessary to keep your child from becoming depressed. Some families whose children have struggled socially in school have turned to homeschooling for a period of respite. Other families may transfer to another area school.

Whatever you choose, the bottom line is this: if your child needs a change, make one.

At the end of fourth grade, we pulled Austin out of our neighborhood public school. He wasn't being bullied, but he struggled to find his place socially. After several joyful years in Montessori school in a multiage classroom filled with friends, Austin had stepped up manfully to the challenge of a new school—driven largely by our need to unload the financial burden of private school tuition.

And so he boarded the bus day after day. He had kids to sit with at lunch, but he was worn down by social pressures. He was unable to break into entrenched groups and felt utterly alone. The stress began to show. By December, he had developed walking pneumonia, missing numerous days of school. He desperately wanted to leave.

He was stoic as the months passed, but my heart hurt for him; my husband Greg and I knew he needed a new environment. So in May, Greg and I headed to a statewide homeschooling conference. We could not afford private school, the local charter schools were full, and we felt Austin—and even little Katie—would benefit from time spent homeschooling.

I found the prospect of homeschooling overwhelming. I worked part-time as a writer and wondered how I could possibly balance deadlines with teaching my children. To be honest, I had never seriously considered homeschooling. But now I felt it was what God wanted me to do.

And so I dove in. For two years—during Austin's fifth and sixth grade years and Katie's first and second grade years—I homeschooled my children. I had a lot of help from my parents, and I enrolled the kids in part-time science and humanities classes at a homeschool learning center that met at a local church—a chance for them to make good friendships and leave our home-based classroom two mornings a week.

Was homeschooling hard? You bet it was. I often worked nights and weekends just to hit my deadlines. And coffee dates with friends were few and far between. Greg sacrificed too, spending evenings after a long day at work (and even some vacation days) helping out with math.

But you know what? It was worth it. I have no regrets. The two years at home were a balm to Austin's weary soul. He regained his zest and enthusiasm, and Katie had the chance to embark on her educational career in an unhurried, relaxed way.

We had some challenging days, but we had plenty of wonderful ones as well. We watched dolphins in Florida and whales in Maine; we drank homemade horchata as we studied Costa Rica; we frequented museums, painted canvases, and read, read, read.

My advice to parents of a child who desperately needs a new school environment? Make it happen. As I write, Austin is finishing his last weeks of eighth grade at a private Christian school. He is happy and has formed strong friendships; in fact, he wrote his eighth grade essay about how much he values the warm environment at his school.

So . . . listen, love, and take action if you need to. I'm rooting for you.

—Kristen

FINAL THOUGHTS

As we conclude this chapter on friendship and fitting in, we want to remind you that you have a great influence on the kind of friends your child will choose. So exercise that influence! Know, too, that the company your child keeps matters. A lot. Those who work with middle schoolers say choosing friends well makes a *big* difference in having the backup support to make wise choices regarding sex, drinking, and drugs (more on these topics later).

And as mom or dad, you can also provide your child with some valuable "parent perspective" as he or she deals with the vicissitudes of adolescent friendship. Never underestimate the value of warm, loving conversations with your child, seasoned with a healthy dose of hard-won parental wisdom.

You can help your child understand that a few close friends are all he or she really needs to make it through middle school successfully. Emphasize *real* friendships, not those that force your child to jockey for social position in a constant and precarious state of disequilibrium. Kids in such friendship circles are both "free and content." Friendship experts Charlene Giannetti and Margaret Sagarese say:

> These children are outside the cool group and have lower status. At times they are teased. Yet their lives and relationships have wonderful commodities, namely security and loyalty. Neither of these are part and parcel for the popular crowd. The clique drama queens and kings rarely feel secure for very long. The loyalty they claim isn't stable. Because it's won by manipulating and intimidating others, it is always in flux.[27]

PARENT TIPS

Use straight talk. Talk to your child about her friendships openly. Make sure you know where she fits in. Remind her that having friends—not being popular—will make her happiest over the long haul.

Make time for the daily download. Take time daily to ask probing questions about social pressures. Make sure your child understands how important it is for him to be true to himself.

Look in the mirror. Monitor what you say about others. If you don't want to raise a gossip, make sure your speech is kind.

Speak early. Let kids know it's easiest to speak up quickly in defense of a friend. Good intentions fade fast as the gossip express picks up speed.

Take time for some self-evaluation. Ask yourself if you like others for who they are or for what they can do for you. Consider what impact your perspective is having on your child.

Pay attention. Look at what your child loves to do. Ask him questions about what makes him happy, and find ways for him to do these activities with other kids.

Chapter Four

ATTACHMENT:
THE KEY TO RAISING EMPATHIC KIDS

"Without empathy, we would have no cohesive society, no trust and no reason not to murder, cheat, steal or lie. At best, we would act only out of self-interest; at worst, we would be a collection of sociopaths."

—Maia Szalavitz, coauthor of *Born for Love: Why Empathy Is Essential—and Endangered*

He had written two *New York Times* best sellers by the time he was eleven years old. He was the friend of a president and one of Oprah's favorite people. Yet he was confined to a wheelchair and breathed through a tracheotomy tube connected to an oxygen supply. His name? Mattie Stepanek.

At a time when "bullying" is a catchword, and we read about the cruelties some children inflict on each other, it is helpful to look at its flip side—empathy. Mattie's mother, Jeni Stepanek, who holds a doctorate in early childhood education, could certainly define "empathy" for us. She honed this beautiful quality in her son Mattie, who had dysautonomic mitochondrial myopathy, a rare form of muscular dystrophy. In his treatment of other people and his desire to be an international peacemaker,

Mattie displayed an unusual understanding of humankind and of suffering, which he wrote about in his collection of poems called *Heartsongs*, published during his middle school years.

Mattie had a ringside seat when it came to the disabling effects of disease and pain; he knew firsthand how depressing it could be to wake up every morning to cope with ongoing illness and endure repeated hospitalizations. He understood that other children with a similar condition sometimes gave in to depression and despair. Yet with all of his disabilities and ongoing suffering, this boy chose to celebrate life. With amazing resilience and incredible hope that defied his doctors' prognoses, he wanted to grow up, marry, and later have grandchildren. He longed to leave a legacy.

And so he did, through his relationships with the people he knew and the millions who saw him on television. And through his five books of poetry that became *New York Times* best sellers. He started to speak his first poems when he was three, and his mother, who is divorced and has the adult-onset form of Mattie's disease, wrote them down. Jeni lost three other children to the disease before she realized she had it and was passing it on. Mattie knew only one sibling, a brother. Out of this life history, he said, "We all have life storms. Times in our lives that are extremely sad, scary, angry. And instead of just suffering through them, and then afterwards just sitting, crying, and waiting to be wiped out by the next one, we should celebrate together that we got through. And when the next one comes along, work through and pull through and celebrate again." This young philosopher's guiding credo: We should "play after every storm."[1]

Mattie, who appeared several times on *Oprah, Jerry Lewis MDA Telethon*, and *Larry King Live*, lived for a time with his mother in a basement in Rockville, Maryland. They were so poor that several churches gave them canned goods. Examining the labels, Mattie discovered they were expired. He later told former president Jimmy Carter that if his books made a lot of money, he and his mom would give "brand new food to the poor even if we have to eat the old, outdated food in our house."[2]

Mattie's concern for others and his international view of world peace led to a deep friendship with Jimmy Carter. In delivering the eulogy for Mattie, who died at thirteen, Carter said that Mattie was "embarrassed" that his books topped Carter's on the best-seller list. He would "sympathize with me and say, 'Well, you know maybe poetry just has less competition than what you are writing about.'" Carter continued, "I've thought a lot about Mattie's religious faith. It's all-encompassing, to include all human beings who believe in peace and justice and humility and service and compassion and love. The exact characteristics of our Savior Jesus Christ. He was still a boy, although he had the mind and the consciousness and the awareness of global affairs of a mature, philosophical adult."[3]

Carter added, "Since I left the White House, my wife and I have been to more than 120 nations. And we have known kings and queens, and we've known presidents and prime ministers, but the most extraordinary person whom I have ever known in my life is Mattie Stepanek."[4]

This physically disabled boy stood on the shoulders of men.

LORD OF THE FLIES

Have you ever wondered why some kids, like Mattie, seemingly possess a deep reservoir of compassion, kindness, and empathy while others appear devoid of these qualities and seem to take perverse pleasure in hurting other children? Some remind us of the boys in William Golding's classic, *Lord of the Flies,* who find themselves on a deserted island after a plane crash and become little savages who murder their own. All are under thirteen years of age. Just as our hearts expand when we hear about a great soul like Mattie, our hearts contract when we learn about children who inhumanly bully or hurt others.

Remember the Florida teen who was set on fire by four other teens, one of whom was a thirteen-year-old middle schooler? Michael Brewer, who lives in Deerfield Beach, Florida, was punished for reporting the four boys who had stolen his father's five-hundred-dollar bike. They said he "snitched." So they doused the fifteen-year-old with rubbing alcohol and set him on fire. He spent months in a hospital on a ventilator with flame burns covering 65 percent of his body. Authorities said that not only were the perpetrators without remorse, but three of the four were laughing about the vicious crime they committed the night they were arrested.[5]

Most of us can hardly fathom this bizarre, nonhuman behavior. We wonder what kind of parenting creates young teens who maim and destroy. We ask ourselves what cultural influences could possibly have helped spawn this horrific behavior. We understand that empathy, compassion, and love do not automatically spring forth in the human breast. Rather, these qualities are either well-honed, neglected, or eradicated in intimate family settings. Although American parents have not been held responsible for their children's criminal behavior for decades, we are, as parents, ultimately responsible for instilling character, self-control, goodness, and kindness in our children's hearts, minds, and souls. Just as Jeni Stepanek nurtured Mattie's optimistic philosophy of life and capacity for empathy, the unknown parents of the four teens who doused Michael Brewer with alcohol and set him ablaze are complicit in the way their sons turned out.

It is from us that our children either develop warmly human capacities or learn to be grotesquely inhuman.

If you're a parent, the buck stops with you.

WHAT IS EMPATHY?

But what, after all, is empathy, and why is it so critical as part of our humanity?

Writer Daniel Goleman, the author of *Working with Emotional Intelligence*, calls empathy "our social radar."[6] He says, "Sensing what others feel without their saying so captures the essence of empathy. Others rarely tell us in words what they feel; instead, they tell us in their tone of voice, facial expression, or other nonverbal ways. The ability to sense these subtle communications builds on more basic competencies, particularly self-awareness and self-control. Without the ability to sense our own feelings—to keep them from swamping us—we would be hopelessly out of touch with the moods of others."[7]

Tanya Beran, PhD, a professor at the medical school at the University of Calgary, suggests that empathy is not just a simple behavior. It is the result of awareness, both of the self and the other person. Beran told us:

> Empathy is a very complex construct. Empathy is not just about understanding someone else's feelings. It's about *feeling* someone else's feelings, but *separating* them from your own. The children have to be able to recognize their feelings, label them, and identify them. They have to be able to do the same thing for other people. So this is quite a challenge for people to do, to identify correctly other people's feelings. And then you have to be able to separate those feelings as belonging to someone else and not belonging to you.[8]

ORIGINS OF EMPATHY

Studies of babies indicate that all of us are born with a capacity for empathy; in fact, scientists believe empathy is innate. Newborns experience distress in response to the cries of other infants.[9] Remember when you went to view your own newborn in the hospital nursery, and one baby started crying and soon there was a cacophony of crying infants? It's our sense of empathy that makes us want to be helpful when others are in emotional or physical pain. Child development expert William Damon describes a thirteen-month-old who took his own mother to aid a crying child.[10] This baby knew that someone—and who better than his own mother—needed to comfort the distressed child.

While we can feel, to some extent, the pain and distress of others in infancy, as we grow our cognition expands, and we begin to understand how to put ourselves in another's shoes. Even as early as age two, we begin to understand that we are not part of a mass of babyhood, but we have a separate self and others' pain is different from our own. According to Damon, between the ages of two and six, children take a quantum leap; now they are not only attuned to another's distress, but children become concerned about "the general plight of life's chronic victims—the poor, the handicapped, the socially outcast."[11] Thus, empathy has twin components—one in the affective or emotional area and the other in the cognitive. In other words, we *feel* the distress of others from birth, but as we grow and our brain develops, we begin to *think* about what they are feeling and can decide how to help the poor, the distressed, and the handicapped.

IT'S ALL ABOUT OUR EARLIEST ATTACHMENTS

The research on empathy shows that before kids *learn* lessons about empathy, they must first *experience* empathy from their parents.[12] Empathy grows out of our earliest relationships; it's part of the language of love and well-being we absorb in infancy and hone as we mature within the context of a warm and responsive family.

Psychologists understand that empathy—that lovely, magical *intuitive understanding* we all yearn for—is linked to our earliest attachments. What do we mean by attachment? *Attachment* simply refers to the enduring emotional bond that babies forge with mother first, then with father, in the first year of life. Psychologists Alan Sroufe and Everett Waters call this bond "a psychological tether which binds infant and caregiver together."[13]

In his classic book, *Attachment*, British psychiatrist John Bowlby wrote about the absolute centrality of the baby's emotional bond with his mother. Bowlby, the only psychiatrist to have twice received the American Psychiatric Association's highest honor, the Adolph Meyer award, has been described as "one of the three or four most important psychiatrists of the twentieth century."[14] He believed that the child's earliest attachment relationship with his mother was the "foundation stone of personality."[15] Bowlby stated that "the young child's hunger for his mother's love and presence is as great as his hunger for food" and that her absence in infancy "inevitably generates a powerful sense of loss and anger."[16]

Sigmund Freud, writing years earlier, also emphasized the singular importance of the mother or mothering figure in a child's life. Writing in *Outline of Psychoanalysis*, he described the relationship a young child has with his mother as "unique, without parallel, established unalterably for a whole lifetime as the first and strongest love object and as the prototype of all later love relationships for both sexes."[17]

MOTHER FIRST, THEN FATHER

This most powerful early relationship with mother first, then father, begins at birth. It is, in fact, the most critical developmental issue in that important first year of life. In *Attachment*, Bowlby wrote that babies begin to fall in love with their mothers between six and twelve months of age, and this attachment relationship puts them on a particular developmental trajectory or path for life. His was a theoretical approach based on the patients he worked with in his psychoanalytic practice in London at the Tavistock Clinic. Bowlby was fortunate in that he met Mary Ainsworth, who in the 1960s became his protégé and colleague.

Ainsworth and her colleagues developed an ingenious laboratory experiment called the Strange Situation, which has allowed psychologists to measure the attachment relationship a child has with both parents. It has been an instrument of choice for decades of infant day care research; in fact, Robert Karen, author of *Becoming Attached*, said it has become "more widely used than any other in developmental psychology" as a tool for measuring infant attachment.[18] It allows psychologists to peer into the parent/child relationship, understanding its mystery and power to shape personality, all intimate relationships, empathy—a life.

PATTERNS OF ATTACHMENT

In her work, Ainsworth found three patterns of attachment: the securely attached, the anxious-resistant, and the anxious-avoidant. Basically, the securely attached baby has learned to trust his mother to meet his emotional needs consistently and sensitively during the first year of life. According to Ainsworth, mothers of these babies have been more sensitive, cooperative, and accepting than mothers of insecure infants.[19]

While the securely attached babies had these dream mothers, the anxious-resistant babies were not so lucky. Their mothers were inconsistently accessible and responsive. Sometimes these mothers were warm and loving, but other times they were cool and rejecting. Because they could not count on their mothers, these babies became anxious and angry.[20] These moms engaged in power struggles with their babies, and when they felt overwhelmed, they often reacted with rejection and hostility.[21]

Finally, Ainsworth and her colleagues found a third group of babies she called anxious-avoidant. These babies tended to avoid their mothers during the highly stressed reunion episodes of the Strange Situation. Ainsworth found, in analyzing her data, that the mothers of the anxious-avoidant babies were not warm and affectionate and basically did not like physical contact. They often rebuffed their babies' bids for attention, and they "seemed to be rigidly containing their anger and irritation."[22] So the baby learns *not* to go to mom for comfort, love, and warmth. He's angry, he stays away from his momma, but he's still needy all the same.

CAUGHT, NOT TAUGHT

In sum, attachment researchers believe that *empathy is caught, not taught.* Alan Sroufe, one of the original researchers involved in the famous Minnesota study, says this, "If you're in a relationship, the relationship is part of you, there's no way around it. You get an empathic child not by trying to teach the child and admonish the child to be empathic; you get an empathic child by being empathic with the child. The child's understanding of relationships can only be from the relationships he has experienced."[23] Graham Music, consultant child psychotherapist and associate clinical director at the Tavistock Clinic in London, agrees. In his book *Nurturing Natures*, Music writes that empathy is acquired through a child's experience with his parents. The securely attached child is able to understand the feelings of others. Not so, the insecurely attached. If the parents are inconsistent, rejecting, neglectful, depressed, or suffer from personality disorders, then the child does not develop a sense of empathy and lacks the ability to stand in the other person's shoes.[24]

Psychologist Tanya Beran agrees. She told us, "To be able to have empathy, you have to have experienced empathy. It's not just cognitive and it's not just a behavior. It's a cognitive-emotional-behavioral experience. That's what empathy is."

But what if one doesn't receive empathy growing into preadolescence? Dr. Beran continued, "I don't think it's reasonable to expect that someone who hasn't been empathized with can turn around and show empathy."

TEACHING EMPATHY IN THE SCHOOLS

But that's just what many schools in America are attempting to do: teach children who haven't experienced empathy to show empathy. Because of the upsurge in bullying across America, schools are stepping in to help students regulate their emotions and learn to be kind and civil to each other. In empathy classes and workshops, professionals are trying to teach kids to take turns, not to hit Johnny or make injurious comments, to see the world through others' eyes, as well as to control their anger.

Although empathy was originally under the purview of parents, with support given by churches and schools, now schools are coming to the rescue because kids are increasingly cruel. Parents aren't the empathy experts they once were. Some schools, like Scarsdale Middle School in Scarsdale, New York, are overtly teaching empathy to their students. For example, a new club invites students to share snacks and board games after school with four autistic students who are in special education classes all day. While many parents are pleased with the new empathy focus, students complain that kids are still mean in the halls and cafeteria.[25]

Nonetheless, empathy training is big news and is spreading nationally. For instance, in 2009, Los Angeles spent nearly one million dollars for its 147 middle schools on a nationally known program called Second Step: Student Success Through Prevention. This program attempts to build character by teaching kids empathy, impulse control, anger management, and problem solving. And on Long Island, Weber Middle School in Port Washington rewarded some three hundred students who had made empathic gestures, like sitting beside a new girl at lunch or helping a frightened student on a rock climbing wall, by inducting them into the Weber Pride club.[26]

Another program called Roots of Empathy is currently being used in three thousand kindergartens, elementary schools, and middle schools across Canada, as well as forty schools in Seattle. As part of this program, kids get to see a mother and a baby interact in an effort to teach students about the origin of human feelings. When the baby cries, the instructor tries to help students understand why the baby could be crying and also how frustrating it can be for a mother who is unable to comfort her baby. Apparently, this attempt to teach perspective (understanding another's point of view) has been successful; some nine studies have shown that Roots of Empathy has helped reduce bullying at school and increased supportive behavior among students.[27]

ATTACHMENT, BULLYING, AND EMPATHY

But if empathy is *caught,* not *taught,* then the effect of training students to be empathic may be only skin-deep. The training is focused on a cognitive-behavioral approach; it does not take into account the *emotional* aspect of empathy and the fact that empathy emerges from an intimate relationship or emotional bond. If empathy flows from a secure bond with parents—and we think it does—then there is no way schools can emulate that. It's like trying to capture the horses long after they have left the barn.

By the time a kid reaches middle school, his empathic response or lack of same is well-established. Current research on bullying and attachment is supportive of this. The securely attached child grows up to become the well-liked, secure middle schooler who has a capacity for empathy that the insecurely attached simply lack. He supports his vulnerable friends and stands up to bullies with force and energy. Robert Karen writes in *Becoming Attached*, "The securely attached children did not allow themselves to be bullied or even pulled into a relationship that had hurtful dynamics. They either found a way to make the relationship positive, withdrew, or met the aggression with just enough force to discourage it."[28]

Studies show that as children reach preadolescence, the "superior relational capacities of the children who had been securely attached in infancy continued."[29] For example, researchers J. Elicker and M. Englund found that 76 percent of the securely attached eleven-year-olds made friends, compared to only 45 percent of those who had been anxiously attached.[30] Robert Karen writes that anxious-avoidant boys tend to be aggressive, cruel, disruptive, and more likely to lie and cheat, whereas anxious-avoidant girls tend to internalize their feelings, becoming depressed and ashamed.[31]

Amanda Nickerson, Danielle Mele, and Dana Princiotta examined 105 middle school students who said they were either defenders or outsiders in bullying situations. They found that attachment to *mother* (but not to father) and the child's capacity for empathy predicted whether or not a middle schooler would defend the hurt child or simply be a bystander, doing nothing.[32] Another study of 110 sixth graders by Megan Eliot, MEd, and Dewey Cornell, PhD, of the University of Virginia, found that those students who indicated attitudes linked to insecure attachment were more likely to be identified as bullies by their peers.[33]

Finally, research conducted in Canada by Laura Walden and Tanya Beran examined 105 students in grades four, six, and eight. They found that students with "lower quality attachment" were more likely to bully and be bullied than those with "higher quality attachment."[34] However, as Beran was quick to point out in an interview, insecurely attached children may be both victim and bully.

So the quality of a child's attachment to his or her parents is predictive of bullying behavior. But we don't hear anything along these lines in the current debate on bullying, do we?

MIDCOURSE CORRECTION

Some of you may be feeling dismay at this point if you have a child who is often a victim or a bully. What, you wonder, can you do if teaching empathy isn't enough? You can make a midcourse correction. The initial part of that change involves remembering the way your parents, particularly your mother, treated you in childhood. How did your parents respond to you when you were hurt or afraid? Did they empathize with you, or did they tell you to be tough and soldier on? The truth is we tend to treat our children as we were treated in childhood until we work through the neglect, the emotional, sexual, or physical abuse, or the emotional deprivation we experienced as children.

In my work as a psychotherapist, I often ask clients, "Who comforted you as a child?" If the person says "my mother" or "my father," then I know that at least one parent was able to be empathic. But when the person says "no one," I understand that my client has grown up feeling alone in the world, as if no one really cared about her feelings or her soul. Usually the client is compulsively self-reliant and seeks comfort from no one. Eventually, I hear my client say that she lives in a comfortless world, and even though she does not articulate it, I understand this is part of why she has come to me—she is looking for understanding, empathy, and comfort. As I try to be empathic, I eventually point to Someone who is better than any human source of empathy, since all humans fail at times.

God, I say to my client, is our ultimate role model when it comes to empathy. I know. Empathy was not much in evidence in my upbringing. Fortunately, I discovered the God of all comfort in childhood and experienced empathy through others whom he sent into my life. And when I became an adult, I worked through the pain I had experienced in life with my mother with a wonderful therapist. That has allowed me to give my daughters more love and empathy than I received. Remember what the stewardess tells you on airplane flights? In case of emergency, put your oxygen mask on first. Then, and only then, are you prepared to help others. This is especially true in parenting. If you had a painful, rejecting relationship with either parent, you need to work this through so that you can be a better parent to your child. In the mental health clinic where I once worked, my supervisor said, "What we don't work out, we act out." This is particularly evident in our attachment relationships with our children. So if your child lacks empathy, look to your own reservoir of empathy first. Once you have dealt with your own longing to be cared for and understood, you will be better able to be empathic with your child.

—*Brenda*

WE MODEL EMPATHY

As we give to the poor, volunteer at rescue missions, or have a ready handout of money or food for the homeless who increasingly line our highways, we are modeling empathy for our children. On the other hand, if we turn a deaf ear to the poor, our children "catch" that life lesson and learn to look the other way when they, too, see the poor and needy.

One mother and her twelve-year-old son saw a six-foot, bearded African American male emerge from the woods near the public library one summer morning. Curious, she asked the librarian if the man lived in the woods, and the librarian responded, "Oh, yes. He has been there for years." The mother then asked, "Well, what has the staff done for him?" The librarian said simply, "Nothing, as far as I know." As she walked to her car, this mother said to her boy, "Let's go to Whole Foods and buy the man lunch." And so they did. When they returned with sandwiches, fruit, and several bottles of water, they found the man sitting on a bench at the edge of the woods. The mother gave him their offering with a sweet message, and then the boy reached in his pocket and pulled out a five-dollar bill he had been saving. "Here," he said, as he handed the homeless man the money.

In Detroit, Michigan, a fourteen-year-old became a local hero after he helped his seventy-seven-year-old neighbor who slipped and fell on a cold wintry night. When Hazel Montrose, who has a heart condition and a bad hip, fell, she pressed the panic button on her car, and her neighbor, Lovell Williams, came running, wearing only his pajamas. He didn't stop for his coat, shoes, or gloves. The boy later told WXYZ radio, "It took five minutes to get her up because she has bad arthritis. I did it to be a good neighbor and friend." Hazel sees it differently; she thinks Lovell is an angel. "Only God sent him. But he said he heard me." She adds, "I am grateful for him and his mother." The reporter said both mother and son are Christians.[35]

And locally, another fourteen-year-old boy we know shaved off all of the hair on his head in solidarity with a family friend, a fellow teen, who is undergoing treatment for cancer. He, his dad (a professor who had recently lost a student to lymphoma), and his stricken friend's little brother "faced the clippers" as part of a fundraiser for St. Baldrick's Foundation—all in an effort to raise money for a cancer cure and to support a friend and sister.

Ah, the positive, moving results of compassion and empathy.

HAVE I DONE ENOUGH?

When Mattie Stepanek lay dying, his mother told Oprah he was in desperate straits. His organs were shutting down, and when he spoke he was gasping for breath. This boy, who had moved millions with his poetry and his great heart, asked his mother, "Have I done enough?" Jeni Stepanek, who had raised her son alone and from her wheelchair, assured him that he had been "the perfect son" and that God would welcome him home. Sensing his agony, she told him it was OK for him to go. Within seconds, Mattie's soul took flight.[36]

We have used the account of this thirteen-year-old to illustrate not only empathy but a greatness of heart that is so antithetical to what we are witnessing in some middle schoolers today. We are struck by the profound difference between wheelchair-bound Mattie and the middle school boys involved in the burning of Michael Brewer. And we wonder about the parents. Jeni Stepanek has created a foundation in her son's name and is a spokesperson for muscular dystrophy. But what about the mothers and fathers in Florida? What will they have to live with for the rest of their lives? And what about the boys—how will they ever overcome their lingering guilt and shame?

Raising kids to possess greatness of heart, compassion, and empathy matters enormously. We comfort our children when they are distressed, and as they grow, we listen from our hearts. As we have seen in the Detroit "teenage angel" and in the Florida case, our empathy or lack of it may have enormous consequences for another human being. Raising a child with a great heart can mean the difference between life and death for a neighbor. Or if we rear a child without empathy, he or she can help create a lifetime of scarring and deep emotional pain for another human being.

Which will it be?

PARENT TIPS

How can you as a parent give and model empathy?

Learn to listen. When your child comes to you hurt and distressed, practice empathic listening.

Offer affection. Those cool middle school boys who can't bear to have you touch them in public? Their hearts are younger than their bodies.

Don't be put off by your daughter's histrionics. Some girls love, love, love drama. They will calm down when they go to college. Stay calm yourself. No shouting matches, please.

Model empathy with the sick, the poor, and the distressed. Don't ignore them. The poor are gifts to you to shape your child's soul and your own.

Do something that's hard for you. Make a meal for a sick friend. Let your middle schooler chop the soup vegetables or mix the cookie dough.

Get help if you need it. Find a warm, caring therapist and let her empathic response be a balm to your soul.

- Do something that's hard for you, like make a meal for a sick friend. Let your middle schooler chop the soup vegetables or mix the cookie dough.
- If you are wounded and never experienced much empathy growing up, find a warm, caring therapist, and let her empathic response be a balm to your soul.

Chapter Five

TWEEN GENIUS

*"Ah, but a man's reach should exceed his grasp,
or what's a heaven for?"*

—**Robert Browning**, poet, *Andrea del Sarto*

Sandy-haired and unassuming, Benjamin Senior has a prodigious memory and an untiring work ethic. He is also a consummate perfectionist, a child for whom "failure is not an option," says his petite and peripatetic mother, Dana, a former social worker who is always on the go helping care for others.

Recently, Benjamin earned the main role in his local community's drama production, *Get Smart*, because, Dana says, "He was the only one who could memorize three hundred lines in one week and pull it off." Identified as gifted early on, Benjamin participated in an elite program in his community's public school system throughout his elementary and early middle school years; to be nominated, students must have scored at or above the ninety-seventh percentile on achievement tests.

In seventh grade, Benjamin won a national science award and traveled to the White House to receive recognition for his achievement. Now homeschooled, Benjamin's passion for science and theater is continuing unabated. He is still driven to succeed in academics but is learning to let his hair down—literally—for laughs and entertainment. "He is scared to fail when it comes to really cerebral issues," says Dana. But he's not afraid to ham it up on stage.

High test scores. Good grades. Awards and recognition. Such are the academic accolades of childhood, and they are music to any middle school parent's ears. We all want our kids to succeed. And with high school just around the corner, college admissions more competitive than ever, and a global job market crammed with talent, kids today face incredible pressures to burnish their academic resumés, to make an impact, to stand out, and to perform.

Even as I am writing about the academic pressures of contemporary middle school on this windy, chilly Saturday afternoon, my son Austin is living it out down the hall. His fourth grade sister Katie is outside enjoying an unencumbered afternoon of playtime. But Austin is closeted in his room, hard at work on a take-home algebra exam he has been told will take him at least three hours to complete. Three hours? Really?

He spent the morning at the computer putting the finishing touches on a PowerPoint presentation for his science class that details the mechanisms by which fireworks light up the sky. Tomorrow afternoon—on Sunday—he will tackle a research paper explaining the software behind Xbox's Kinect system.

While fascinating on some levels, this seems like a crushing amount of homework for an eighth grader to complete in one weekend. Fortunately, this workload is an anomaly—most of Austin's weekends generally involve a few hours of homework. And to be fair, the project and paper were assigned weeks ago; Austin's adolescent procrastination has surely upped the ante.

His school is intent on preparing him for the rigors of high school and beyond, for which I am grateful. As a longtime education writer, I'm all too familiar with the data on school failure. And I understand how pivotal the middle school years are in putting kids on the path to success. But as a mom, I also know Austin is still a child and needs sufficient time to play and unwind. Reconciling these two realities nowadays is no easy task. In the meantime, I am motivating him with the promise of a youth group ski trip next weekend and a Twix bar the minute he wraps things up.

—Kristen

As a parent of a middle schooler, you undoubtedly wrestle with some of these same issues. Just how much homework is enough? What makes for an appropriately rigorous middle school curriculum? What characteristics enable students to succeed? How can you help your child do her best? And are kids today under *too much* pressure?

HOMEWORK: FRIEND OR FOE?

Despite all of the advances of modern pedagogy, homework endures. Why? It works. An array of studies confirm what most parents and teachers know intuitively: homework boosts student achievement. It reinforces what kids learn during the day and gives them an opportunity to test out their newfound understanding at home.

How much homework is enough during grades six through eight? Experts generally recommend between one and one and a half hours of homework per night for middle schoolers, depending on what grade they're in. Duke University researcher and author of *The Battle Over Homework*, Harris Cooper—dubbed "the nation's top homework scholar" by *Time* magazine[1]— has conducted an extensive research review of over sixty studies on homework. His findings lend credence to the "ten-minute rule": beginning in first grade, teachers should increase the amount of take-home work incrementally by ten minutes a day for each year a child is in school. Under these guidelines, middle schoolers in sixth through eighth grade should complete between sixty and eighty minutes of homework daily; high schoolers should be assigned between one and a half and two hours per day.[2]

When it comes to homework, more isn't necessarily better. Even in high school—a time when some kids today say they are shackled with up to five hours of homework daily and seldom hit the sack before midnight—research shows that more than two hours of nightly homework yield *no* real improvement in achievement. In fact, too much homework is "counterproductive" for students of all ages.[3] That makes good sense to parents who know that a burnt-out, overworked child is too tired to learn well.

PARENTS ON HOMEWORK

What do middle school parents tell us about homework? Their estimates of their child's homework time vary, but they mostly range from one to two or even three hours per day. To be sure, some kids are doing even more than this, logging hours that more closely resemble those of cramming college freshmen.

Variation in total homework time is to be expected, hinging on schools' and teachers' attitudes toward homework and procrastination on the part of students, as well as on the fact that some students take more care and time with their assignments than others. But if your middle schooler is routinely assigned more than three hours per night, that's too much. And if your son or daughter becomes worn down from chronic homework overload, it's time to become an advocate for reasonable limits and schedule a meeting with the teacher.

For busy parents, part of the homework battle is finding undistracted time and a quiet place for kids to work. Rebecca Draper, who teaches special education students at Margaret Pollard Middle School in Chatham County, North Carolina, says her seventh grade daughter, Olivia, has benefited from staying after school and doing her schoolwork in her mother's classroom. Says Draper, "When she came directly home, she was working until about

9 P.M. every night. That was her fault because Olivia is a person who distracts herself completely with everything going on around her. But since I've made her start staying at school with me, she finishes within about two hours. At school, there's no TV, there's no little sister Sally. It's just Olivia, and so she can focus."

Other parents say they are zealous about protecting all-important weeknights from outside obligations so kids have sufficient time for their studies. Terry, the mother of a middle schooler, says, "We try to limit nighttime commitments and events during the week. I honor that time after dinner as time to do homework."

If a child's bedroom (and workspace) is fully outfitted with gadgets and distractions, parents say they have a harder time tracking homework time. What should take two hours may end up taking far longer. Says one mother of an eighth grade girl, "Because of technology, it has gotten very complicated to be able to tell how much homework my daughter has. Even though she goes to her room to do her homework, she has a cell phone, she's texting, or she's talking on the phone. Now that she has her own computer, she could be on Facebook all night long."

IS SELF-DISCIPLINE OR SMARTS THE KEY TO SUCCESS?

Even when kids faithfully complete their homework, we all know that some do better than others. What makes for a good student? Conventional wisdom would seem to dictate that smart kids—those genetically blessed students with lots of high-functioning gray matter—are preprogrammed for success. Clearly, intelligence is a significant factor in academic achievement, and we would never argue otherwise. But self-discipline and the ability to delay gratification—factors that are within our control—matter more. These are valuable internal traits that compel a child to tackle the distributive property of mathematics, for example, before watching television.

Psychologist Martin Seligman and his colleague Angela Duckworth affirm the powerful role of self-discipline in predicting academic success.

As their study of eighth graders at a public magnet school showed, "Highly self-disciplined adolescents outperformed their more impulsive peers on every academic-performance variable, including report-card grades, standardized achievement test scores, admission to a competitive high school, and attendance."[4]

What's the bottom line? Work on inculcating self-discipline in your child. How? Drs. Seligman and Duckworth conclude: "We believe that many of America's children have trouble making choices that require them to sacrifice short-term pleasure for long-term gain, and that programs that build self-discipline may be the royal road to building academic achievement."[5]

TEACHING CHILDREN TO WORK

While Dr. Seligman's advice might spawn a bustling industry of school-based self-discipline programs, we believe the "royal road" to academic achievement need be none other than the family hallway—especially if it leads to the cleaning closet.

Moms and dads, you can build your own self-discipline program.

For generations, parents have taught children about self-discipline by requiring that they do chores. Most kids don't milk the cow or chop wood anymore, but they can still walk the dog, set the table, do dishes, fold laundry, or take out trash. And as they work, they build self-discipline.

They also learn how to delay gratification. The psychological research linking delayed gratification with success in children is abundant and well-established; work helps here, too. Kids inculcate the importance of delaying gratification as they rake and bag soggy leaves *first*, knowing they can see friends *after* chores are done. Parents who require their children to help out around the house also reinforce the inescapable reality that life, well lived, involves an abundance of hard work. These kids learn, as did inventor Thomas Edison, that "genius is 1 percent inspiration and 99 percent perspiration."

Armed with responsibility and self-discipline, kids reap dividends with their schoolwork. Teacher Rebecca Draper is a firm believer in the link between chores and school success. Even for her special-education students, some of whom are autistic, she says at-home chores help them learn better. That's because, says Draper, chores teach kids that "there are some things you just do." She requires her own two daughters to clean their bathrooms every week. Draper says, "If Olivia and Sally mess up the bathroom and get toothpaste everywhere, they have to scrub it." Neglecting their responsibilities brings real-world and painful consequences, she says. "If they don't clean, they don't get their allowance."

Victoria Lynn Fielder, a veteran middle school teacher in Columbia, South Carolina, agrees on the importance of home-based responsibilities, especially as kids gear up for middle school. In a newspaper interview on "teacher tips" for parents, she said:

> Having more daily chores—helping to prepare meals, being respon-
> sible for packing sports gear, planning out summer reading require-
> ments, even neighborhood jobs such as babysitting and lawn care—
> can help budding adolescents learn to plan ahead, budget their time,
> and keep organized. These are essential foundation skills that will
> help rising middle schoolers take on the responsibilities of middle
> school more successfully and ease their transition.[6]

How do you respond to your ornery middle schooler who glares at you and insists mowing the lawn on a hot summer day amounts to slave labor? Try the tart reply of columnist Ann Landers: "Nobody ever drowned in his own sweat."

IN MATH, A IS FOR EFFORT

There are perhaps few subjects in school where effort and performance converge more powerfully than in math. However, such thinking is contrary to the prevailing attitude toward mathematics success in the United States—one that portrays math achievement primarily as the product of innate intelligence. This deeply entrenched belief caused the National Mathematics Advisory

Panel to lament America's widespread "resignation about mathematics education" that "seems rooted in the erroneous idea that success is largely a matter of inherent talent or ability, not effort."[7] In fact, this impressive panel—stacked with scholars, mathematicians, psychologists, and professors—affirmed the power of a little elbow grease:

> Children's goals and beliefs about learning are related to their mathematics performance. Experimental studies have demonstrated that changing children's beliefs from a focus on ability to a focus on effort increases their engagement in mathematics learning, which in turn improves mathematics outcomes: When children believe that their efforts to learn make them "smarter," they show greater persistence in mathematics learning.[8]

When the Math Panel polled the nation's Algebra I teachers about their top challenge in teaching math, they said it was "working with unmotivated students."[9] Teachers love—and can do wonders with—a motivated student.

So effort triumphs.

ALGEBRA FOR EVERYONE?

What areas of mathematics content should middle school students master before they enter the heady days of high school? A chorus of educators affirms the importance of taking Algebra I by eighth grade. Part of the reason for this emphasis on Algebra I in middle school is that mastering algebraic concepts is foundational for later math achievement. Warren Gould, the director of the middle and upper schools at Trinity School in Durham, North Carolina, says algebra gives students "the keys to the kingdom."

Students who complete Algebra I in middle school are more likely to stay on track to pursue more advanced math courses in high school, such as calculus. This in turn affects college success: students who go on to complete a course of Algebra II more than double their chances of graduating from college than kids who do not take advanced algebra.[10] Middle school, and its mastery of algebraic concepts, is quite literally a make-or-break time for kids, prompting the Math Panel to point out, "The sharp fall off in mathematics achievement in the U.S. begins as students reach late middle school, where, for more and more students, algebra course work begins."[11]

Nationwide, more schools are embracing the push for middle school algebra. Gifted specialist Jami Burns says, "I think the curriculum is funneling down now. It used to be that some eighth graders took pre-algebra. Now we're trying to get every eighth grader doing algebra."

We support Algebra I in eighth grade for kids who are ready. But not all are. Eighth grade math teacher Jaime Knox cautions:

> In one part, I think it's a great thing. It's what I did. For the student who is driven and enjoys math, it's great. But there's another part of me that sees the students and watches a lot of the parents push them to be in Algebra I in eighth grade. Because of the new rule that students have to take four math classes in high school, [this practice] can be very difficult for students who struggle with math, especially when they come to their senior year and they're taking AP courses and math is not their strong suit.

So as a parent, it's critical to work closely with teachers, using their feedback and assessments to determine the best math placement for your child. Forging ahead without having the basic skills in place guarantees frustration and discouragement. If kids need more instruction and time to master basic algebra skills, then they ought to get it.

TO READ OR NOT TO READ?

What about reading? Middle schoolers who read well and often fare better academically than those who do not. In fact, research shows that reading frequency is strongly related to reading comprehension and academic achievement. But kids today are reading less: just half of nine-year-olds read every day for fun, and less than a third of thirteen-year-olds are daily readers.[12]

Why does our literary indifference matter? As writer Mark Twain put it long ago, "The man who does not read good books has no advantage over the man who can't read them." This is still true today. Children who don't read regularly for enjoyment don't hone their reading skills.

To be a good writer, one needs to read. A lot. Ultimately, poor readers have fewer options professionally and earn less money than their peers who read competently and voraciously.[13] And nonreaders are less prepared for the world of work. As a report from the National Endowment for the Arts indicates, "Employers now rank reading and writing as top deficiencies in new hires."[14]

National reading scores indicate we have cause for concern. Less than one-third of eighth graders are proficient readers.[15] Boys are particularly at risk. Many parents say their daughters love to read, and, in fact, girls are significantly more likely to read well than boys. Boys, long dominant in math, are losing their edge there as well: girls not only lead boys in reading in every state, but they have also closed the boy-girl math gap.[16]

Fortunately, there's a lot parents can do to encourage reading. For boys, parents should be flexible in reading content. Middle school boys are drawn to books about sports, science fiction, fantasy, or history. Boys like excitement, and as *New York Times* columnist Nicholas Kristof writes, they're mesmerized by books with an adventure or "gross-out" factor: "Indeed, the more books make parents flinch, the more they seem to suck boys in."[17]

What's a sound, attainable reading goal? Parents ought to aim for having kids read at least twenty-five books a year in middle school, recommends the Making Middle Grades Work initiative.[18] To do that, books need to be accessible at home, whether from the bookstore, the school, or the public library—even downloaded onto a portable e-book reader for the digitally inclined.

A RACE TO NOWHERE?

But as we encourage our kids to do their best, we must be careful. As parental anxiety grows—some of us are losing our jobs and struggling financially—we must not displace our worry on to our kids and their school performance.

Kids can crack under too much pressure.

One California mother has lashed out at what she sees as a widespread pressure to achieve—pressure that is costing many American kids their childhoods. Corporate lawyer and mother of three, Vicki Abeles, a newbie filmmaker, channeled her worry over American schooling's grueling pace into a documentary called *Race to Nowhere*. Abeles's was propelled into action several years ago after her twelve-year-old daughter landed in the emergency room with a stress-related illness. Abeles' husband, Doug, an accomplished orthopedic surgeon, says, "It got to the point where my seventh grader had more homework than I did in medical school."[19]

During filming, Devon Marvin, a thirteen-year-old honor roll student in Abeles' California community, committed suicide after receiving a poor grade in math.

In the film's trailer, a curly-haired girl with braces laments, "I can't really remember the last time I had a chance to go in the backyard and just run around." A teen boy says, "School is just so much pressure that every day I would wake up dreading it."

Abeles is angling for systemic change. American kids, she says, are inundated with pressures, but they are unprepared for the world of college and work. In an interview with Katie Couric, Abeles said, "Our competitive performance-oriented culture and education system are creating a generation of kids who are depressed, anxious, and in many cases have checked out altogether. We have such a narrow definition of what a successful young person looks like today."[20]

Has Abeles touched a nerve? We think so. The burnout she references may not be widespread yet—at least not in the middle school years that precede Advanced Placement coursework and college admissions. Most of the families we talked to had children who seemed to be coping well with middle school academics.

But the stress is there, and it's real. One eighth grade boy we interviewed said, "I don't dread school. But there *is* a lot of pressure." A middle school teacher in a highly educated city told us, "The kids are worried about college. You know what I mean? You're twelve! Enjoy being twelve! It's OK if you want to watch cartoons still. It's OK!"

EXPANDING OUR DEFINITION OF SUCCESS

What about that narrow definition of success that Abeles mentions? Not all children are capable of acing their tests and schoolwork. Many kids—even with substantial effort and parental support—won't *ever* earn straight A's or other coveted achievement accolades.

That needs to be OK.

As a parent, you should not mindlessly push your child. You know when your child is working hard and giving it her all. You have a lot to guide you as you form healthy and reasonable expectations of her performance: standardized tests, teacher feedback, your child's level of frustration or ease with homework, and areas of intense personal interest or aptitude.

So encourage and work with the child *you have*. Set realistic guidelines. Understand that school achievement (or the lack thereof) will not render the final judgment on your child's success as a learner.

Isaac Newton, Thomas Edison, and Winston Churchill all turned in subpar performances in school, yet no one questions their intelligence or their valuable contributions to mankind. Churchill, who suffered from a speech impediment, wrote of his time at Harrow School near London, "I was, on the whole, considerably discouraged by my school days." Traditional schooling provided meager opportunities for him to showcase his incisive mind and marvelous memory (although he once won a prize for his 1200-line recitation from the poem collection *Lays of Ancient Rome*).[21] But real-life and international leadership during a seminal time in world history? Now *that* was a different story.

REDEFINING INTELLIGENCE

Both psychologists and educators have suggested we broaden our narrow definition of intelligence. Almost thirty years ago, Harvard psychologist

Howard Gardner proposed the idea of "multiple intelligences." In his later book, *Intelligence Reframed*, Dr. Gardner outlined the multiple facets of intelligence as follows:

- Linguistic intelligence
- Logical-mathematical intelligence
- Musical intelligence
- Bodily-kinesthetic intelligence
- Spatial intelligence
- Interpersonal intelligence
- Intrapersonal intelligence[22]
- Naturalist intelligence and existential intelligence (added later to Gardner's original list)[23]

Those possessing linguistic intelligence are the writers, lawyers, and poets among us, says Gardner. People who possess ample quantities of logical-mathematical intelligence tend to become the mathematicians and scientists. These first two kinds of intelligence, according to Gardner, "are the ones that have typically been valued in school."[24]

But what about the others? They are no less valuable. Dancers, actors, and athletes, writes Gardner, possess high levels of bodily-kinesthetic intelligence, for example, while pilots or architects utilize spatial intelligence.[25]

Do you recognize your child in Gardner's list? You may have a child who possesses marvelous and untapped musical potential, or perhaps you have a future psychologist on your hands who has interpersonal savvy in spades.

Intelligences are not mutually exclusive, of course, and Gardner writes that "human beings possess a range of capacities and potentials—multiple intelligences—that, both individually and in consort, can be put to many productive uses."[26]

How can you help your child achieve his best? Find out where he has a special aptitude and give him lots of opportunities to pursue his gifts.

EARLY WARNING SIGNS

But what about the red flags which signal that are truly struggling in school? How can parents help? Watch sixth grade closely. This is the year when early warning signs are visible and intervention is essential.

Dr. Robert Balfanz, a research scientist at Johns Hopkins University who studies risk factors for dropping out of school, has found that *future dropouts can be identified as early as sixth grade*. Believe it or not, the warning signs are already there.

Dr. Balfanz and his colleagues have found that an early SOS is most worrisome: "Although all distress signals should be taken seriously in the middle grades, schools should pay special attention to students who send a signal in 6th grade. The earlier a student first sends a signal, the greater the risk that he or she will drop out of school."[27]

Dr. Balfanz's study of fourteen thousand students in Philadelphia, Pennsylvania, found that sixth graders with just *one* of the following distress signals had "at least a three in four chance" of dropping out when they reached high school. Here are the four areas he says parents and teachers should monitor:

- A final grade of F in mathematics
- A final grade of F in English
- Attendance below 80 percent for the year
- A final "unsatisfactory" behavior mark in at least one class[28]

Watching these areas closely gives parents and teachers powerful indicators about which kids are at elevated risk. Once problem areas are identified, schools and parents can act; Dr. Balfanz recommends steps such as schoolwide attendance programs or attendance contracts that students sign, or for more entrenched problems, targeted help from a team of school professionals or social services.[29]

PARENTAL TOUGH LOVE

What about the middle schooler without learning issues? Parents might need to step back and allow children to make mistakes along the way. Ultimately, kids need to own their academic successes and failures themselves.

Warren Gould views the middle school years as a time when kids should be allowed to bruise their knees. He says:

> It's always really difficult when the parent cares more about the academics than a student does. And I've seen plenty of instances of a parent working really hard to keep a student organized, keeping track of their assignments—lots of hair pulling going on at home. And it sets up an unhealthy relationship between the parent and the child—a kind of enabling that just delays the reality check, the inevitable.
>
> I think the middle school years are the perfect time for a little parental tough love and to say, "We're going to set up some systems for you. I'm not going to completely remove myself from this, but in partnership with the school, we're going to give you a fairly low safety net. And if you aren't doing well, how you feel when you aren't doing well will be instructive for you."
>
> So let's learn *now* what it means to have good study habits and why that's important, rather than still trying to pull the child up the mountain when he gets to ninth or tenth grade.

THE JOY OF LEARNING

As we wrap up this chapter on academics, we want to take a step back and look at real achievement. Is it a child who outguns his peers on every academic measure? Some parents would say so. But we would argue that academic success is achieved when a child loves learning, is intellectually curious, and has a vibrant imagination. Maybe he gets A's. Maybe he doesn't.

But we shouldn't allow a fear of college admissions or career success to define our view of what constitutes a sound education. These things matter. But they aren't everything.

To learn well, kids need downtime. They need time *every day* just to be. In fact, boredom may be just the catalyst they need to pen a poem, write a story, or paint a picture.

Creativity cannot flourish in a life with no fallow time.

Lazy, rainy days in the attic spent with his brother Warnie, prompted C. S. Lewis to write stories about talking animals who inhabited the imaginary land of Boxen. The Boxen tales were the precursors to the enormously popular *Narnia* series. Dr. Art Lindsley, a senior fellow at the C. S. Lewis Institute, writes of Lewis's childhood:

> C. S. Lewis' earliest memories involve "endless books" in the study, dining room, cloakroom, in the bedrooms, and piled as high as his shoulder in the attic. On the often-dreary days, time would be spent in reading and in imaginative games involving "dressed animals" and "knights in armor." These were the subjects of his first novel, *Boxen*, written at the age of twelve.[30]

This twelve-year-old novelist wasn't building his resumé as he shuttled breathlessly from one activity to the next. Instead, as he whiled away hours in the attic, he mused, imagined, and learned.

And that, we would argue, is what academic success is really about.

PARENT TIPS

Protect sleep. Pediatricians indicate that children in the middle school age range need nine to nine and a half hours of sleep per night. Try to make sure your child hits this mark most of the time.

Create a quiet zone. Establish a quiet workplace without noise or other distractions so children can complete homework undisturbed.

Become an advocate. If your child is spending more than three hours per night on homework, request a meeting with the teacher and advocate for assignments that respect the "ten-minute rule."

Safeguard weeknights. Protect evening time during the week so children can be home, completing homework and studying for tests.

Emphasize effort, not smarts. Praise your child's work ethic, not intelligence.

Take time for twenty-five. Make sure your child has regular access to books, reading at least twenty-five per year.

Set high but reasonable expectations. Expect the best from your child. But work with the child you have; don't force her to be someone she can't possibly be.

ID intelligence. Identify what your child is good at, and give him many chances to hone skills in this area.

Stay involved. While kids should take the lead in interfacing with teachers when they have problems or issues, parents need to stay in the loop as well. Show up for parent night, schedule periodic parent-teacher conferences, and help out at school.

Intervene early. If your child's performance starts to slide, find out why quickly. Don't wait until failure is deeply entrenched to take action.

Go high-tech. Invest in a keyboarding or computer skills class. If schools do not provide computer classes, investigate the local public library; many provide such courses for free.

Chapter Six

WHERE'S
THE FIRE?

"The time to relax is when you don't have time for it."

—Sydney J. Harris, American journalist

When my daughter Kristen's children were under five, I was visiting her one day when she became super stressed about her day's agenda. Having raised Kristen and Holly in a pretty relaxed manner, I asked her, "Where's the fire?" She gave me a startled look, thought for a moment, and laughed. Soon some of her friends were asking each other, "Where's the fire?" Since then, I've noticed that many women in their thirties and forties are in constant motion. One woman said that she found herself running after disembarking from the metro in Washington DC on her morning commute. Everyone around her was racing, so she did too. Then she asked herself, "Why am I running? I have plenty of time to get to work." Because their lives are so fragmented, women tell me they have no free time for themselves or the niceties of friendship. As a psychologist, I know that women who *do not replenish their souls at the well of female friendship can feel pretty empty inside. And then there's the man in the family, who may work twelve hours a day, help out with the kids at night, and play chauffeur, coach, and Boy Scout leader on the weekends. When do dads find respite and rest?*

—Brenda

Living in the Triangle region of North Carolina, an area which has more PhD's than most of America, we have observed that dual-income parents of school-aged children live as if they were fleeing a house on fire. Juggling two jobs, music lessons, church activities, food shopping, and multiple after-school sports, these parents often look addled and stressed. When we talk to mothers of middle schoolers and teens at church as we women huddle together, nursing our cups of morning joe, we hear anxiety rippling through their voices as they recount their crammed, jammed schedules—their out-of-control lives.

And it's not just mothers in the workplace who live on the run; mothers at home have been on the go ever since the Mommy Wars ended in the mid-nineties. They volunteer, run the PTA, go to book clubs, attend Bible studies—all good activities—and live in their cars until it's time to collect kids after school. Then they wait in the carpool line chatting on their cell phones, planning for the days to come. Then it's on to myriad lessons and an errand or two. The day is far spent when the weary American family finally straggles home.

We wonder if all this frenetic activity is not an escape from loneliness—after all, nobody's home in America's neighborhoods—and an attempt to grasp at self-worth in a culture that only values the workplace. Raising children, after all, is a trivial job that just about anybody can do, right?

Tell that to a psychologist.

TOO BUSY FOR CHILDHOOD

What is the impact on the children who may long to come home after school and play with friends in the neighborhood, but whose lives are so heavily scheduled that when mom arrives in the driveway, there's little or no time left in the day? Play, as the famous psychologist Piaget said, is the work of childhood. Our children are forgetting how to interact casually with friends and instead turn to solo activities, like gaming, social networking, or television, while mom cobbles together a fast-food meal of frozen pizza and bagged salad. But something precious is quietly vanishing in all this frenetic activity: not only are parents losing touch with their children because their lives are, simply put, crazy, but women are missing out on the healing power of friendship. Men are too. Moreover, children are failing to experience childhood. That's a whale of a lot to lose.

LIFE WITHOUT MARGINS

Dr. Richard Swenson, author of *Margin,* contends that Americans are currently living lives without margins. What does he mean by that? He describes a marginless life as one filled with fatigue, hurry, anxiety: he says it is a "disease of the new millennium."[1] This physician, who blames "modernity" or "progress" for the increased stress in our lives, has seen patients for years who come complaining about symptoms that result from their stressful lives. Swenson chronicles *psychological symptoms* (depression, anxiety, difficulty making decisions, anger, hostility), *physical symptoms* (rapid pulse, increased blood pressure, ulcers, headaches, weight change, insomnia), *behavioral changes* (bossiness, irritability, withdrawal, changes in sexual desire, compulsive behaviors), and the end result, *burnout.* Burnout simply means that when our loads get too heavy and life overwhelms us, we begin to shut down: we dread going to work; we feel we're on a treadmill and can't get off, we stop caring.[2] About anything.

Have we described you? We hear from people that daily stress is a given. A university physician talked about how the stress of having to see too many patients per hour spilled over into her relationship with her daughter. She simply couldn't switch off her tension and anxiety when she walked in the door at night. A mother at home spoke to us about the stress of driving her children to all of their after-school activities and said that she did not have time for a one-on-one conversation with each of her three children often—once a month at most. Her middle school daughter complained about this, but the mother had not yet addressed the child's need for intimacy.

NATIONAL STRESS

Of course, life without margins has worsened because of the Great Recession of 2008, with its far-reaching fallout. For many families across America, there's a real fire blazing. And in the words of the 1983 musical cult classic by the one-hit wonders, the Talking Heads, this one's "burning down the house." Currently, Americans have to deal with enormous outside pressures and stresses—job losses, the drop in housing prices, major financial setbacks and hits to their 401(k) retirement plans, foreclosures, and the soaring prices of food and gas. All are taxing our ability to cope, to pay bills, and to survive.

Add to this mix the fact that the marketplace has experienced an exponential change. The workplace has become a country without borders. With laptops and smartphones demanding a response around the clock, there is precious little time for the demands and joys of family life. It is now possible to live in San Diego and manage computer experts in Bangalore or London. Not only is it possible; increasingly, it is the norm.

Said one mother of a middle schooler, "When I was growing up, my dad put in his forty hours at the office and arrived home for dinner at 5:30 P.M. Now the workplace requires that you work until the job is done. My husband may have a conference call at 11 P.M. because he has clients on the other side of the world. Not only is this intrusion disruptive to any kind of family life, it's incredibly stressful."

Technology, like Wall Street, never sleeps.

As a consequence, we are feeling the effects of stress in all areas of our physical and emotional health, in our marriages, and in our relationships with our children.

TOXIC DIET

Moreover, we're eating a diet that's toxic for us and our children. Instead of cooking real, unprocessed food loaded with nutrition, we're feeding ourselves an artery-clogging diet and setting our kids up for poor heart health and obesity. If you don't believe us, just watch the movies *Super Size Me* or *Fast Food Nation*. Are you aware that in 1970 Americans spent about $6 billion on fast food, and in 2001 the figure rose to $110 billion dollars? We now spend more on fast food than we do on higher education.[3]

Just look at what has happened to the family breakfast. According to Sharon Hwang in the 1700s, breakfast consisted of thick slices of bacon, stewed antelope steak, cornmeal or bread, and coffee.[4] In the 1800s, as American wealth increased, breakfast consisted of hearty meats (ham, beef, bacon, sausage, or chicken), along with hot breads and even gravy. In the late 1900s, with both parents increasingly in the workforce, speed and convenience became the name of the game, so boxed cereals, fast food, and boxed pastries became the norm.[5] Now we see ads on television of kids sitting down (without grownups around) to munch frosted Pop-Tarts before they rush off to school just as their blood sugar soars.

Is it any wonder that they are hyperactive and overweight?

Giving up unprocessed, real food that takes time to prepare is just one evidence of the increasing stress in American homes. In addition, many of us struggle with sleepless nights, excess pounds, and joylessness.

We are a stressed-out nation. In August of 2010, the APA conducted an online survey of 1,134 adults, ages eighteen and older, including one hundred parents of children ages eight to seventeen. The APA also surveyed another 937 parents of children in this age range, and a Youth Query survey was conducted online for 1,136 young people ages eight to seventeen.[6] Respondents

(76 percent) said they were stressed about money, work (70 percent), and the economy (65 percent).

Parents also reported that family responsibilities were a major stressor. So why don't parents simply change their behavior? According to the survey, most said that lack of willpower and time constraints undermined their ability to make important lifestyle changes.

THE KIDS AREN'T ALRIGHT

While the majority of parents in the APA survey did not believe their children were affected by their stress, data proved otherwise. Nearly three-fourths of the parents of teens and tweens said their stress had little or no impact on their children; yet 91 percent of the children said they were quite aware of their parents' stress. 34 percent of the children said they knew their parents were stressed when they yelled.[7]

"Even though children know when their parents are stressed and admit that it directly affects them, parents are grossly underestimating the impact that their stress is having on their children," states psychologist Katherine C. Nordal, PhD, the APA's executive director for professional practice. She adds, "It's critical that parents communicate with their children about how to identify stress triggers and manage stress in healthy ways while they're young and still developing behavioral patterns. If children don't learn these lessons early on, it could significantly impact their physical health and emotional well-being down the road, especially as they become adults."[8]

While parents can be de-stressors for their children, the APA survey found that they are not getting the job done and that stress is having a profound effect on children's health. Currently one-third of American children are overweight. These overweight children said they worried a great deal as opposed to children of normal weight (31 percent vs. 14 percent). Moreover, children who believed they were overweight were more likely to say that their parents were often or always stressed (39 vs. 30 percent). And overweight children were also more likely to report health problems: trouble falling asleep, headaches, eating too much or too little, feeling angry, or getting into fights—all behaviors related to stress. Overweight children admitted they used food to make themselves feel better when they were worried or stressed.[9]

One famous psychologist who knows how to measure the impact of marital and family stress on kids is Dr. John Gottman at the University of Washington. This is what he says about how stress affects kids:

> We found that we could actually measure how parents were getting along in two ways. We could either ask them how happy they were— how much conflict they were having—or we could take a 24-hour urine sample from their kids and measure how many stress hormones, particularly adrenaline, were getting secreted in the children's bodies.
>
> So if you're fighting, your kids are secreting adrenaline. And if they're secreting adrenaline because they're stressed out, one of the things that happens to them is that the first and most sensitive system to reflect this stress is the attentional system—the kid's ability to focus attention, the kid's ability to shift attention when they want to, and the kid's ability to sustain attention. And part of what we're seeing in all of this diagnosis of hyperactivity is, in part, a reflection of increased family stress, increased stress between parents. So the attentional system is really a very sensitive indicator of whether kids are stressed out.[10]

Have you or your child's pediatrician ever thought that your child's hyperactivity could be related to marital stress?

WHAT IF YOU LOSE YOUR JOB?

What if your worst fears are realized and you or your spouse loses a job? Even then, you still have lots of choices in how you deal with this crisis. You can choose whether you stay in panic mode (of course, you will panic initially) or whether you confront your predicament with pluck and courage. Losing a job can induce feelings of failure and a temporary loss of identity. You are no longer a manager, a teacher, or an executive. You have joined the ranks of the unemployed.

Losing a job can cause you to ask: What went wrong? Am I good enough? Am I capable? It also arouses fear that you won't find another job for some time, that the money will run out, and that you may lose your home. It doesn't help that the evening news shows middle-class people in bread lines, and newspaper headlines remind us of current unemployment figures.

If this happens, the first major antidote to fear and inner terror is to realize you are not alone in your current situation. If you believe in an infinite, personal God who loves you, and if you believe that he cares about all aspects of your life, then you can give your anxieties to him and believe he will pull you through.

It's hard not knowing how you're going to pay your bills. But it's also an opportunity for God to prove himself faithful. I have had a front-row seat in watching God's provision for my family. My husband Greg was out of work for a couple of months in 2010.

We had no small amount of fear and trepidation about what could happen. But you know what we learned? Living on God's dime can be kind of exciting. Sure, it was stressful. But we saw God come through for us in unexpected ways. Our first weekend of unemployment, my sister gave us a coupon to dine out at a Durham restaurant. Another friend passed on four tickets to a Durham Bulls baseball game. And we received three hundred dollars in gift cards to Amazon.com—all tangible evidence of the care of God and others.

Sometimes late at night, I wondered if we would lose our house. I knew we wouldn't last on our savings account for many months. But the bills got paid—somehow. On numerous occasions, I went to the mailbox only to find gifts of serendipitous generosity—from my father and stepmother, from my mother-in-law, and from other sources. My mother and stepfather kept my children in shoes and clothes, met multiple other needs, and took us on our only vacation during a hot, hard summer. And my sister paid Katie's monthly dues at a swim club so she could train weekly.

God encouraged me with Scripture—even on a car's license plate on a particularly dark day: JER 3227. I had my Bible on the seat next to me at the stoplight and looked up Jeremiah 32:27: "I am the Lord, the God of all mankind. Is anything too hard for me?"

Surely by now I know the answer to that.

Greg did find another position at a wonderful company. One week later, the company implemented an across-the-board hiring freeze. How's that for God's perfect timing?

—Kristen

KIDS ARE LIKE SPONGES

We need to remember that our children are like sponges: they hear our words, they register our tone of voice, and they see our body language—the grim, worried look, the far-off gaze, the rigid posture. They do not have the life experience or cognitive capacity to understand situations like we do, but they pick up a lot. They are barometers in gauging our moods, our stresses, and our emotional availability; they know when they can come to us with their anxieties or when they cannot because we are lost in our own world of worry.

How can you help your child deal with the stresses in her life? One single mom whose girls have had to cope with divorce, joint custody, and middle school, told us that since she works full-time, she always makes time to have one-on-one conversations with her three daughters during the days they are with her. When they were young, she started spending ten minutes alone with each child, plus "tuck in" time. Now that they are older, she takes a walk with each child along the pathway behind her home.

HOMEGROWN STRESS

One day as I drove her home from school, Katie said to me, "Mimi, what if Daddy doesn't find a job and we lose our home? What if we become hobos?"

Surprised and saddened that Katie was afraid of homelessness, I said, "Katie Bee, as long as Papa and I are alive, you can always come and live with us."

That seemed to comfort her as we continued driving along, listening to music on the Disney Channel and talking of other things. Then about a week later, she and Austin came to our house to spend the night so their parents could have some time together. About an hour after she went to bed, I looked in on her to see if she was asleep. Katie lifted her head and said, "Mimi?"

"Yes," I responded.

"I can't go to sleep."

I went into the bedroom, sat down, and asked Katie if something was bothering her.

"Mimi," she said. "Where would we all sleep if we came to live with you? Your house only has three bedrooms."

Aware that she had given my offer some thought, I assured her that we could not only turn Papa's office into a bedroom for Austin, but the playroom could be converted into her family's living room.

Silent for some moments, Katie said quietly, "Mimi, I know you say we can come and live with you, but would you want us to come and live with you?"

Deeply moved, I stroked her arm and said quietly, "Katie, I would love for you and your family to live with us." And I meant it.

Hearing that, sweet Katie let out a long sigh, rolled over and quickly went to sleep.

—Brenda (aka Mimi)

DEALING WITH STRESS

Whatever the stresses in your life—a new job, a lost job, insufficient funds, divorce, marital conflict, health issues, and/or a lack of margin—it is imperative that you find a way to handle your stress without allowing it to damage your mental health or hurt your children.

When patients come to me with their complaints and very real stressors, I usually ask them a question I learned from immersion in William Glasser's Reality Therapy at Johns Hopkins: Is what you're doing helping or hurting you?[11] A central premise of Reality Therapy is that all of us make choices all the time whether we're aware of this or not, and often we don't like the consequences of our choices. Or our choices get us into trouble.

To date, I have never had a patient tell me her choices were helping her. After the client says, usually without hesitation, that her choices have produced real hurt in her life, I ask the next question: What new choice would you like to make? It is a principle of Reality Therapy that we are capable of changing our lives, one small choice at a time. It is not required that we change our whole lives at once, but that we make small, incremental changes that create a new lifestyle and new perceptions over time.[12]

—Brenda

So we want to ask you: Are your life choices helping or hurting you? Life is all about choices. And one key choice is how we spend our time. We are allotted the same amount of time each day. If we spend our time working, running, vegging in front of the television or computer, or texting on our phones, we may realize one day that we have lost something precious—our children's childhood. While we were frenetically running, our kids quietly tiptoed out of the house and left childhood behind. Their once clamorous voices have fallen silent.

They have grown up and gone.

LIFE WITH MARGINS

It doesn't have to be this way.

When Dr. Richard Swenson felt that his marginless life as a physician exacted too high a personal price, he made a drastic decision. He decided, after two years of serious thought and discussion with his stay-at-home wife, to work only three days a week.[13] Swenson, who said that he practiced in a great community, enjoyed his colleagues, had never been sued, and had a loving family, grateful patients, and "a growing faith," felt he had what he wanted from life except for margin. He eventually left his academic and clinical work at the University of Wisconsin to pursue the "exploration of cultural medicine and world system problems." He and his family became avid travelers, working from locations around the world.

"I lived sixteen years without margin: college, medical school, residency, and practice. And since the decision to cut back my involvement in medicine, I have lived several decades with margin. *I can say with certainty that if margin were taken away from me now, I would beg shamelessly to get it back.*"[14]

What would your life look like if you made new choices? What kind of gift would that be for your child—to know you had time to relax together, time to be? If your current choices aren't working, you can create new ones. Why do this? These middle school years are perhaps your last chance to profoundly shape and influence your child.

YOUR BEST AND LAST CHANCE TO INFLUENCE

Rita Callahan, a petite, attractive mother of thirteen who lives in northern Virginia, says she believes that middle school is the last time kids will be so dependent on their parents. She states:

> In middle school, you have a great opportunity to take a child through every situation that will come into their lives in high school. The child is still dependent. If you miss this opportunity in middle school, you really miss it. Once they hit high school, they're so busy and they drive and there are so many activities, that you're not their primary go-to person. So I really use that time when they get in the car after school when they tell me about their day, to say this is why we do things. I try to guide them—especially with the boy issues. That's when they see how you're going to react. If you yell at them, they keep things from you. And I don't want that in high school. I want them to be more open.

LET'S HEAR IT FOR THE FAMILY DINNER

In addition to reconnecting with your child after school, you can use the family dinner as a uniquely effective de-stressor in your family's life. And research shows it is a powerful influence on whether or not your child will use drugs (see Chapter Nine). The shared, daily family meal is important because it is perhaps the only time the whole family comes together in a twenty-four-hour period. The experience of eating with parents provides an anchor in your child's life; it keeps him from feeling isolated and alone.

One of the most impressive mothers we interviewed for this book says that family dinners have been nonnegotiable in her home for years. Nilda Melendez, whom you have met before, grew up in an intact family in Puerto Rico, and is the mother of nine children, ranging in age from eight to twenty-four years. A mother at home, Nilda, whose husband works for the Department of Defense in Washington DC, says that family dinners occur daily, whether they have to wait until 9 P.M. for everyone to assemble (usually only in summer) or until 7 P.M. during the school year.

"This time is sacred," says Nilda. "That's when my husband and I ask, 'How was your day?' or 'How was that test?' Our children talk and talk and talk. We talk about politics, about what's going on in the world," says this woman who admitted that her children have stayed strong, making wise choices about drugs, alcohol, and premarital sex.

A PERSONAL NOTE

I'd like to end this chapter on a personal note. Early in our marriage, Don lost his job and was unemployed for four long months in the dead of winter. Christmas was bleak that year. The girls got any money we had, and we charged our fifty-dollar gifts for each other.

Our meager savings account was soon emptied, and we felt stressed to the max. Don, a lawyer who had left his job at Boeing in Seattle after the company failed to reward him for his ace-negotiation of a 2.7-billion-dollar contract, had tried diligently to find another job in Asheville, North Carolina. To no avail. One day, when we were at the end of our resources, Don had lunch with the vice president of one of the local banks. I shall always remember his face when the vice president dropped him off at our home. Without saying a word, Don let me know that he hadn't gotten the job. As we walked in the house, I said, "What will we do now?"

Don replied, "There's only one thing to do. Call Boeing." It was hard for him to swallow his pride, pick up the phone, and call his former boss, Dale. But we were desperate. Before he dialed the number, Don and I prayed and asked God for a positive outcome. We had about one hundred dollars in the bank. Dale was not only warm and friendly, but he asked Don if he could be in the office on Monday. It was now late Friday afternoon. Don said he could, but with real emotion in his voice, he asked Dale for airfare.

Truth was, we couldn't afford to pay for his flight to New Jersey. After a brief silence, Dale said, "I'll have a ticket waiting for you at the airport."

That was when Don and I learned to believe God when he says that he will never abandon us, leave us, or forsake us, but will provide for us like a father.

Funny thing, Holly and Kristen do not remember that time as particularly stressful.

—Brenda

PARENT TIPS

Make sure you and your spouse have a regular date night to focus on the marital relationship. Make time for each other and keep that time sacrosanct.

If you are a single parent, go out with the girls, your buddies, or on a date. You need time to just be you.

Have a weekly family time and take turns choosing the activity. Play basketball, board games, or go on outings.

Spend more evenings at home. Get more sleep. Rediscover downtime and relaxed time. Learn to say no to activities that will be there when the kids are older and need you less.

Slash expenses and learn to live on less. As Dr. Phil says, "There are no fixed expenses."

Finally, get control of your life. Don't allow your family to be buffeted by cultural forces and other people's expectations. Decide what gives you a less stressful, higher quality life. And practice saying "no." You are in a special season of life with your middle schooler, and these years will soon be gone forever. Make them memorable.

Where's the fire in your family's life? You have just put it out.

Chapter Seven

HOME INVASION, PART ONE— MOBILE PHONES AND GAMING

"Communication and socialization in our kids' world is increasingly moving from face-to-face to face-to-cyberspace."

—**James Steyer**, CEO of Common Sense Media

Six-thirty on a Monday morning: flailing adolescent hands, heavy with sleep, reach out to silence the incessant beeping of the alarm. What's next on the agenda for the just-awakened modern middle schooler? Not orange juice and oatmeal. For many a technologically equipped teen, the day begins with a bleary-eyed interface with friends, made possible by the trappings of technology. In fact, some kids never disconnected at all, instead passing a fitful night of slumber punctuated by the sound of an incoming text.

If today's tweens and teens, dubbed "digital natives," aren't texting, they're gaming, posting comments on social networking sites, or chatting with friends online—all in a grammatically challenged techno-vernacular that only a fellow native can decode.

In little more than a decade, technology has reconfigured childhood.
Some of the changes technology has ushered in are wonderfully enriching
and useful; others are not. Successfully balancing this duality is a challenge
that *every* middle school parent we have talked to—from the technophile who
feverishly awaits the latest app to the technologically averse Luddite who
hasn't checked e-mail in months—must confront.

IT'S A HOME INVASION

In this, the digital age, technology—and the media it pipes into kids' lives—is
everywhere. For many parents, it *feels* like a "full-blown home invasion," says
Faith Burnham, a pastor's wife and mother of two.

As the parent of a modern middle schooler, you are bombarded daily by
decisions about technology. What should you buy for your child? When to
buy it? How should you restrict content? Time? Texting? Applications? And
how can you, as a parent, already pressed in by the demands of contemporary
culture, stay abreast of technology that is constantly evolving?

Every nanosecond, it seems, something new and wonderful hits the
market. Laptops. Smartphones. Digital cameras. Tablets. Gaming devices.
And your child needs them. Now! Well, actually, yesterday. For this generation of parents—digital "immigrants" who navigated middle school without
computers and cell phones, and whose adolescent gaming prowess hinged on
mastering the single-button Atari joystick—it's a lot to take in.

If you're feeling overwhelmed, you're not alone. Many parents tell us
they are running as fast as they can, but are always playing catch-up. Middle
school parents also worry about the downside of constant connectivity.
Susan Johnson, mother to seventh grade Julie and eighth grade Sean, worries, "Things have changed so much for our kids. Because of technology,
kids never have a break from their peers." Gone are the days when kids
would unwind and disengage from peers at the end of the day. Virtual bonds
of technology mean many middle schoolers stay connected with friends
around the clock, providing endless opportunities to rehash the day's events.

Middle schoolers today are coming of age in a culture more saturated with digital distractions than ever before. But one thing hasn't changed: As the parent, *you* are still the gatekeeper for your child. Even in this digital age, *you* get to decide what flows in and out of the walls of your home. You *can* erect strong, sturdy walls to protect your child.

Know this, too: technological trends will change with the tides. Remember the early cell phones that looked like bricks and weighed as much? The one-time domination of Friendster and MySpace? Or when You've Got Mail not only served as a cultural touchstone, but also signified the millions of users connected to their AOL e-mail accounts? Despite the ever-shifting panorama of technological innovation, the principles of good parenting endure.

Before we dive in, it's helpful to know this: Just how pervasive is media in kids' lives?

MEDIA: THE OTHER PARENT

Survey research from the Kaiser Family Foundation shows American children ages eight to eighteen now spend an average of seven and a half hours per day with media from devices such as cell phones, iPods or MP3 players, computers, and television.[1] Middle schoolers—kids in the eleven to fourteen age range—are the heaviest users of all, averaging almost nine hours per day in media use.[2] For all but the sleepiest of teen and tweenie sack rats, this is as much time as they spend in bed! These shocking findings prompted the Kaiser Family Foundation to dub media "the other parent" because of the extensive influence it now exerts over children's lives.[3]

Many kids are multitasking maestros, flipping back and forth between different kinds of media simultaneously. They use their phones to text their friends while they play video games or watch television. Or they listen to music on an MP3 player while they post comments on their Facebook wall. When such "media multitasking" is totaled, it drives kids' daily media consumption up to almost eleven hours.[4] That's nearly half of the hours in the day and clearly most of the time those adolescent eyes are open—unless, of course, we factor in the time they're rolling those orbs at mom and dad!

What about rules? While some parents set clear guidelines, many do not. Generally speaking, parents are more inclined to set rules about *what* children watch or play than they are about *how much time* they spend doing it. In fact, only about a third of kids had any rules about the amount of time they could devote to watching TV, using the computer, or playing video games.[5]

MOBILE MIDDLE SCHOOLERS

How have we gotten to a place of media saturation? Part of the reason is that mobile devices are so readily available now, and they're more affordable than ever. To tweens and teens, handheld gadgets have become must-have accessories—a social status symbol that they believe cements their coolness. Once acquired, mobile devices travel with kids everywhere—to school, to soccer practice, to a friend's house, to the bathroom, and even to bed. Say Kaiser's researchers:

> The story of media in young people's lives today is primarily a story of technology facilitating increased consumption. The mobile and online media revolutions have arrived in the lives—and the pockets—of American youth. Try waking a teenager in the morning, and the odds are good that you'll find a cell phone tucked under their pillow—the last thing they touch before falling asleep and the first thing they reach for upon waking.[6]

So vaunted is the cell phone that for many teens it has become their most cherished possession. Data show some "teens consider the loss of a cell phone more dire than the loss of an internal organ."[7] Can you believe that? Phones have become an antidote to adolescent boredom. They are a go-to prop, filling awkward silences as kids wait for rides. (Any mama sleuth who patrols the parking lot after middle school lets out knows the drill: doors open, phones out.) Kids see phones as a way to fit in and be like everyone else. Truly they are objects of adoration—and sometimes grooming. We've even seen a middle schooler lick her phone!

The mobile love affair generally begins in early adolescence; it is during middle school that most kids acquire a cell phone. More than two-thirds of middle schoolers (eleven- to fourteen-year-olds) now own mobile phones.[8] And phone ownership is now trending even younger. Many eight-year-olds now own cell phones; some get phones as young as second grade.

The trend for children to acquire cell phones at ever-younger ages dovetails with the move many families are making to ditch landlines completely. The latest data from the Centers for Disease Control indicate that more than *one out of five* U.S. households do not even have a landline and use mobile phones exclusively.[9]

PARENTAL SUPERVISION AND CELL PHONES

Once kids have their phones, parents vary widely in their approaches to supervision. Some parents tell us they allow their kids unlimited access. Other parents force kids to disconnect, particularly at bedtime. Some allow texting; others do not.

Susan Johnson tells us she is emphatic about monitoring her children's cell phone usage. "Both of my kids' cell phones have parental controls," she affirms. "Their phones are shut down at 8 P.M. and turn on at 7 A.M. During that time, they can call 911 and mom and dad. Those are the only numbers allowed. The charger is in a closet in the playroom," strategically chosen for its location away from slumbering teens.

A sizeable minority of middle school parents are postponing the purchase of a cell phone altogether. Lisa Nagle, a vivacious mom to seventh and eighth grade girls in South Bend, Indiana, has traveled the globe with her family, so her girls are unfettered by the boundaries of geography. But they still don't have cell phones. "At this point," she says, "they don't really need them."

Lisa may change her mind in the future, "as a safety issue so we could get in touch with the girls." But for now, she is intent on waiting until they are older. Another mother told us she and her husband have decided their seventh grade daughter will have to wait: "There are very few places she goes when one of us is not there. That could change, but there would be a lot of limitations on it—no texting. I just don't even want to start *that*!"

CELL PHONES FOR SAFETY

Safety is the key reason parents purchase phones for their kids in the first place. Parents want to be able to reach their children on the spur of the moment, whenever they are apart. Almost all parents (98 percent) of teen cell phone owners say "a major reason their child has the phone is that they can be in touch no matter where the teen is."[10] One mother-father duo whose fourteen-year-old daughter babysits a lot told us they purchased a cell phone in part to be able to reach her. Some of their daughter's babysitting clients had dispensed with landlines altogether, making staying in touch more difficult.

The safety issue rings true to Carla, who says her protective husband, Sam, first bought their daughter Abby a cell phone in third grade. It was a stripped-down version—one, she says, that only dialed about three numbers. Several years later, in sixth grade, Abby got her first real phone. Carla says, "It has just gone crazy from there. My husband bought it because he wanted to text her and get in touch with her. But I was not happy."

Now in eighth grade, Abby has her phone "all the time, unless she's in trouble," says Carla. She has lost phone privileges a number of times, when she was "inappropriate or not communicating well with us. But she is very unhappy without her phone. She'll pull out all the stops and use the guilt card, particularly the social one."

When she has had her phone taken away, Abby says to her parents, "You're making me socially isolated, and I'm not going to have any friends." Abby is not alone in attributing social cachet and power to her phone; kids see huge social implications for cell phone ownership. One set of parents we interviewed recently purchased a smartphone for their seventh grade son, telling us, "He feels really cool about it."

TETHERED TO TEXTING

Once they go mobile, how do kids use their phones? If your child has one, you already know: it's the texting they love. Unlike parents who generally favor voice communication, middle schoolers let their fingers do the talking. And are they ever busy! Some teens become so habituated to texting behavior they find it hard to stop—even for sleep.

> Jackie Ferrara is addicted to texting. This summer, night after night, the lanky 14-year-old texted with friends for hours on end, sometimes not going to sleep until well after the sun was up. She'd interrupt her evening showers to check for messages, and at night she'd lie in bed with her phone pressed against her thigh to make sure she'd be alerted to any new messages.[11]

Jackie's case, chronicled in The *New Jersey Star-Ledger*, may seem extreme—she "sends and receives up to 10,000 text messages a month."[12] But actually, she's in good company. One-half of teen texters aged twelve to seventeen send at least fifty texts daily; one-third send more than one hundred texts each day; and 15 percent exceed two hundred texts a day.[13]

Which means, almost half of teen texters are sending an incredible three thousand to six thousand texts per month.

When confronted with this statistic, one parent of four children—three of whom own cell phones—nods knowingly and affirms, "That sounds about right."

For middle school girls, texting is a virtual lifeline to friends—even more than it is for boys. This will come as little surprise to mothers of teen girls, many of whom wonder if the phone is an electronic appendage. Girls in seventh to twelfth grades spend almost two hours each day with their fingers glued to mobile keyboards, texting away, while boys spend about forty-five minutes less than that texting in a typical day.[14]

How are parents handling kids who are tethered to texting? Some give them free rein. Carla says she and her husband Sam were "naïve" when they got a phone for Abby. She notes, "We signed up for the basic plan that we both had. Neither one of us texted much. Well, when we got the first bill we flipped out at how expensive it was because of all of the texting. And so we immediately switched to an unlimited texting plan." Carla doesn't know how many texts Abby sends per month, but says, "I'm sure it's high." Does she check Abby's texts? "No," sighs Carla, "but I question the wisdom of that."

Although generally not text-aholics like girls, boys can also get sucked into excessive texting. One father told us his son went crazy when he first got a cell phone in eighth grade. After he and his wife received their first phone bill (they had not yet signed up for an unlimited texting plan), he called the provider to ask for a printout. His son, they learned, was texting incessantly with a girl; the two had exchanged some six hundred text messages over a period of a few days. Their dialogue, said this father, consisted mostly of one-liners. "It was ridiculous: What you doing? Nothing. What's up? Nothing. It was meaningless." Their son soon wised up and became more temperate in his texting.

SLEEPLESS IN TEXTING LAND

What about after hours? Researchers are finding, to their dismay, that some tween and teen cell phone owners don't disconnect even for sleep. Ongoing sleep research at John F. Kennedy Medical Center's New Jersey Neuroscience Institute has revealed that such "overnight hypertexting" is insidious, harmful—and common.[15] Jackie Ferrara, the teen texting addict referenced in the last section, is a patient at the JFK Medical Center, driven to seek help for migraine headaches.

Dr. Peter Polos, one of the sleep medicine doctors conducting research, says, "Mobile phone use after lights out is very prevalent among adolescents. Its use is related to increased levels of tiredness. There is no safe dose and no safe time for using the mobile phone for text messaging or for calling after lights out."[16]

Dr. Polos and his research partner, pediatric neurologist Dr. Mike Seyffert, have found that some teens are texting for hours after they go to bed at night. Some of these nocturnal texters are little tykes as young as eight. That's a big problem, because as these early behaviors become ingrained, they become deeply entrenched—harder and harder to change. Of these texting aficionados, Dr. Seyffert says, "In the first year of college, they are flunking out because they can't separate themselves from the technology."[17]

His remedy? It's pretty basic: "Throw the phones away, turn the computers off, get the televisions out of the room, and let our kids sleep."[18]

HANG UP AND LIVE

Throw the phones away? Seriously? We know from interviews, as well as survey data, that many middle school parents have already purchased phones for their children. In fact, many of you reading this chapter have made that decision and are now looking for guidance. Others of you are seriously contemplating a cell phone purchase for your child. And some of you have decided to wait—for now.

Where do we stand? We believe providing a middle schooler with a cell phone is *crazy*!

It is enormously time-consuming for parents to provide the appropriate and necessary oversight to monitor a tween or early teen cell phone user. We also believe putting a cell phone in the hands of an impulsive middle schooler is potentially harmful. (We'll say more about this later.) And the truth is, with rare exceptions, most kids this age—transported nearly everywhere by a parent or older teen with a driver's license—do not need a cell phone. Their orbit simply is not that large.

But that's our view. What do others say?

Principal Debra Scott says:

I think the generation that is coming up now is so wired in to everybody and everything. And I think they've come up with that expectation of being able to get in touch with everyone at any time. I see my next-door neighbors giving cell phones to their eight-year-olds so they can be in touch with them. Even when my children were growing up, I just did not think until they were driving that we needed that contact. . . . The mentality has shifted now to, "What do you mean? I can't do without it." Even with parents, even though we have phones in every room in this building, the parents [say], "I have to be able to get up with my child. What do you mean they can't pull their cell phone out?" A lot of times when we catch them with cell phones, it's the parent who has texted them.

When asked about parents who purchase cell phones for safety, Warren Gould says, "I'm sorry, I don't buy it. I don't think this world is any less safe than it was in the 1950s. I don't see the reason to put a cell phone into the hands of a child before he gets into high school at the earliest."

About younger cell phone owners, educator and best-selling author Rosalind Wiseman says, "If you have a child between the ages of five and twelve walking around with a cell phone and it has any other capabilities beyond calling you, their grandparents, or 911, you have lost your mind."[19]

For those of you who have already given your middle schooler a mobile phone and regret your decision, we would tell you this: **You are the parent and you can take it away**. If you feel that your child would not accept your decision, we have a question for you: Do you pay the monthly bills to the wireless provider? If so, you get to decide.

Todd and Anna Patrick exercised their parental prerogative and took their sixth grade daughter Kelsey's cell phone away. Says Anna:

She got to the point where she was just very distracted as far as her homework or doing anything inside the house. You'd say "wash up the dishes," and you'd have to say it four times because she'd be washing and she'd walk away and go and text and come back. But then what I also noticed was if I asked her for the phone because she was being

distracted, she would delete all of her messages. And I'm like, "What
is that you're texting that you don't want us to see?"

Six weeks after she lost her phone, says Anna, Kelsey "wants to know when
she's getting it back. And I've said we're not sure when that's going to be."
Kelsey has accepted her parents' decision, but, Anna says laughing, now Kelsey
"wants to get a job for the summer. She wants to buy her own phone!"

What, you may ask, is at the root of our opposition to cell phones for
middle schoolers? First, we believe eleven- to fourteen-year-olds are too
young and impulsive to temper their use of a tool that can be incredibly
time-consuming and has such wide-ranging capabilities. While there may
be some responsible middle school cell phone owners, we agree with seventh
grade teacher Amanda Klee: "I would say that 99 percent of kids abuse it—
texting all day long, calling friends, probably meeting people who are out of
their age range."

Phones and texting vacuum up hours of teenagers' time—time they're
not spending on critical face-to-face conversation and interaction with *you*,
exercising their bodies, doing schoolwork, and sleeping those essential nine-
plus hours pediatricians say they need each night.

It sounds pretty obvious, but it's still true: There are only so many hours in
the day. Technology, with all of its marvelous advances, will never change that.

THE GREAT SAFETY ILLUSION

We would also ask you to consider this: Are cell phones, especially the souped-
up versions, *really* keeping your kids safer? James Steyer, head of the watchdog
group Common Sense Media, has said that most parents give a child a cell
phone to keep them safe, "but that ignores the great majority" of ways in
which kids actually use their phones.[20] The truth is, cell phones can introduce
many images and interactions into a child's life that are profoundly unsafe.

We'll talk at length about the prevalence of sexting later, but you should
know that it is a growing and widespread problem in middle schools across

the United States. Cell phone texting is also a favored tool for modern meanies to engage in cyberbullying. Even though you may believe your child might not engage in this kind of behavior, you can't protect him or her fully from harassment and bullying from other children via text message.

SMARTPHONES? NOT SO SMART FOR MIDDLE SCHOOLERS

And parents who give their children a smartphone—essentially a handheld minicomputer as well as a phone—are opening up a world of mobile Internet consumption and interaction that they can't possibly regulate, even with the help of filters and other controls. Experts say kids, far savvier than most of their parents, are quite adept at bypassing controls put in place by parents, and they often do so out of the house while pinging away on smartphones and laptops. John Whitaker, head of the Georgia Bureau of Investigation's Child Exploitation and Computer Crimes Unit, said in a newspaper interview, "There is no real way for parents to monitor it all."[21]

Because of their location services capabilities, smartphones can introduce additional risk. When kids (or parents) use a GPS-equipped smartphone to snap photos and then post them publicly online, they give away detailed location information. Why? That photo has a geotag that reveals both the longitude and latitude coordinates for where it was taken.

Say your middle schooler picks up his smartphone, snaps a photo of a pet at home, and posts it on Twitter. He has just enabled a voyeur to "pick out your house within fifteen feet. That's pretty accurate," says Sharon Vaknin of CNET News.[22] Unless you or your child disables the GPS setting before you say cheese, that smartphone photo will be geotagged.

One news report found that hackers can learn a lot about your child from geotagged photos: the location of her bedroom, where she hangs out, and where she goes to school. Checking Facebook, Craigslist, Photobucket, and Twitter for children's photos, and then searching by various city names, NBC reporters ascertained kids' home addresses and play areas.[23]

Mike Chudik, a school resource officer interviewed for the news report, says of public geotagged photos: "Basically, what you're doing is you're telling the bad guy where I live, where I recreate, my likes, my dislikes, what my mom or dad look like. . . . The online mapping is phenomenal."[24]

And when *you* use your smartphone to take photos, deactivate the geotagging feature beforehand; even then, only post kids' photos privately. You don't want location information, accompanied by a picture of your smiling child, in the hands of a predator.

LOCATION, LOCATION, LOCATION

While you might appreciate having location services settings on your smartphone, do you really want Apple, Facebook, Google, advertisers, or others in the data business knowing where your child is?

Additionally, GPS-equipped smartphones enable the use of location-based applications, such as Foursquare, where users can "check in" to share where they are. And on Facebook, users no longer even need a smartphone to broadcast their location. In 2011, the social networking site announced new features allowing users to add their "location to anything from anywhere, regardless of what device you are using, or whether it is a status update, photo, or Wall post."[25]

Should middle schoolers use location-based social applications? No, no, no. While location-sharing may be trendy, it's unwise for middle schoolers. The privacy implications of this for children are obvious, huge, and beyond worrisome.

What's the lure? Foursquare, for example, not only allows users to connect with friends, but it also serves as a game with rewards. Check in during visits to Starbucks five times, for example, and you'll get a "barista badge."[26]

While these kinds of applications may appeal to you as parent, they aren't for your middle schooler. We agree with Internet expert Anne Collier, who says Foursquare and other geolocation apps are "for young adults, not kids."[27]

(Kids can download location-based apps on an iPod Touch, too, so make sure you know what's on your child's mobile device.)

CELL PHONE BRAIN DRAIN

Even for parents who don't allow middle schoolers to text, or who have chosen to forgo smartphones, we still have a concern about regular cell phone use among children. Why? Scientists have yet to render a definitive judgment on the long-term safety of cell phones—even for adults. To date, the research on adult cell phone use has been mixed; some studies have found no increased risk from the radiation emitted by cell phones, while others have shown an elevated risk of cancer on the side of the head closest to the phone.

In May 2011, the World Health Organization, after an extensive research review, classified cell phones as "possibly carcinogenic to humans." That puts cell phones in the same category as DDT, the now infamous pesticide, and exhaust from gasoline engines.[28]

Data released in 2011 from the National Institutes of Health revealed "increased activity in the part of the brain closest to the phone antenna" after just fifty minutes of cell phone use.[29] No one knows yet whether this elevated activity is harmful, but some doctors are worried, particularly about kids. Dr. Keith Black, the head of Neuro-Oncology at Cedars-Sinai Medical Center in Los Angeles, is one of them:

> Black is concerned about kids' increased use of found that since their less-developed skulls and brains are more susceptible to the radiation. A cell phone, he says, "is really a microwave radiation antenna. The amount of radiation you get from it is directly related to [the] distance it is from the head." He recommends a headset and says texting is probably OK.[30]

We don't know about you, but we don't find these words particularly comforting. We think about the care parents employ when roaming the aisle at an all-night grocery to find medicine for a feverish child, or the time they spend perusing the sports aisle at Target for the safest bike helmet. And *these* aren't even items kids use every day.

We would also ask you this: On the occasions when your teen does phone home, does she always wear a headset? Seriously, have you *ever* seen a middle schooler blithely chatting away on a headset (or speakerphone) while the phone is transmitting?

If she doesn't, she's likely receiving more radio-frequency energy than is safe. Apple recommends that its iPhone, for example, be kept five-eighths of an inch away from the body while transmitting in order to comply with acceptable emission standards. BlackBerry's manufacturer says the devices need to stay about an inch away; the one-inch rule holds for Motorola mobile devices.[31]

Dr. Devra Davis, founding director of the toxicology and environmental studies board at the National Academy of Sciences and author of the 2010 book *Disconnect*, has grave concerns about cell phone use among children. Why? She writes:

> The brains of children have a pretty high fluid content compared to those of adults. This is why shaking young children is so dangerous—literally their brain matter can be sloshed around. Children's skulls and bone marrow are thinner and much more absorptive than those of adults—a fact that explains why children's heads can absorb double or more the radio-frequency energy of adults' heads. . . . Bone marrow can take in ten times more radiation in children than in adults. . . . These advances in our understanding of the young brain have not had any impact on the way that cell phones are tested or rated. Yet.[32]

According to Dr. Davis, at least a dozen countries have issued warnings against cell phone use by children. To date, the United States has remained silent.

CELL PHONES, CHILDREN, AND RISK

It was the text forwarded 'round the world: at last, good news on kids and cell phones. In 2011, Swiss researchers released data, published in the *Journal of the National Cancer Institute*, which found that children who used mobile phones regularly were no more likely to develop brain tumors than nonusers. The study, of almost one thousand children ages seven to nineteen in Denmark, Sweden, Norway, and Switzerland, seemed to provide definitive proof that cell phones were harmless.[33] But did it?

Not exactly. A subset of 163 children (for whom actual phone company data were available, and not just self-reports from parents and kids) proved otherwise. For these children, owning a phone longer increased their risk of brain tumors.[34] Moreover, this study's design was flawed: children were classified as "regular" cell phone users if they made at least one phone call a week for a six-month period.[35] We may not be scientists, but we find this to be an unrealistically low threshold of use.

In a press release, Dr. Davis said:

> This new JNCI [Journal of the National Cancer Institute] report represents an astonishing, disturbing, and unwarranted conclusion. Of course, the researchers found no link between children's brain tumors and their reported cell phone use. Brain tumors can take ten years to form and young children certainly have not been heavy cell phone users for very long. There has been a quadrupling of cell phone use in the past few years that this study could not possibly capture. . . . In fact, the JNCI researchers downplay their own finding that children who owned phones the longest had an increased risk of cancer.[36]

WHAT TO DO?

At a 2008 congressional hearing organized by Rep. Dennis Kucinich, Davis writes, experts expressed concern about children's cell phone use. Cancer biologist Dr. Ronald Herberman indicated that he had issued a warning to his more than three thousand staffers at the University of Pittsburgh Cancer Institute: "Don't use a [cell] phone next to your head. Use a speakerphone or earpiece and restrict children's use."[37]

Also testifying at the hearing was epidemiologist and former dean of the School of Public Health at the University of Albany, Dr. David Carpenter. Both Carpenter and Herberman said they supported national warnings on cell phone use for children. Dr. Carpenter said, "I think evidence is certainly strong enough for warnings that children should not use cell phones. I think failure to do that is going to lead us to an epidemic of brain cancer in the future."[38]

Dr. Davis stops short of calling for a discontinuation of cell phone use among children. She does support warning labels on phones and the use of headsets, speakerphones, and texting. (Phones emit less radiation while transmitting texts; texting also increases the distance between the head and the phone.) While texting, phones should not be held in the lap. Dr. Davis urges the use of landlines "whenever possible" and advises that children should not put phones in their pockets when they are turned on; nor should they (or any of us) sleep with powered-on phones on nightstands or under the pillow.[39]

After reading this, you may still choose to provide your middle schooler with a cell phone. But we want you to know the risks—as they are understood by a number of medical experts.

We should say that we have nothing against mobile phones. In fact, we both use them ourselves (on speakerphone, generally). But we do believe that what is appropriate for an adult is not necessarily so for a child. Middle schoolers are children, not mini-adults.

GAME ON

What about video games? Almost all middle schoolers play them. Data show that 97 percent of teens in the twelve to seventeen age range play games on the Internet or computer, or on portable gaming devices or consoles. Console games are the most popular, with 86 percent of teens gaming on Xbox, PlayStation, or Wii.[40] Most kids play a range of games, as do adults.

Some play alone or with an on-site friend. Others use their consoles to engage in "live" gaming with partners online.

Among young teen boys, first-person shooter games (including those in the Call of Duty franchise), in which players arm up to shoot and kill, are wildly popular. In fact, the Call of Duty: Modern Warfare 2 game ranks as one of the most profitable games ever. The installment that followed Modern Warfare 2, titled Call of Duty: Black Ops, earned a record-breaking $650 million+ worldwide in its first five days on the market in November 2010. According to Eric Hirshberg, the top executive at the game's publisher, Activision, such sales represented "the biggest five-day launch in entertainment history across any media."[41]

Many of these first-person shooter games have earned a mature (M) rating for violence, blood, and gore, but that has not kept parents from snatching them up in droves for preteen and teen boys.

Recently, Austin asked us for a popular first-person shooter Xbox game for Christmas. He arrived at the negotiating table armed with data, prefacing his request with a long list of friends who were already proud and satisfied owners. These kids all have thoughtful parents I respect. So I drove to my local gaming and electronics store with an intent to purchase. As I pulled the game off the shelf and headed to the checkout line, I flipped it over to scan the rating. My heart sank as I saw it was rated M for maturity—because of blood, drug references, intense violence, and language—and had a recommended age range of 17+. As I paid the cashier, I expressed my concern over whether this game—essentially equivalent to an R-rated movie—would be appropriate for my son. The store clerk assured me I could return the game if I changed my mind.

Later that night, I expressed my misgivings to my husband Greg. We researched the game online and concluded it would be damaging to Austin, particularly given the fact that he would likely spend hours practicing and perfecting his skills if he owned it. Several days later, I returned the game, mentioning my reasons to the young, savvy cashier. To my surprise, he validated my choice, noting, "A lot of parents cave, but this game is pretty intense."

When Austin learned of our decision days later, he was crushed—and mad. He wanted this game fiercely. All of the boys at school talked about it, he told us. He also was bothered by what he said was an uninformed decision on our part: neither Greg nor I had ever actually played the game. Conceding his point, we rented the game several weeks later and took turns playing it with him.

We found the game disturbing. As targets die, they collapse and bleed. Some cry out in pain. When Austin, Greg, or I was hit, the split screen splattered with realistic-looking blood, turning my stomach.

Our decision, fully informed this time, remains unchanged. This M-rated game is graphic, violent, and, we believe, harmful.

—Kristen

MEDIA VIOLENCE

What do the experts say? Dr. David Walsh, *Why Do They Act That Way?* writes, "Scientifically speaking, the notion that media violence harms kids is an open-and-shut case"; research has found that "violent video games increase levels of aggression hormones in teen players. While their onscreen personas kicked, punched, cut, and shot their way through enemies, testosterone and adrenaline levels rose significantly in the bodies of the players behind the controls.... The strength of the evidence linking media violence to youth aggression is stronger than the evidence linking lead poisoning with mental retardation and more definitive than the case linking secondhand smoke with cancer."[42]

Those are pretty strong links. The American Academy of Pediatrics takes a hard line on media violence, noting in their policy statement, "Research has associated exposure to media violence with a variety of physical and mental health problems for children and adolescents, including aggressive and violent behavior, bullying, desensitization to violence, fear, depression, nightmares and sleep disturbances."[43] Have you ever noticed how you have trouble going to sleep after a particularly intense or violent movie? It's the same with our kids.

Need more proof? The Academy says the media violence-aggression link actually trumps the relationship between calcium consumption and bone mass.[44] Everybody knows calcium depletion is hard on your bones.

Violent media games, it seems, are even harder on your son's mind and spirit.

CONTENT MATTERS

When you purchase these games for your son, you virtually guarantee that he will be immersed in these images over and over again, day in and day out. Dr. Michael Rich, associate professor of pediatrics at Harvard Medical School and the director of the Center on Media and Child Health in Boston calls himself the "world's first mediatrician." He responded to a parent question about shooter games on his blog by saying:

> Video games, which present environments and conditions to which the player must respond in certain ways to do well, function as "behavioral scripts" which the player practices over and over. Interactive electronic media that immerse participants in a "virtual reality" are among the most effective teaching technologies we have. What children do, they will learn. Content matters. Therefore, as a pediatrician, I would steer parents and kids toward video games that are sports-, logic-, or strategy-based, instead of those that center on violence.[45]

Are there plenty of well-crafted, exciting video games out there that don't saturate kids in a world of graphic violence? Sure there are. They may not be the latest hit games your son's friends are talking about at school, but there are other options. And think about this: Are we as parents to look to what is popular as the arbiter of what's good and right? *That* is a slippery slope indeed.

We recommend that parents proceed with a strong dose of caution when making choices about gaming content. Video games, rightly conceived, can provide fun downtime for kids. But keep close tabs on time and restrict gaming to weekends, when homework and school have been set aside for the week. "Live" gaming should also be monitored closely.

GAME ON . . . AND ON . . . AND ON . . .

What about those tween and teen gamers who just can't stop? While gaming can be a normal recreational outlet for middle schoolers (with the all-important caveat that parents monitor content and time closely), it can morph into an obsession. A 2011 study of more than three thousand elementary and middle school kids in Singapore, published in the journal *Pediatrics*, found that almost 10 percent of these kids exhibited gaming habits considered "pathological." This percentage is consistent with data on gaming addiction in other countries.

The Singapore study is particularly compelling because children's gaming habits were tracked over a two-year period. What were the risk factors researchers identified for juvenile gaming addicts? Greater impulsivity and less empathy, social competence, and ability to regulate emotions. Not surprisingly, kids who spent more time playing video games were more likely to go on to become addicts; these kids averaged a whopping thirty-one hours a week on games.[46] That means that these children were allowed to spend more than four hours a day gaming—*before* they spiraled into addiction!

Once begun, the gaming habit is hard to kick: according to the Singapore study, "Most pathological gamers (84 percent) are still pathological gamers two years later." These were also unhappy kids—they were more depressed, anxious, and socially phobic, and were poorer performers in school than their non-addicted peers.[47]

The Singapore study confirms yet again the link between violent games and behavior:

> Children who began consuming more violent games also began to have more normative beliefs about aggression, hostile attribution biases, and aggressive fantasies and to engage in more physically and relationally aggressive behaviors (they also became more likely to be victims of aggression).[48]

What should you look for if you think your child might be a gaming addict? According to psychologist Dr. David Walsh:

> Video game addicts exhibit all of the same tendencies that people who are addicted to drugs or gambling do. They lie about how much they play. They eschew social contact in favor of their games. They play compulsively. Some even engage in dishonest behavior to support the habit. . . .
>
> You should be concerned if your child repeatedly breaks family rules about when and how much game playing is allowed, withdraws from friends and activities to spend time playing, sneaks and lies about game playing, neglects schoolwork and other responsibilities, or throws temper tantrums when limits are imposed.[49]

Before we close out this chapter, we want to leave you with some wise words from our interview with clinical psychologist Dr. Charlie Cooper, the CEO of HRC Behavioral Therapy. He spoke about addictions in general, as well as gaming:

> At the most generic level, addictions all serve the same purpose, and that is that they give short-term comfort, satisfaction, relief, excitement—short-term gain—and the only reason we call them addictions is that there's long-term pain that comes later. [The long-term pain]

depends on the addiction. So if it's alcohol, it's cirrhosis of the liver. If it's gambling, it's poverty. If it's gaming, it can be social isolation, it can be changes in propensity to violence, it can be truncated social development—social skill development can be far below par. It can be academic problems. Different addictions obviously have different kinds of costs. And the cost of many of the computer-based addictions is distortion in normal allocation of time because people are spending way more time on the game than they are on good things that are healthier for them.

Kids (and even savvy adults), while not outright addicts, can still abuse games. Dr. Cooper told us about a period of time in which *he* gamed excessively. He said:

> Somebody that's abusing a substance or an agent or an activity or whatever might not be dependent on it, but might go through an episode in which they have a really bad time. I went through an addictive period in an absolutely marvelous computer game that I haven't even seen on the market for years. I think it was called the Amazing Machine or the Incredible Machine. It was a great game for cognitive development, actually . . . it was a great brain-teaser. But I tell you I wasted a whole lot of time. There was a period of time when I wasn't doing much else except that.

His gaming affected his family and sleep, says Dr. Cooper. "I was up until two or three in the morning on it."

So, moms and dads, that gives you all the more reason to monitor video game time and content closely. And if you believe your child could be addicted to gaming, seek professional help. If, after you have intervened, your child still cannot attain balanced gaming habits, *throw it all away*—games, consoles, everything. Don't let your son (or daughter) waste irretrievable childhood hours addicted to video games.

PARENT TIPS

Maintain tech-free bedrooms. Keep computers, laptops, televisions, and gaming equipment in common areas.

Keep bedtime boring. If you purchase mobile devices such as a cell phone, smartphone, MP3 player, Nintendo DS, or iPod Touch for your middle schooler, collect them *all* at bedtime so kids can sleep.

Restrict violence. Don't purchase games that are riddled with violence. If games are borderline or questionable, rent and preview them before buying.

Round up ratings. The Entertainment Software Rating Board—the group behind the Everyone (E), Teen (T), and Mature (M, 17+) ratings—has detailed ratings available for parents on its Website. Check them out before making purchases at www.esrb.org/index-js.jsp.

Establish gaming blackouts. Ban gaming during the school week. Allow kids to play only on the weekend, when school and homework are done for the week.

Regulate time and content. When kids are gaming, know *what* they're playing, *with whom* (if gaming is "live"), and for *how long*.

Arm up with information. Subscribe to media alerts and newsletters from parent-friendly groups, such as Common Sense Media (www.commonsensemedia.org) or Focus on the Family's Plugged In Online site (www.pluggedin.com).

Chapter Eight

HOME INVASION, PART TWO— SOCIAL NETWORKING AND THE INTERNET

"The reality is that nothing on Facebook is really confidential."

—David Kirkpatrick, author of *The Facebook Effect*

Just minutes after logging on to her Facebook account, your seventh grade daughter can scan her News Feed, catching up on the latest updates from her friends. After she uploads photos that showcase her crazy dance moves from Saturday night's party, she can post a comment about the ridiculous amount of math homework she still has to finish. And then she can update her status to show she's finally "in a relationship" with that cute boy from PE class. For the in-the-moment adolescent, Facebook offers an irresistible blend of immediacy, connection, and digital fame.

How did it all start?

A WORLD OF FRIENDS

Founded in 2004, Facebook is more than the world's leading social networking site: It's a global phenomenon that's changing how we interact with others. Now virtual friendships connect more than eight hundred million active users around the world, half of whom visit Facebook every day.[1] The site has even expanded our techno-lexicon—less than ten years ago, the word "friending," used as a verb, would have produced a blank stare. Now everyone knows what it means; how many "friends," we wonder, do our peers have? One hundred? Two hundred? For those at the top of the social networking food chain, the answer can be one thousand or more. So it's a very public barometer of how "connected" you are: more friends, more status.

Are Facebook and, to a lesser degree, other social networking sites, transforming how middle schoolers (and even younger kids) communicate? You bet. Many parents might be surprised to learn how much. *Consumer Reports'* 2011 "State of the Net" survey of more than two thousand U.S. households found that twenty million minors under the age of eighteen had used Facebook in the past year. Of these kids, seven and a half million had subverted Facebook's age requirement and were younger than thirteen; more than five million Facebook users were ten or younger.[2]

Many parents are in the dark when it comes to their kids' social networking habits. A national poll by Common Sense Media of seventh through twelfth graders found that more than half of teens check social networking sites more than once daily; yet only a quarter of their parents realize that.[3] Not only are kids on social networking sites more than their parents think they are, but some are signing on without parental consent: 12 percent of teens with Facebook or Myspace accounts say their parents don't even know they have one.[4]

PARENTS SPEAK OUT ON FACEBOOK

Among parents who give kids permission to use Facebook, some say they track online disclosures by "friending" their child. Rick, a father of two, says he tries to "stay a little bit ahead" of his kids' use of technology; he and his teenage daughter are Facebook friends. Lisa and her husband John, parents to eighth grade Laura, also track their daughter's Facebook posts as friends.

Even with mom and dad in the Facebook loop, kids can still be exposed to content that can be hurtful. Lisa says of Laura, "A few of her friends got together and were talking about each other and having fun without her. It hurt her feelings. Social networking brings it to a very public level." Sandi, a mother of four, adds, "Kids are making plans on Facebook. So they know where everybody is and what everybody is doing. [Kids] are even more aware now if they've been left out or excluded." Plus, *other* kids know, too, which can reinforce feelings of stigmatization in the real world.

One father who permitted his eighth grade daughter to have a Facebook account says she eventually decided to quit on her own because she felt ongoing social pressures. He says, "I was so proud of her. It was an area where she was constantly feeling judged or not fitting in or evaluating how many pictures were posted of her." This father is astute about the one-upsmanship endemic to Facebook. David Kirkpatrick, author of *The Facebook Effect*, writes that "'friending' had an element of competiveness from day one."[5]

One mother who gave her daughter a Facebook account in sixth grade told us:

> For the most part, it has been a positive thing and has opened up some great discussions about what's appropriate to type and put on Facebook, and what's not. But I am concerned that she spends a lot of time just navigating around Facebook—not even looking at profiles of people she knows, but looking at profiles of people she doesn't know. It's frightening to me what she can access on Facebook. You can be a sixty-year-old man and post a picture of a seventeen-year-old boy and pretend that it's you. I'm now realizing Facebook is a can of worms.

FACEBOOK AND MIDDLE SCHOOLERS

Should middle schoolers, many of whom are *under* the age of thirteen (the minimum age requirement to get on Facebook) have a Facebook account in the first place? We don't think so. Some middle schools agree with us. Trinity School of Durham, North Carolina, for example, has published the following statement on Facebook in its parent handbook:

> Parents are advised that Facebook prohibits students under 13 from using its site. While Trinity prefers not to involve itself in students' online behaviors, from time to time it must deal with discipline issues that arise from students' activities on such online sites. It is the Middle School's position that social networking sites are inappropriate for middle schoolers, who lack the maturity, judgment and skill with language to use them in a healthy manner, and that use of such sites should be delayed until students at a minimum are in [high] school.[6]

Tony Orsini, principal of Benjamin Franklin Middle School in Ridgewood, New Jersey, made national news by sending an e-mail to parents of students in his school, pleading with them to keep their middle schoolers off Facebook: "Please do the following: Sit down with your child (and they are just children still) and tell them that they are not allowed to be a member of any social networking site. Today!" Kids' interactions via Facebook and other forms of technology have proven to be a hindrance for staffers at Orsini's school. He said, "Our guidance counselors spend most of their time dealing with things that didn't happen in school."[7]

Even First Lady Michelle Obama opposes Facebook for younger kids; her tween daughters Sasha and Malia do not have Facebook accounts. She told Matt Lauer on NBC's *Today* show, "I'm not a big fan of kids having Facebook. It's just not something they need."[8]

Parents should also know that kids who lie to get on Facebook often miss the site's protections for minors aged thirteen to seventeen. Middle school social worker Lisa DeCesaris says that underage kids commonly add ten years to their age. "So instead of being twelve, suddenly they become twenty-two." She continues, "If they add ten years to their age, they've bypassed all of those safeguards and now they're just considered an adult."

FACEBOOK'S DATA TRAIL

In a conversation with students at Wakefield High School in Arlington, Virginia, President Obama expressed concerns about the long data trail left by Facebook use, saying:

> I want everybody here to be careful about what you post on Facebook, because in the YouTube age, whatever you do, it will be pulled up again later somewhere in your life. And when you're young, you make mistakes, and you do some stupid stuff. And I've been hearing a lot about young people who, you know, they're posting stuff on Facebook and suddenly they go apply for a job and somebody's done a search.[9]

Some schools are racing to educate students about the far-reaching implications of material they post on Facebook.

Just this morning, I attended a seminar on social networking and the Internet at a local middle school; students viewed a YouTube video on the extensive "digital dossier" they amass over years of online posting. The kids then broke down by grade; two accomplished and articulate seniors explained to the seventh graders why they both had decided several years ago to forego Facebook—too much drama, too much time.

—Kristen

Amanda Klee worries that Facebook use by young adolescents is fraught with far-reaching implications. "If you've had Facebook since you were twelve years old—and you're probably making poor choices on it—then how are you ever going to get a job?"

And it's not just prospective employers who are reading Facebook posts. Here are a few of the other people who might be checking out your child's Facebook wall: parents, teachers, coaches, admissions officers at colleges, law enforcement officers, and online predators.[10]

In May 2011, one seventh grader, Vito Lapinta Jr., was questioned by the Secret Service about Facebook posts he had made warning President Obama about the possibility of suicide attacks following the killing of terrorist Osama bin Laden. Vito, who says he was "very scared," is trying to be more judicious about what he posts on Facebook.[11]

Nothing your child posts online is truly confidential.

PRIVACY SETTINGS

At this point, you're probably wondering about privacy settings. Are they effective? The answer, of course, is yes, and if you have decided to allow your middle schooler on Facebook or other social networking sites, he should use them. Facebook users can share with anyone (set to public); friends of friends, the "maximum audience for minors," according to Facebook; friends; or a customized audience, such as a specific group.[12] (Know, however, that some tech-savvy children have used the group function to filter the data they share with their parents, while giving the illusion of openness, as you'll see below.)

About two-thirds of teens, or 64 percent, say they use privacy settings, according to survey data from TRUSTe, the top provider of Internet privacy seals. However, 60 percent of teens in TRUSTe's survey also said they used "privacy controls on social networks to hide content from specific friends, including parents." And not all of teens' "friends" are people they know: 42 percent said they "accept social network 'friend' requests from strangers."[13] While privacy settings do restrict the audience that can view your child's information, they are not foolproof. When a teen (or anyone, for that matter) posts material online, even using privacy settings, he loses ultimate control over who sees it. Why? As Facebook advises teens:

- Remember that any information you post—whether in a comment, a note, or a video chat—might be copied, pasted and distributed in ways that you didn't intend.
- Before you post, ask yourself: Would I be OK if this content were shared widely at school or with my future employer?[14]

For the 36 percent of teens who don't use privacy settings, the opportunity for embarrassment is far greater. As TRUSTe, the authority on online privacy, says, "The Internet never forgets."[15] The group advises parents:

> If your teen uses Twitter, for example, and chooses not to make their tweets private, then this information can be indexed and recorded on the public Web by various third parties and search engines. As a result, it may be visible later to teachers, employers or potential employers, or college admissions officers—even if your teen has deleted the original tweets and the Twitter account itself. Online it's very hard (if not impossible in some cases) to put the cat back in the bag and things your teen posts online today could come to haunt them years down the road.[16]

LESSONS FROM GOOGLE

What about other social media platforms? It simply isn't possible for us to give you a comprehensive list of the sites your middle schooler might find alluring. Even if we tried, such a list would soon be obsolete. But we do want to share "lessons learned" about online privacy from Internet giant, Google. In 2011, Google released its newest networking product, Google+, but its foray into social media has been far from smooth.

Google's now-defunct networking tool, Buzz, once popular with many middle schoolers and elementary school–age kids we know, is a case in point.

When Buzz was rolled out in February 2010, all current Google Mail users (Gmail) were automatically enrolled in the network. And Gmail users' address books "were essentially published for all to see."[17] This prompted the Electronic Privacy Information Center to file a complaint with the Federal Trade Commission; Google has since settled.

In its Buzz rollout, Google also failed to ensure that users were thirteen or older. In the summer of 2010, Google rectified this omission, and began asking for a birth date as part of Gmail registration. But many underage kids were already on the site, and their parents may have had no idea they were too young.

Clearly, this has been a messy, invasive process from the beginning. Here is a 2010 statement from Google spokesman Scott Rubin, responding to a critical *Los Angeles Times* blog post about Buzz and kids' privacy risks:

> We designed Buzz to make it easy to have conversations with your friends about the things that interest you. Keeping kids safe online is very important to us. You must have a Google account to use Buzz, and we require all new users to provide birth dates to keep children under 13 from signing up for Google accounts. Since we launched Buzz, we've listened to the feedback from our users and have made many product improvements to address their concerns. . . . Even as we roll out these changes, we think it's important to remember that there's no substitution for parental supervision to keep kids safe on the Internet.[18]

Sound familiar?

Google certainly isn't alone in its privacy missteps. The bottom line is that sites are only as good as their online security. While we have the illusion of privacy and security, professional hackers are always trying to exploit Internet loopholes. And when a site makes major changes to the functionality, there is always the opportunity for more Internet breaches. You should know, too, that tracking privacy settings is not a one-time activity. If you allow your child to use social networking sites, you need to be prepared to stay abreast of any changes to the privacy policies on the sites you permit your child to access. Since its inception, Facebook, for example, has updated its privacy policy multiple times.

In addition to Facebook and Google, other platforms are acquiring behavioral data on your children whenever they set up user accounts. The words your children post, the pictures and news they view, the applications they use, and the time they spend—all create a rich treasure trove of behavioral data that can be used for marketing and other purposes.

LUCKY NUMBER THIRTEEN

So, what's magical about age thirteen in the online world? Thirteen is the age at which kids' personal information is no longer protected by law. The Children's Online Protection and Privacy Act (COPPA), passed by Congress in 1998 and effective since 2000, "applies to the online collection of personal information from children under 13."[19] Personal data such as a child's name, e-mail address, home address, or telephone number is covered under COPPA. For kids under the age of thirteen, Website operators must make "reasonable efforts" to notify parents and obtain their consent before they collect or divulge kids' personal information.[20] But once a child turns thirteen (or lies and says he's thirteen), all of this changes.

"The minute you're thirteen in this country, you're an adult when it comes to privacy," said Jeff Chester of the Center for Digital Democracy in a Fox News interview.[21] A number of groups are pushing to change that, asking Congress to expand protections for thirteen- to seventeen-year-olds who are still minors. And in the wake of its startling survey findings on underage Facebook users, *Consumer Reports* is calling on Facebook to "beef up its screening to drastically reduce the number of underage members and make its privacy controls even more accessible."[22] Clearly, social networking sites have a lot more to do to protect kids' privacy. We hope they do it.

Ultimately, however, you are responsible for your child's online activities.

INTERNET SAFETY

What about Internet content? This can be a tricky area to navigate. Unlike phones and social networking, it's impossible to shut down the Internet in middle school since most tweens and teens today must use it to access online class agendas, write papers in Google docs, research assignments—some on a daily basis.

How do parents police the Internet? Some purchase Internet filter software to block pornography or other harmful content. Other parents choose monitoring software so they can track kids' online activities. We interviewed Jason, a tech-savvy father of two homeschooled boys, ages eleven and fourteen, about his approach to Internet safety. This is what he told us:

> One of the first things that we did was install the Net Nanny application which I've been really pleased with because they seem to do a really good job of keeping it updated for threats, plus you can customize the settings even as far as entering keywords—which of course it just looks for in the metadata. You can just block specific sites and say, "No, I'm not going to allow this site." You can also just flat-out say, "I'm turning off Web browsing completely" if it's too much out of hand. Thankfully, we haven't had to resort to that.
>
> We are in the process of setting up everyone in the house with an account so when you get on a computer [Apple], you will have to log in to your account. By doing that, I can, with the Apple software, restrict how long you are allowed to be on your account per day. So I set an hourly limit for everybody. Because the boys use the computer for homeschooling, this is really going to force them to economize their time. When that time's up, that time's up. You're not getting an extension.
>
> As administrator, I can go and see exactly what they've been doing. Did they get an e-mail, were they chatting with somebody, were they on Word, were they on Excel, were they visiting a Website

that I told them not to? Then I can actually take that [information] and make adjustments either to their account setting or to the Net Nanny application—and say, "All right, you're visiting this Website way too much. I'm going to stop it."

Other parents tell us they don't install filtering software, but are vigilant about checking their kids' browser histories and talking about what's appropriate. One father of two boys and two girls said, "We don't police the Websites. I don't put a filter [on the computer]. I do go in and check their computers. I see that their histories are still intact, so they're not erasing their histories." Recently this father had a retreat with his teen boys to watch a video on pornography and talk through the perils of viewing sexual images.

We urge parents to talk with kids about the dangers of Internet pornography. This is one more serious reason parents must be vigilant about monitoring Internet use. We have already heard from middle school parents whose eighth graders are addicted to pornography.

EXPERT ADVICE ON SAFETY

Cyber-expert Parry Aftab has three simple suggestions for parents on Internet safety:

- Find out what your children are doing online and understand the risks posed by the technologies and services you and they are using.
- Determine what choices you have to address those risks and make the choice that works for your family.
- Understand what technology and parental-control tools exist to help you enforce those choices.[23]

We would add this: you cannot rely just on tools or software to police your middle schoolers. *You* need to stay abreast of your child's online activities. We know this can be exhausting. As one father of two teens told us, "It takes so much energy to track all that stuff. When there is other stress—financial, physical illness – that's the first thing to go. The attitude is, 'If the kids aren't bothering me, then I'm going to leave them alone.'" But leaving kids alone in the virtual realm is profoundly unsafe.

We don't want to scare you, but we do want you to be aware of online risks. Here's some advice for kids about online safety from the New York State Internet Crimes Against Children Task Force:

- You may not know the truth about someone you first meet online . . . you can be lied to or betrayed.
- Predators will use information obtained from children to gain trust and friendship.
- Warning signs are: someone who tries to isolate you from family or friends, turn you against your parents, makes you keep secrets, threatens you, or sends you inappropriate material.
- Beware of anyone who wants to "go private" or meet you.
- Check in with friends before posting information or photos about them.
- There is no such thing as a private conversation online. It doesn't matter if you are communicating with a friend on Facebook, Twitter, or Skype; anyone can copy and paste your conversation and images.
- Use privacy settings.
- Use strong passwords and keep them confidential.
- Remember that any picture you post online can be downloaded by anybody and copied and pasted online forever.
- Kids (along with the help of a parent) should report: anyone who sends revealing photos or videos, talks to them about sex, or asks to meet offline.[24]

TELEVISION AND MOVIES

Last—but not least—there are the old standbys of media content: television and movies. These forms of media can provide opportunities to enrich and uplift, but must be tracked closely. One father-son pair has regular movie nights together, where they select a movie, pull out the popcorn, and engage in end-of-the-week male bonding. Family movie nights can give parents and kids a great time to relax and reconnect. So, too, can television shows with appropriate content. One family, whose members love to cook, enjoys watching programs together that feature culinary celebration, such as Bobby Flay.

But television and movies can also introduce more questionable content. Shows like MTV's *Jersey Shore* are popular among middle schoolers. And MTV continues to push the envelope with the uber-revealing and shocking show about teen life, *Skins*—a program which prompted the Parents Television Council to call for an investigation into potential child pornography.

As you make decisions about movie and television content, remember that kids are always learning while they're watching, for good or for ill. As psychologist Dr. David Walsh has said: "If you believe that Sesame Street taught your four-year-old something, then you'd better believe that MTV is teaching your fourteen-year-old something."[25]

MEDIA AT HOME

Our principles at home mirror those we advocate in this book. Austin does not have a cell phone; he finished middle school never having owned one. According to his tally, he and only two other boys in the entire eighth grade did not have mobile phones. Did he like our decision? Absolutely not. He protested regularly, but ultimately he respected us. He will not get a phone until high school, and even then he will have to abide by restrictions on its usage.

Nor is Austin on Facebook; he does not seem to mind waiting until he is older. After Austin turned thirteen, we allowed him to open a Google

Mail account for e-mail and use Gmail's networking tool, Buzz. At the time, I had no idea that Buzz's networking capabilities were so extensive. We have since had plenty of discussions about what is appropriate to write in cyberspace. We do have an Xbox gaming system in the house. We implement a weekday blackout on Xbox gaming Monday through Thursday. Austin does look forward to playing Madden NFL games on Friday afternoons! Our only gaming system is located in our family room, right next to the kitchen, so I can see what he is playing, and for how long. Austin also has an iPod Touch which he uses primarily to listen to music and play occasional games.

Have we made mistakes along the way? Absolutely. In addition to our naiveté and ignorance about Buzz, we purchased the iPod Touch without knowing Austin could use it to go online. We have since updated its settings to turn off Internet browsing. What about gaming? Initially, we allowed Austin to play the popular M-rated first-person shooter games at his friends' houses even though we had decided not to purchase these games for our own home. We soon realized this was inconsistent and confusing. Our subsequent decision to restrict all M-rated gaming was met with intense antipathy from Austin. The initial conversation, conducted on the way home from school one day, resulted in Austin's walking part of the way home. I let him out at the entrance to our neighborhood so he could cool off and learn to speak more respectfully. I can report that the fresh air and exercise did him good!

Austin does not have a laptop of his own and uses a computer in my home office for his schoolwork and time on the Internet. We will not allow him to have a computer in his bedroom, and he knows that. Has all of this been hard for Austin? Absolutely. Has it been hard for us? You bet. But we have felt strongly about protecting him during these impressionable middle school years. He doesn't appreciate our rules now and thinks we're way *too strict. We understand and sympathize, but also know, as parents, we have to stand on our convictions as we raise our boy.*

The real irony is that I grew up without a TV and hated it. I felt different and wanted to be like everyone else, just like Austin does. At the time, I promised my health-conscious, media-averse mother that MY children would swill Coke, eat Doritos, and watch TV all day long. They would, I told her, be just like their peers.

Guess what? The joke's on me. Past really is prologue, as they say.

—Kristen

HOME AS A REFUGE

What has been the impact of our cultural media and technology "home invasion" on the family? William Powers, in his best-selling tome, *Hamlet's BlackBerry*, says it well:

> The home has traditionally been a shelter *from* the crowd, within which human beings experienced life in a different way from how it was experienced on the outside. For the individual, home has always offered privacy, quiet, solitude. For those living in couples, families, and other cohabiting groups, it also afforded an intimate sort of togetherness that's possible only in shared isolation.
>
> The crowd drives us away from the reflective, the particular, and the truly personal. At home we could be more human.
>
> High-speed, around-the-clock digital connectedness has already diluted these vital aspects of home life. The more connected our house became in the last decade, the less it provided the sense of peace and soul nourishment I associate with "home." What was once a happy refuge from the crowd is becoming a channel for crowd delivery. The

walls are membranes through which a tide of people and information flows in and out around the clock.[26]

As a parent, you can push back this home invasion. Your home can be a "shelter from the crowd," not a "channel for crowd delivery." Even in this digital age *you* still get to make choices. Technology has altered irrevocably the way we communicate with the outside world, but the immediate and detached connection it creates is no substitute for the face-to-face connectedness that takes place in the home.

It's time to make our homes places of refuge, places where they engage in meaningful connections.

Places where they can be fully human.

How to do this? First, let us say what we are *not* suggesting. We do not advocate banning all media and technology from the home. Technology is a necessary and valuable part of modern life. But we are not the pawns of technology either. There *is* a difference between technology we use in our professional and academic lives and what we use in our recreational lives. The lines today are too often blurred. Middle schoolers today are *bingeing* on recreational media and technology, and it is spilling over into every facet of their lives. For some of them, it *is* their life.

They're wired. They're tired. And with all of the junk they're consuming, they have no space to play, to imagine, or to think. To be.

CONTROL ACCESS

So what's the answer? You have to shut some of it down. Say no. Of course it's not realistic to power everything down. But remember this: while many of the tools of technology are good, they are *not* all age appropriate for middle schoolers.

If you are already standing strong, we applaud you. And if, after reading this chapter, you are prompted to make changes, we salute you. Your kids may hate you (and us) as you seek to erect new media walls in your home.

That's OK. Someday, they will thank you. (And they might even write a book with you saying you weren't so strict and weird after all! Stranger things have happened.)

Regulating your child's media and technological usage will yield long-term dividends. Research shows that parents who make and enforce rules about media drive down kids' overall consumption. Kids who use the least amount of media do better in school compared to those who are tethered to media during most of their waking hours. They're less bored. And they're happier.[27]

PARTING THOUGHTS

Finally, as parents, we must engage in some self-examination. As author Rosalind Wiseman has observed, "The BlackBerry doesn't fall far from the tree."[28] Are *we* constantly tethered to technology—texting, browsing, posting—while our impressionable children watch and wait?

"Who has time for all this selfish entertainment?" asks one father of four, referencing our cultural obsession with media and technology. Given the day's fixed twenty-four-hour limit, he wonders, "Where are you going to do good? Where are you going to engage with another human? How are you going to produce and contribute to the world?"

What this father speaks to is our very humanity—our ability to connect with others on an emotional level.

That's what's at stake. *The essence of who we are.*

PARENT TIPS

Obey the rules. Kids must be thirteen to join social networking sites, such as Facebook. We advise waiting until high school *at the earliest* for Facebook.

Monitor social media and Internet usage closely. If older middle schoolers use social networking sites, monitor content and time carefully. Same goes for any time spent browsing the Internet.

Install Internet guardrails. Many parents choose to install Internet filtering software or set up parental controls. But the best guardrails are conversations parents have with kids about safe ways to use the Internet as well as family rules, consistently enforced, that govern Internet use.

Know your stuff. Don't purchase technology for kids until you, as parent, understand it yourself. If you didn't get it right the first time around, stop now and find out what your child can access.

Don't just throw out the bad; bring in the good. Use media as a teaching tool. View uplifting movies and have rich discussions. Play sports games on Xbox or Playstation with your child. Bowl together on your Wii. Download dance tunes and jump around.

Keep it clean. Make sure content is age appropriate and not harmful. What we look at matters.

Unplug. Turn off the recreational media spigot sometimes—for the day, for the week. Schedule time for nondigital family fun.

Chapter Nine

GROWING UP
AT WARP SPEED

"Girls are getting sexier earlier. That's not a good thing."

—Leonard Sax, MD, PhD, author, *Girls on the Edge*

"Kids are growing up quicker. Parents are less available and are finding it harder to enter their kids' worlds. As kids become increasingly connected through electronics and social media, they grow less connected to their parents. This creates an environment where children easily wander into more risky behaviors."

—Mark Piehl, MD, pediatric critical care physician and medical director of WakeMed Children's Hospital, Raleigh, North Carolina

She stood in the doorway of the office where I sat conducting an interview with the mid-thirties middle school counselor. The blonde fourteen-year-old with a well-endowed woman's body was clad in short shorts, a low-cut pink tank top with bra straps showing, and a loose-fitting beige jacket,

completely open at the front. While she set up an appointment with the counselor, I couldn't help but stare at her bare legs and cleavage.

After she left, I asked the counselor, "Don't you have a dress code at this school?" and listened as she proceeded to tell me that, yes, the school had a dress code. Shorts were acceptable, along with tank tops as long as bra straps were covered. What about cleavage? Well, that wasn't supposed to be visible. And this girl, was she dressed in an acceptable manner? I asked. "She was borderline," said the counselor, obviously uncomfortable. Then she noted that it was twelve o'clock and apparently no teacher had felt the student was inappropriately dressed, or she would have been sent home. "Well," I said, "I'd hate to be a fourteen-year-old boy sitting beside her in math class."

—*Brenda*

Too sexy, too soon. The sexualization of girls begins in this culture as early as infancy and continues throughout high school. Through the media they absorb and the clothing available for little girls, our youngest girls are bombarded with the message early on that sexy is good. Sexy is the way to be. Little girls, especially after they leave size 6X behind, enter a whole new world of thongs, push-up bikini tops, dresses that are cut low, shorts that show buttocks, and skirts so tight they cannot possibly run and play in them. And if you ever watch the television show *Toddlers & Tiaras*, you will see young tots dressed like racy women with mascara, bleached hair, lipstick, and all that glitters. As they come onstage with their sexy moves, you can view their mothers slightly offscreen, hands on hips, mimicking the suggestive dances they have taught their little daughters.

Ours is a culture that attempts to turn girls into hookers and boys into voyeurs and—if they are immersed in violent video games—thugs. Is it any wonder that we have heard from parents and teachers about dating in elementary school and oral sex at the middle school dances and football games, or read about girls servicing boys on the bus and in the classrooms of middle schools?

Sex is in the air our children breathe, the water they drink, the television ads and shows they watch, and the retail stores they visit.

Recently, Abercrombie, the children's division of Abercrombie and Fitch, marketed a padded bikini top for girls as young as eight years of age. The top, ostensibly designed to cover up breast buds, was originally pitched as the "Ashley Push Up Triangle." Apparently, the retailer dropped the words "push up" due to parental outcry. Back in 2002, Abercrombie's underwear for girls age eight to fourteen was labeled "eye candy" and "wink wink." Again, parents objected and these products were removed.

While Abercrombie may be among the most aggressive retailers selling sex to mothers and their daughters, this company is not alone. Have you been to your favorite store lately and tried to buy something for your middle school daughter that is not a strapless dress, a skintight skirt, or six-inch jean shorts? It's tough to find clothes that cover them up. Some moms call today's clothing for young girls "hooker wear," as they comb the stores for appropriate clothing for their daughters.

THE APA RESEARCH

In February of 2007, the American Psychological Association (APA) released an executive summary called "Sexualization of Girls," indicating that sexualizing girls is not only rampant in American culture, but it is harmful to both sexes. The APA suggested that "sexualization" occurs when a person's value comes only from his or her sexual appeal, when a person is sexually objectified (meaning that she is viewed as a "thing for sexual use"), and when a person is held to a "standard that equates physical attractiveness with being sexy."[1] According to the APA, virtually every form of media—from television to music videos, movies, magazines, sports media, video games, the Internet, and advertising—sexualizes girls more than boys. In fact, the APA study found in study after study that women more often than men were portrayed in a sexual manner (in revealing clothing with body postures and facial expressions implying "sexual readiness").[2]

The study mentions Skechers' "naughty and nice" ad with Christina Aguilera dressed as a schoolgirl with pigtails and an unbuttoned shirt, licking a lollipop.[3] And what about the Victoria's Secret models who prance around in bra and panties after the evening news? With their beautiful bodies and ample cleavage, they send messages to both girls and boys about the deliciousness of sex. What does it do to a young girl when those around her, as well as her culture, tell her she has to be "too sexy, too soon"? It robs her of innocence, violates her mind and her body image, and puts her on a treadmill of boy-pleasing early in life when she cannot possibly know who she is.

Small things like that.

In truth, the sexualization of girls robs them of childhood and takes them away from skill development, academic pursuits, and athletic accomplishments and sets them up for big-time problems later on. Like eating disorders to capture the *impossibly thin* body, low self-esteem, and debilitating depression.[4] In sum, the sexualization of our girls affects their cognitive development and emotional health, as well as their attitudes and beliefs about themselves, boys, and sex. And we contend it sets them up to give sexual favors to boys and even men—from oral sex to intercourse—for the asking at a time in their lives when they should be funneling their energies into wholesome, life-affirming pursuits.

WHAT ABOUT BOYS?

What does this sexualization of girls do to boys? First of all, it creates a huge distraction. Can you imagine what boys thought who went to school that day with the girl described at the beginning of this chapter? And we know there were others, maybe not as attractive or well-endowed. The boys in this middle school were exposed hourly to *girls as sex objects in every class!* How could they possibly concentrate? And, really, we know that teenage boys often think about sex anyway. Why up the ante?

In addition, a lot of middle school boys are either not that tuned into girls, or they may still be relatively innocent if they have not been allowed to watch sexy movies or television shows. When girls dress and act in sexually provocative ways, it can be troubling to boys. They may not know how to deal with their emotional and sexual responses or their arousal. Remember, the females they know intimately are their mothers and sisters. How to mesh this with all the sexual distractions at school? Plus, it colors their view of girls as sex objects rather than as people to be known for who they are.

Your sons need your tutelage and protection just as your daughters do.

MOMS AND DADS, ARE YOU PART OF THE PROBLEM?

Think about it, moms and dads, when you drop your daughters off at middle school. Don't be fooled by the oversized jacket that can be left in the locker all day. One father told us recently that he checks his daughter's school bag to make sure she isn't taking short shorts or a low-cut top to school; this was after her older brother snitched on her.

Teacher Tommy Jones addressed the male teacher's dilemma when a female student shows up at school scantily clad. "I have to tell some kids—and some of my fellow teachers (guys) won't do it: 'Sweetheart, you need to put on another shirt. Or do you have a jacket?' And sometimes I'll try to be nice and say—'because I'm telling you boys are boys, and you're a young lady. I don't think this is the image you want to portray.' And I'll ask them, 'Did your mother drop you off wearing that?' And they won't ever answer that question!"

Jones continued:

Usually they have a jacket with them or a different pair of pants. This is sensitive because here I am a male teacher asking a girl to cover herself up. Sometimes it's just easier to ask a woman to do it, but not everybody will, and then you get to seventh or eighth period, and they go, "Well, no one else said anything about the way I'm dressed." As they get to be eighth graders, the sexual part is more mental or cognitive and they know it, versus the sixth and seventh graders who are pretty clueless.

Moms, we need to ask you: Are you complicit in the sexualization of your daughter through the messages you give her about physical attractiveness and what she should wear? Do you place a high premium on being thin and popular? Many of the people we interviewed reminded us that it is the mother who generally buys her daughter's clothes. Dannah Gresh, founder of the ministry Pure Freedom, writes, "Since the girls do not have jobs, it's the moms who willingly fork out their credit cards to buy the tools of destruction for their daughters."[5]

Of course, marketers and retailers want you to whip out your credit card, since girls eight to twelve years old spend five hundred million dollars a year, and tweens have forty-three billion dollars of spending power nationwide.[6]

Since you, mom, rule when it comes to your daughter's wardrobe (unless dad plays the role of inspector general), we ask: What's going on? If a mother opens her wallet and knowingly turns her daughter into a sex object, what's happening at a deeper, unconscious level in her own psyche? Is it just that mom wants her girl to be popular in a way she wasn't, or does this have something to do with an unresolved sexual past? Think about it. The stakes are high when you put your daughter on a particular sexual trajectory, allowing her to dress in a suggestive manner. Are you sure you want to do this even if she cries and says every other girl dresses this way? At the extreme end of the spectrum is the mother from the show, *Toddlers and Tiaras*, who dressed her three-year-old daughter as Julia Roberts in her hooker role in the movie *Pretty Woman*.

On the other hand, if you are like many mothers we interviewed who are dismayed at what's available in the department stores, we suggest you protest locally and, if possible, nationally. Dannah Gresh protested the current state of girls' clothing when she created "The Modesty Project" and in 2009 marshaled some forty-seven thousand mothers and daughters to sign the "Modesty Project Petition," which was sent to the Council of Fashion Designers of

America, as well as the American Apparel and Footwear Association, to make them more aware of how fashion influences the lives of young girls. This created quite a stir, and *Women's Wear Daily* and *USA Today* "told the world" about The Modesty Project.[7]

We support all the mamas in this country who are fed up with the sexualization of their girls.

SEXUAL EXPERIMENTATION

Since girls have become sexualized in this culture, is it reasonable to assume that middle schoolers are experimenting with sex?

Though she hears rumors and gets calls from parents, principle Debra Scott doesn't think her students are sexually active, though she does worry about where some of her kids are going with their Flip cameras when they're outside making videos for their science class. "There's this little nook back there where the elementary principal was so nice to put a carpet and bean bag chairs, and it's out of view of our cameras, and I'm thinking, 'Here I'm worried about sex and you're putting out a rug and pillows?' As a principal, I see the red flags and I think, what corners are they getting into and what are they videotaping?"

Researchers report that the percentage of middle schoolers engaged in risky sexual activity is still relatively small. A 2010 Guttmacher Institute study by Christine J. De Rosa and her colleagues on the prevalence of sexual intercourse and oral sex among 4,557 middle school students found that overall 9 percent had ever had intercourse, 8 percent had had oral sex, and 5 percent had had both.[8]

In their 2010 Youth Risk Behavior Surveillance study, the Centers for Disease Control and Prevention (CDC) reports that 5.9 percent of students had sexual intercourse before age thirteen, with more boys having had sex than girls (8.4 percent vs. 3.1 percent).[9] Based on what we have heard from school personnel and parents, we believe these studies underreport the problem. We have been confused at times by the discrepancy between what the data show and what those on the front lines have reported to us. We hope that your middle schoolers are not sexually active. Perhaps you are like one mother we interviewed who said her sixth grade son is clueless, and her eighth grade daughter goes "Eeww" whenever her mother talks to her about sex. But even if your children are in the majority of abstaining middle schoolers, they will *hear* about what other kids are doing, and it will impact their inner world. This same mother, Leslie, who lives in Charlotte, North Carolina, said that when her daughter was in seventh grade, they had this conversation:

> "You wouldn't believe what the girls say they are doing with the football team."
> "Well, what are they doing?" Leslie asked.
> "Mom, I can't even talk about it," the daughter said. "They're doing IT!" she exclaimed in exasperation.
> "So the girls are having sex with them?"
> "Yes, that's IT."

One mother told us she is grateful that her eleven- and thirteen-year-old middle schoolers are not interested in sex, said that when she lived in California, she knew that some seventh grade girls in her daughter's school "were servicing boys in the movie theaters."

Our point is that even when parents try to protect their children in our over sexualized culture, the kids will hear about what other kids are doing and sometimes this rocks their world. One father told us that a girl in his daughter's class announced that she lost her virginity in seventh grade; she came to class high in eighth grade. He and his wife were troubled and were trying to help their daughter deal with these revelations.

SEXUAL FALLOUT

When middle schoolers become sexually active, not only are parents and school administrators concerned, but researchers express alarm. In fact, when researchers at the University of Texas School of Public Health found that middle schoolers as young as twelve were engaging in risky sexual activity, it created a national stir. Christine Markham, PhD, examined sexual behaviors among middle school students in a large, southeastern U.S. urban public school district, in one of the few studies to look at specific sexual behavior. The study found that although most seventh graders had not engaged in risky sexual behavior, some already had—multiple times. In fact, 12 percent of the students had already engaged in vaginal sex, 7.9 percent in oral sex, 6.5 percent in anal sex, and 4 percent in all three types of intercourse.[10]

According to Markham, "These findings are alarming because youth who start having sex before age 14 are much more likely to have multiple lifetime sexual partners, use alcohol or drugs before sex, and have unprotected sex, all of which puts them at greater risk for getting a sexually transmitted disease (STD) or becoming pregnant."[11]

Those who work in schools with middle schoolers have told us that more kids are sexually active than ever before. Counselor Linda Reyner says, "It's just not questioned" anymore that kids are having sex.

Middle school social worker Lisa DeCesaris agrees that sexual behaviors are drifting down to younger kids. She says:

> Doing this work has been such an eye-opener. Before I was a social worker, I was a high school English teacher. I taught mostly high school sophomores, and I remember when I started teaching thinking to myself, "None of these kids are having sex." And then by the time I finished teaching seven years later, by the time I went back to grad school for social work, I thought, "All of these kids are having sex." And then I started doing social work in a middle school, and I thought to myself, "Oh, none of these kids are involved in sexual activity." And the past twelve years have really changed my thoughts on that. I certainly don't think they're all having sex, but I do think that kids are becoming sexually active at a younger age.

"ORAL SEX: THE NEW GOODNIGHT KISS"

What about oral sex? Some students have witnessed oral sex on the school bus or in the classroom. For example, at Haycock Intermediate School in Southern California, a seventh grade girl engaged in oral sex with an eighth grade boy while a film was being shown in the classroom. Other students filmed the sexual act on their cell phones. Where was the teacher? He was present but apparently just ignored the couple.[12]

Sadly, the topic of oral sex and teens is not new and has been around for years. Physician Leonard Sax, author of *Girls on the Edge,* says, "I have talked with many girls and young women whose main sexual experience, from age 14 onward, has been providing oral sex, with the girl on her knees servicing the boy. . . . I have been stunned by the detached tone in which some girls describe oral sex. 'It's no big deal,' is the recurring refrain. A girl who knows how to give 'good' oral sex can raise her status in the eyes of boys, without risking pregnancy or even making eye contact."[13]

So common has oral sex become in the teen culture that it is called "the new goodnight kiss." In fact, Claire Shipman and Cole Kazdin did a *Good Morning America* special on "Oral Sex and Casual Prostitution," based on the documentary by Canadian filmmaker Sharlene Azam about the secret sexual lives of today's tweens and teens, some of whom are as young as eleven years old. In addition to her documentary, *Oral Sex is the New Goodnight Kiss,* Azam wrote a book under the same title about the epidemic in teen and even tween sexual promiscuity.

Azam told *Good Morning America* that oral sex is as common as kissing for teens and that casual prostitution—being paid at parties to give sexual favors—has become commonplace. Azam says that teens don't think oral sex is any big deal. In fact, they don't consider it sex, echoing what we heard from middle school counselors. In this documentary, eleven-year-olds talk about having sex and exchanging sexual favors for money, clothes, or even homework "and then still arriving home for dinner with the family." The girls talked about pressure to "do anything" to stay in a relationship with a boy. While the girls interviewed said they liked the "no strings attached" behavior, Azam believes otherwise. "A lot of girls are disappointed in love, and I think they believe they can hook up the way guys do and not care. But unfortunately, they do care."[14]

What did Azam find when she looked at the parents of the girls engaging in risky sex? She discovered that they were completely *unaware* of what their daughters were doing. Further, Azam believes that for parents, ignorance is bliss. "Parents don't want to know," she says, "because they really don't know what to do. I mean, you might be prepared to learn that, at age twelve, your daughter has had sex, but what are you supposed to do when your daughter has traded her virginity for $1,000 or a new bag?"[15] She continues, "We're not talking about marginalized girls; we're talking about the prettiest girls from affluent families who thought nothing of trading oral sex for cash, cell phones, handbags at sex parties or hotel rooms." The girls were shocked to find that Azam described what they did as prostitution, since were they not women walking in off the streets.

Azam believes that though her documentary involves girls across Canada, the same thing is happening in middle schools and high schools in the United States. "It's a hidden problem," she says.

What can parents do? Azam says, "You almost have to parent double time. You have to be engaged constantly or the kids are at risk."[16] Since kids do not believe that they are doing is in the same realm as losing their virginity, they obviously need to have parents talk to them about the risks, emotional and physical, of engaging in sexual behavior.

We need to tell our daughters that whenever boys and girls cross the line sexually, different standards prevail. As one disenchanted girl said, "When boys engage in oral sex, they get popular; when we do, we get labeled."

It was ever thus.

SEXUAL SIDE EFFECTS

The late Bernadine Healy, MD, former head of the National Institutes of Health and columnist for *U.S. News and World Report*, suggested that, from a medical perspective, oral sex is not risk-free sex. She said that parents must provide young people with "graphic medical information and stern parental and medical guidance" about the dangers of oral sex.[17] She understood that some young people believe oral sex preserves virginity—technically—and allows for "risk-free intimacy." However, from a medical perspective, oral sex is unsafe sex. Healy wrote:

> People seem clueless that sexually transmitted diseases such as herpes, gonorrhea, chlamydia, and human papillomavirus can take hold in parts of the oral cavity during sex with infected partners and that STD-ridden mouths are likely to transmit disease to uninfected genitals. HPV is a particularly scurrilous threat, since it incubates silently in the back of the mouth and is linked to a dangerous form of throat cancer in both men and women similar to the one that arises in the cervix.[18]

Healy continued by saying that there has been an increase in oropharyngeal cancer, which develops in the tonsils and the base of the tongue, and the rise is linked to changing sexual practices, particularly the rise in oral sex. "That our children might be at growing risk for this deadly cancer is particularly unnerving," said Healy. "Health surveys indicate that well over half of American teens now engage in oral sex, with about 10 to 20 percent claiming 'technical virginity.'"[19] Healy, who was one of America's most prominent physicians, advocated abstinence from both vaginal sex and oral sex.

Caitlin Flanagan, writing in the *Atlantic Monthly*, laments the plight of America's girls:

> And here are America's girls: experienced beyond their years, lacking any clear message from the adult community about the importance of protecting their modesty, adrift in one of the most sexualized cultures in the history of the world. Here are America's girls: on their knees.[20]

What about the side effects of "real" sex?

In an interview, Dr. Mark Piehl told us sex is surprisingly prevalent among young adolescents and that the concept of "safe sex" is an illusion. "Kids may be given a false sense of security when they are told they can have safe sex. Many sexually transmitted infections, such as herpes, human papilloma virus (HPV), and HIV, are permanent and incurable. Of these, HPV and herpes are not reliably prevented through condom use." Moreover, kids are far less likely than adults to use condoms consistently or correctly, says Piehl.

Dr. Piehl says that young girls disproportionately suffer the consequences of early sexual activity, for several reasons. Compared to older girls and adults, adolescent girls are at greater risk of contracting STIs, they are most affected by the burden of unwanted pregnancy, and they may suffer more emotional consequences of early sexual activity.

"Condoms can do nothing to protect a young girl's heart," adds Piehl.

THE LINGERING EMOTIONAL PAIN

Psychologists know that the effects of early sexual experience don't simply go away; they linger, creating shame and a distorted self-image that some girls will carry for years. In fact, pediatrician Meg Meeker says that girls who engage in sex in their early teenage years are at higher risk for depression than girls who don't. She calls depression a "sexually transmitted disease," meaning that sex *causes* the depression in young girls.[21] Early sexual experiences put girls on a path many find hard to get off. When they begin having sex at thirteen and fourteen, they become geisha girls or little wives and fail to learn how to relate to males in a nonsexual way.

Kathie Lee Gifford addressed other consequences of early sexuality in an interview with *MSNBC's TODAY* Moms blog. The talk show host decried television shows like *Skins* that flagrantly advocate sex among teens. She said:

On so many of these shows, you never see an STD that results from it, you don't see the depression the girl goes through when the guy—after he has used her—rejects her. So she starts mutilating herself, and she starts hating herself because she feels unloved, and then she gives herself away to everybody in hopes that somebody will love her. Maybe not the one who rejected her, but somebody. And it starts a whole path of depression and rejection and despair that ultimately leads to not just pregnancies but teen suicides.[22]

The consequences of early sexual experience just roll on.

BOTH SEXES GET HURT

Do boys suffer when they engage in early sex? Of course they do. You might believe they are not harmed as much as girls. After all, folk wisdom says that boys are driven by hormones and want sex—indiscriminate sex—while girls long for intimacy in their sexual relationships. Well, we are not so sure this stereotype is true.

The evidence is that early sexual experience has consequences for both boys and girls. Joe McIlhaney, MD, an obstetrician and coauthor of the book *Hooked: New Science on How Casual Sex Is Affecting Our Children,* told us that "sex is a primary stimulator and molder of the brain. When we have sex, the body secretes the hormone dopamine, and that makes one want to do it again and again. That's one of the primary reasons to abstain from sex when you're young, because it becomes addictive." He adds, "The body also secretes the hormone oxytocin, that some label the love hormone—a hormone that seems to contribute to a girl's trusting a man she is intimate with and also bonding to him emotionally." Then comes the breakup. McIlhaney continues, "When young people break up, MRIs show that the pain center of the brain lights up. Emotional and physical pain are felt in the same brain center." McIlhaney believes that when kids have multiple breakups, they seem to contribute to their losing their ability to forge lasting connections or attachments with the opposite sex. In addition, they sometimes become depressed and some become suicidal.

We contend that boys and later men want to think well of females in their lives. It's all there in the Courtly Love literature of the twelfth century. The knight went on a quest for the female he admired from afar, usually the most important woman in the castle. He wanted to engage in heroic pursuits for his lady love. He did this, not necessarily for sexual conquest, but for the longing that burned in his heart to be heroic and gallant—to be deserving of this mysterious female he had put on a pedestal.

Since this is so, many middle school boys are surprised and even flummoxed by the aggressiveness of modern girls who pursue and text them constantly. Like the sixth grade girls in one school who texted the boys in their class and asked them to meet near the woods during recess. Or the seventh grade girls who pursued one boy so relentlessly his mother cried, "Enough!"

Girls should appeal to the best in boys—the heroic—and should value themselves highly. The fire that burns in the male breast is quenched when the female stoops low and gives away the most intimate part of herself. No secrets or mystery here. It is all free for the asking. This will change how boys view girls. Forever. They will see females primarily as objects of sexual desire. And some boys will grow up to become young men who are disrespectful, violent, and even brutish with women. We see this happening today on college campuses around the United States. Recently, Yale University was sued under Title IX for allowing sexual harassment and assault against students, primarily women, to go unpunished on campus. The lawsuit was ignited when members of the Delta Kappa Epsilon fraternity chanted "no means yes" and "yes means anal" in October 2010.[23]

BEWARE THE EMPTY HOUSE

What can concerned parents do to help their child avoid early sexual experiences?

At this point, we need to address a topic parents seldom talk about anymore, but which is really the proverbial elephant in the living room: the empty house. Sex has got to occur somewhere. What better place than the empty house? Today, millions of middle schoolers and high schoolers return home after school, insert a key into the lock, and enter a house that is lonely and devoid of adult supervision.

When we asked one teacher how many kids at his public school (where one-third are labeled "gifted") came home to empty houses, he answered, "A lot of them. Even the wealthy ones. To me that's scary because I know I've heard students say—whether they've said it directly to me or not—there's money left on the table, or there's a note, 'Order a pizza. I'll be home at 9.'"

Does this happen often, we asked? The teacher replied, "For some it becomes a pattern, it becomes a habit, and the kids learn how to live life on their own. . . . Some kids can be completely diligent and disciplined, and others don't have the structure set in place yet. And yes, it's sad."

A lot can happen in an empty house.

At the very least, you have a kid spending hours alone. Feeling lonely. Feeling blue. Feeling afraid when darkness falls. That's why some kids have sex in the afternoon or invite friends in to drink or use drugs. The empty house can be a sterile, cold, and lonely place. It can also be a dangerous place for young teens.

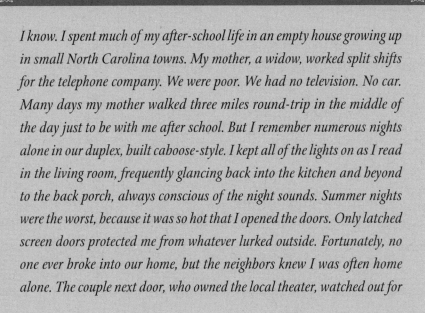

I know. I spent much of my after-school life in an empty house growing up in small North Carolina towns. My mother, a widow, worked split shifts for the telephone company. We were poor. We had no television. No car. Many days my mother walked three miles round-trip in the middle of the day just to be with me after school. But I remember numerous nights alone in our duplex, built caboose-style. I kept all of the lights on as I read in the living room, frequently glancing back into the kitchen and beyond to the back porch, always conscious of the night sounds. Summer nights were the worst, because it was so hot that I opened the doors. Only latched screen doors protected me from whatever lurked outside. Fortunately, no one ever broke into our home, but the neighbors knew I was often home alone. The couple next door, who owned the local theater, watched out for

me, but I grew up hating the empty house. I didn't turn to alcohol or sex, but I internalized a lot of loneliness.

Years later, when I had my daughters, I decided that I would not bequeath them the legacy of the empty house. As a single mother, I tailored my work life so that I could be with Holly and Kristen when the school bell rang. After I remarried, I worked as a writer from home and planned my doctoral work at Georgetown University so that I could be home with the girls after school. Even in the late '80s, I was one of the few mothers inhabiting a home in my neighborhood in the afternoons. Today Kristen, who works from home as a writer, has also chosen to BE THERE with her children after school, a decision that makes my heart sing.

—Brenda

It's important that your child come home to an adult who cares about his or her well-being. If you or your spouse cannot be there, why not engage the services of a neighbor or member of your extended family? Edna, an Australian grandmother who lives near her only daughter's family, pops her head in the door to say "Hi" to her seventeen-year-old grandson who comes home to an empty house. She tells him, "Oh, I know you're fine here alone, but I just wanted to check in and hear about your day." Her employed daughter, Jennie, says she is grateful for her mother's help.

VIRGINITY LIVES

Now for some good news. In March of 2011, the National Center for Health Statistics reported that 27 percent of men and 29 percent of women ages fifteen to twenty-four said they had *never* experienced sex. This is up 22 percent for both sexes since the government's last survey, released in 2005. While no middle schoolers were included in this survey, we hope that the frenzy ignited by the sexual revolution in the 1960s is cooling off and that modesty and abstinence will make a comeback.[24] In a recent article in *USA Today* entitled "Is Dating Dead?" 72 percent of college students said they had "hooked up" (a euphemism for mild to flaming sexual activity), while 23 percent of both men and women, ages eighteen and nineteen, said they had never had sexual contact with another person.[25]

Thankfully, in some corners of America, virginity lives.

DRUGS AND ALCOHOL

Sexual experimentation is just one area of concern; parents are anxious about substance abuse as well. One father said, "I worry about drugs and alcohol. With drugs it appears to me to be limited to certain groups of kids. It's not like it's pervasive throughout the school. But alcohol is more pervasive. It's usually because the kids are home, there's no adult, and there's a liquor cabinet. Once they get into that, a whole host of things follow."

How widespread are drugs in middle school? In the *National Survey of American Attitudes on Substance Abuse XV: Teens and Parents*, the Center for Addiction and Substance Abuse at Columbia University found that some 23 percent of twelve- to thirteen-year-olds currently attend schools where drugs are prevalent, an increase of 39 percent over 2009. Those middle schoolers who attend schools where drugs are readily available are thirty-three times more likely to have tried alcohol and one to three times more likely to have tried marijuana. No twelve- to thirteen-year-old used marijuana in a drug-free school, whereas 10 percent did so in a drug-infested school.[26] The bottom line? Get your child out of a drug-infested school or fight tenaciously to clean up the school.

But for those kids who do drink alcohol, when do they *really* start to drink in this culture? A study conducted by John Donavan, an associate professor of psychiatry and epidemiology at the University of Pittsburgh Medical Center, found that some 7 percent of fourth graders reported that they had had an alcoholic drink in the past year. But the largest jump occurred between fifth and sixth grades, just at the time kids begin middle school.[27] Although some kids try marijuana before age thirteen, alcohol is the primary drug of choice for children, and they usually get their first drink at home, served by their parents.[28] And while elementary school children see drinking as wrong, in middle school attitudes change because of the presence of older children.[29]

If you happen to be a parent who feels it's best if you introduce your child to alcohol at home, think again. A new study finds that teens who drink with an adult present are more likely to have later problems with alcohol than those whose parents tell them not to drink until they are twenty-one.[30] The study tracked 1,945 seventh graders from Australia and Washington State for three years. They were asked questions, like how many times they had experienced harmful consequences from drinking, such as "not able to stop once you had started" and "had sex with someone you later regretted." Australian teens, who were more likely than their American counterparts to drink with adult supervision by eighth grade (66 percent vs. 35 percent), were also more likely to have experienced harmful consequences from underage drinking.

Bottom line? Draw a line, support the law, and tell kids to say no alcohol until they are of legal drinking age, at the very least.

FAMILY FIRST

What helps teens say no to drugs? You guessed it: a happy family. Kids with close family ties (parents who seldom argued, who listened, who went to church at least once a month, and ate family dinners five times a week) were inoculated against substance abuse, whereas those with weak family ties were open season. Strong family ties protect kids against tobacco, alcohol, and marijuana use. Period.[31]

A powerful antidote to experimentation with substance abuse is *the humble family dinner*. Researchers have found that twelve- to thirteen-year-olds who have frequent family dinners (five or more per week) when compared to those who have infrequent family dinners (two or fewer per week) are:

- Six times *less likely* to have used marijuana.
- Four and a half times *less likely* to have used tobacco.
- Two and a half times *less likely* to have used alcohol.[32]

Isn't it amazing that dinner with you at the end of the day can anchor your child to a good and decent life, giving him a sense of belonging?

It is simple, yet profound.

SUMMING UP

Can you see just how significant your role is in your children's lives during these pivotal middle school years? They will take their cues from you in the clothing and sexual arenas, as well as in the area of drugs and alcohol. Remember, your attitudes, practices, and presence rule in their lives. Hey, it won't be easy. But your kids are worth it. During these middle school years, you have a Big Job: you need to be a vigilante, a tutor, a listener, a clothing stylist, a substance abuse expert, a detective, and a teacher of morality and spirituality.

And if you have unresolved sexual issues from your past that would hinder you from teaching your child about sexual morality, now is the time to confront and deal with your shame and low self-worth. Otherwise, you will be hamstrung in dealing with your child. One mother who had buried her own promiscuity began accusing her innocent thirteen-year-old daughter of sexual misconduct. Not surprisingly, the girl eventually got into trouble and had a baby in her late teens. So deal with any guilt or shame. Then you will be better able to set limits and sexual boundaries for your child.

While cultural forces would try to steal your child's innocence and lead him down a path toward STDs and addiction, *yours* is the more powerful voice your child hears. If you are physically and emotionally accessible, there's a far greater chance your child will listen to what you say, and comply. Finally, to stand against cultural pressures, your kids need to know that you love them with passion and abandon, and God does too.

More from Kathie Lee Gifford:

You know, kids just want to be loved, but they look for love in all the wrong places because they don't believe inherently that God loves them just the way they are. And that's the best message any of us can give to our children: "You don't need to have that jerk on the football team tell you you're beautiful. God tells you you're beautiful. God tells you you're beautiful from your toes up, and more than that, inside you're beautiful and he has a great plan for your life if you'll only trust him for it. Don't fall for the big lie the world gives you that if you do this, and this, and this, and this, you're going to have it all. No, you're going to have a pregnancy, you're going to have an STD, you're going to have misery in your life, you're going to have despair. OK? Now you have the freedom to make that choice." God gives us that. . . . I get mad at parents who don't tell their kids the truth.[33]

So tell your children the truth about the high cost of sex outside of marriage. Take a stand. Never waver. And your children will listen, and many will wait for sex inside a loving and committed relationship. Then they will not only make you proud, but they will have a better chance at finding lasting love as an adult.

PARENT TIPS

Remember your own adolescence and the way you handled sex. Deal with any regrets and don't let the past co-opt the present.

Tell your child THE TRUTH about drugs, sex, and alcohol. Don't leave it to the school or his friends to educate him.

Don't give your child alcohol at home for any reason.

Monitor your middle schooler's friends. If they are a bad influence, encourage your child to find new friends. This is easier said than done. But do it anyway.

Take your child to places where others will support your values: church, youth group, homes of parents you know and respect. Stand firm.

Chapter Ten

BULLIES,
BYSTANDERS,
VICTIMS

"Hurt people hurt people."

—**Holly Emanuel**, middle school principal

"Bullying has become a tidal wave of epic proportions."

—**National Crime Prevention Council**

"You don't deserve to live."

"God should never have created you."

"Why don't you just go kill yourself? You would do everybody a favor."

"I would laugh if I watched you hanging."

"I'll go get you the gun if I can watch you blow your brains out."

These are terrible words, right? Even for an adult, such messages are painful to read. We wish we could tell you these statements were hypothetical—missives we conjured up to illustrate the crushing power of adolescent malice.

But they're not. They're real. Kathleen, a fourteen-year-old girl, was on the receiving end of all of these words from girls at her public school. Cara, a "second mom" to Kathleen, told us about her young friend's victimization—perpetrated, she says, because "a bunch of girls ganged up and decided to make her life a living misery." Cara says:

> It was amazing the things that were being said to this girl. . . . She was at the point where she wanted to kill herself. We talked about it a lot. I was *very* concerned about her. . . .
>
> The teachers tried to intervene, but their methods were, "Well, let's have some sensitivity training for the kids doing this. Let's tell them it's not nice." The problem is that a lot of kids, for whatever reason, just don't seem to have the same sensitivity to their peers. It's like they're little kids that like to burn the ants with the magnifying glass.

OF BOYS AND BULLIES

If you're a parent of a daughter, hearing about Kathleen's victimization must surely make your blood boil. It certainly had that effect on us. What about boys? Tiffany and Scott, parents to a blended family, told us about the protracted bullying their son Daniel experienced as he rode the bus home from school last year in sixth grade. A boy bully brigade mocked and ridiculed Daniel, but one boy in particular instigated the bulk of the nastiness. Here's what Daniel's stepmom Tiffany says he endured:

> It was really bad language, put-downs, insulting stuff. It wasn't, "You're a loser." It was, "You're a f****n' fat SOB." At one point, one of them was saying he [Daniel] had sex with his mother—awful stuff. It was clearly crossing a significant line there.
>
> Our original rule was, "You don't fight. You try a more appropriate way of dealing with it." We had gone to the school. They had tried a lot of things—they had had the boys come in and sign this

contract [with Daniel], and they had suspended one of the kids who had bullied him—a whole host of interventions. But it didn't stop. Ultimately, [Daniel] was taking a totally different bus that was stopping a considerable distance from our house and walking home in order to avoid contact with this boy. I told him [Daniel] that I did not want him to instigate trouble. But if this boy said anything to him, he had permission to say something back—to tell him to shut up and leave him alone, to up it a bit. I said, "Word for word, physical to physical. If this boy touches you in any way, shape, or form, you lay him out!"

So [Daniel] rode the bus. They had a strong verbal confrontation. It never did progress to the physical, and the boy started to back down when he realized that [Daniel] was going to defend himself.

Can you relate to Tiffany's story of bus rides fraught with fear and tension? We know many of you have children who have been subjected to the cruel taunts—and even blows—of other students. Maybe it has happened at school—in the hallways or in the cafeteria. Perhaps it has happened online. We're sure of this: it's happening a lot. In fact, stomping out bullying has become a national cause célèbre; President and Mrs. Obama even hosted a White House conference on bullying prevention in early 2011.

GROUND ZERO IN THE BULLY WARS

If you have a middle schooler, you already know what we're going to tell you: middle school is ground zero in the bully wars. Some of your kids are taking cover right now, their hair singed by the flaming salvos and epithets lobbed across the schoolyard—actual or virtual—by modern meanies.

We want to encourage you by telling you it gets better as kids get older. It doesn't go away, of course, but bullying reaches its peak in late childhood and early adolescence. How common is it? According to the American Academy of Child and Adolescent Psychiatry, roughly half of all kids will be bullied at some point during the K–12 years, 10 percent of them on an ongoing basis.[1]

Girls are prone to bully verbally while boys often act out physically. But as you can see clearly from Daniel's example, boys engage in verbal nastiness, too. And girls have been known to land some punches as well. One guidance counselor who works with middle schoolers told us bullying is a "topic that needs to be hit time and time again." She says, "I think bullying occurs at all schools in different forms, depending on the school culture."

WHY, WHY, WHY?

Bullying has always been with us. But studies indicate it has reached epic proportions. You can't read or watch the news these days without hearing some sad story about a bullied student. Most commentators focus on *how* to respond to bullying.

But don't you want to know *why* it's increasing? In Chapter Four, we talked about the importance of parent-child attachment in the development of empathy. Since parents socialize children—teaching them their earliest and most powerful lessons about how to relate to other human beings—they are the architects of empathy. Or not. Actually, bullying and empathy are flip sides of the same coin. An empathic child is no bully.

Why are kids less empathic and therefore more prone to bully? We contend it is because more kids today are walking around with insecure or ruptured attachments to their parents. In the wake of parental divorce, many are growing up without one of their parents, or at best spend protracted time away from mom or dad, shuttling back and forth between parental homes. And parents—often both mom and dad—are working more than ever, which means kids spend many hours with caregivers in day care starting when they are infants, and then in after-school care or on their own in empty houses as they get older.

So who is teaching this generation how to be human? For too many, it is an unpredictable and constantly shifting parade of people.

Kids who aren't close to mom and dad are at risk—for low self-esteem, meanness, and bullying. Obviously, other factors play a role, too. Kids who

witness violence and hostility at home learn destructive lessons about regulating their emotions. And a school culture that tolerates or tacitly condones
bullying is problematic, too.

But parents are the first and best anti-bullying program around. A kid
who feels loved and close to his parents is highly unlikely to bully his peers.

So, what about that bullying triumvirate of victims, bullies, and
bystanders?

VICTIMS

Who becomes a bullying victim? We have already stated in the empathy chapter that insecure kids can be both victims and bullies. Now let's differentiate
between the two. Victims are often kids whose appearance or behavior devi-
ates from standard or expected norms. Bullied children lack social power and
have fewer friends than kids who are not bullied. Victims may be overweight
or look slightly different. Bullied kids are generally more prone to depression
or anxiety—*but not always*. They may also be more sensitive and have trouble
defending themselves or standing up to others.[2]

Some bullied children are mistreated because they irritate other kids.
Karen, whose daughter Rachel is in seventh grade, says Rachel tells her stories
of one girl at school who is routinely picked on because she isn't savvy about
responding to her peers' attempts to redirect her behavior. Karen tells of one
recent incident:

> [Rachel] had a substitute gym teacher and the girls went in the locker
> room. Some of them wrote on the lockers and a couple of them stole
> a girl's bra. They threw it in the trash, and she couldn't find it. They
> said to the girl that she didn't need one anyway—that she looked like
> a boy. This is one of the girls who doesn't respond to social cues. She
> doesn't stop doing things when you ask her to stop.

Karen says she has talked to Rachel about how to respond to this girl, under-
scoring that Rachel should not take out her frustration through meanness.

Instead, says Karen, she should just explain that this girl's behavior is bothering her. Karen says, "I tell her, 'It's different to say, "You're annoying me" versus saying, "You have big funny ears, and I don't like the way you look."'"

BULLIES

Like victims, bullies are also more likely to suffer from mental health problems. A British study of almost seven hundred kids ages twelve to sixteen found that bullies were more likely to be hostile, depressed, and anxious. These kids are also more prone to live on the edge—they were more likely to have been offered alcohol than non-bullies. And bullies often hail from homes where they live with a single parent, foster parents, or extended family.[3]

These aren't happy kids.

Bullies may be strategic about their choice of a target, honing in on those more vulnerable kids who are unlikely to tap into a strong support network at school. Research shows that "bullies tended to hold a negative view of themselves, suggesting they pick on others to feel better about themselves, and they may especially single out those who have trouble fitting in for other reasons."[4]

Kids who bully are not only at risk during their school years. Male bullies are more likely to go on to become criminals as well. One study found that almost 60 percent of boys identified by researchers as bullies in sixth through ninth grades went on to be convicted of a crime by the time they were twenty-four; some 40 percent of these boy bullies had three or more convictions by the time they turned twenty-four.[5]

BYSTANDERS

Who is the bystander? No foolproof profile exists. It can be anyone or everyone. Chances are pretty good your middle schooler will be a bystander at some point—if not today, then probably tomorrow. According to the National Crime Prevention Council, a majority of U.S. teens (six out of ten) "witness bullying at least once a day."[6]

This exposure to bullying takes a toll. In her book, *The Bully, the Bullied, and the Bystander*, educator Barbara Coloroso writes, "Bystanders are also affected by bullying. These onlookers may observe the bullying, walk away, jump in as accomplices, or actively intervene and help the bullied child. All of these options come at a price."[7]

Increasingly, school-based anti-bullying efforts are focused on mobilizing and educating bystanders. At one school we visited, sixth graders signed a "Bystander's Pledge" promising the following:

> When I see a bullying situation at [school name], I pledge to put a
> stop to it. I will either REPORT, SUPPORT, or STAND UP.

Educational psychologist Dr. Michele Borba has developed a Bully-BUSTER acronym for parents and educators to use as they train bystanders on bullying-intervention strategies. According to her blog, Dr. Borba used this technique to work with middle schoolers on a *Dateline* special:

B: Befriend the victim
U: Use a distraction (to divert attention)
S: Speak out and stand up (show or state disapproval)
T: Tell or text for help
E: Exit alone or with others (bullies love audiences)
R: Give a reason or a remedy (say *why* the action is wrong and *what* to do)[8]

We applaud efforts to educate bystanders to do the right thing. As one mother of a sixth grader said, "Just being a bystander is participating." However, we worry about shifting the responsibility for mediation to kids. Encouraging students to report bullying is fine. But in today's school culture, it isn't always safe to do so. Ultimately, adults need to be the ones to step in and put a stop to it.

WHAT BULLYING IS . . . AND ISN'T

In this chapter, we've offered some clear-cut examples of what bullying *is*. No one would dispute the fact that Kathleen and Daniel were bullied. But we also want to share with you what bullying *isn't*. When your daughter is told on Monday morning that she looks fat in the new jeans she purchased over the weekend, she isn't being bullied—though this ill-conceived remark will likely make her self-conscious. And when one boy lashes out at another, telling him he's a loser because he doesn't make the buzzer-beater shot at the end of a tied game, that's not bullying, either. Bullying is not a single event or even a nasty post online, upsetting as these may be. Here's how one middle school principal defines bullying:

> I don't think parents understand our definition of bullying, which is something that has happened consistently over time. Being shoved in the hall or being called something in the hall is bad, and we try to address it, but if we spent all our time on that we would get nothing done.

Parents need to be careful to assess whether bullying is ongoing and harmful, or whether it represents "the natural progression of changing friends" that those who work with kids, like the principal above, know and understand is a normal—if painful—part of middle school. Sporadic name-calling, or a falling-out with a cherished friend, calls for a heart-to-heart with mom or dad, not a visit to the principal's office. Parents may be able to help kids patch things up with a friend if a misunderstanding becomes entrenched. And some things smooth over with the passage of time.

But fixing friendships is not the province of school administrators.

Other times, when a friendship isn't on the line, and a classmate is acting in a way that's just plain mean (but not on a recurring basis), it may work best for a child to defend herself, and then turn on her heel and head in the other direction. Karen says:

> Last year at a dance, a girl had it out with [Rachel]. They were very competitive. She said, "You can't dance" to Rachel. This girl's parents were going through a divorce. Rachel and I had to work on how she

could stand up for herself without getting in the dirt—saying things like, "I don't like it when you talk to me that way," or "You hurt my feelings."

One sixth grader, Leila, said meanness is a problem in her school, and actually it's the boys who dish it out a lot. She says, "It's usually not the girls but sometimes the guys will like call you 'fat' and stuff and just like say things that are really rude." What's the best way to deal with this? "Kind of laugh about it and move on," she says.

Experts recommend using three specific criteria to evaluate whether or not your child is being bullied:

1. The bully intends harm, pain, or humiliation to the victim.
2. There is an imbalance in power between the bully and the victim (this can be physical or social).
3. The aggression is perpetrated repeatedly and over time.[9]

If these three criteria are being met, moms and dads, it's time to head in to school and advocate for your child. You do not want full-on bullying to proceed unchecked, as the emotional (and physical) costs to your child can be extremely high.

We would also add that parents should track closely with their child's moods, since both bullying victims and aggressors are more prone to mental health disturbances. If your gregarious middle schooler suddenly becomes troubled and sad, retreating to his room for long stretches of time, it's time to get in there and find out what's going on. Take your child for counseling if the low mood persists.

BULLYING'S CYBER-TWIN

If bullying is so painful, what about cyberbullying? What is it anyway? The Cyberbullying Research Center defines it as "willful and repeated harm inflicted through the use of computers, cell phones, and other electronic devices."[10]

Cyberbullies may send their victims intimidating or nasty texts or e-mails. They may spread vicious rumors online. Some even impersonate a victim on a social networking site—ever easier to do since kids swap passwords so readily. In recent years, cyberbullying has risen exponentially. National Crime Prevention Council survey data indicate 43 percent of teens had been victims of cyberbullying over the past year.[11] Cyber-lawyer Parry Aftab, executive director of the site WiredSafety.org, indicates that 85 percent of middle schoolers have been cyberbullied at least once.[12] These numbers are rising and they're all too high.

Girls are more likely to engage in online bullying than boys. Leigh Hodge, mother of sixteen-year-old Alana, says her daughter was bullied both in person and online while she attended a private Christian middle school. During eighth grade, the bullying became widespread—one group of girls told another girl online they couldn't wait to start throwing chairs at her the next day to kill her.

Leigh took action. She says, "Finally, I got to the point where I went in and said, 'It's got to stop.' But the teachers weren't experienced at handling it, especially the after-school online stuff." Eventually, she and her husband threw up their hands in frustration and withdrew Alana, enrolling her in another private school for ninth grade.

That was just the beginning of their cyberbullying nightmare. The summer before ninth grade, Alana went on Facebook to become acquainted with some of the kids in her new school. But the site quickly became a vehicle for trashing Alana's reputation. Says Leigh:

> Everything starts out benign on Facebook. [But] when one girl saw that [Alana] was coming in and she was a pretty girl, she was going to do everything that she could to either make [Alana] her pawn and expect [Alana] to be her shadow and do everything that she said. Well, that's not my daughter.
>
> So [this girl] started the bullying in school. . . . And the rumors became vicious—I'm talking rumors about my daughter being

sexually active every weekend. . . . These girls said she was doing stuff with every junior in the back seat of the car.

Begun in school, the rumors were posted online as well. Alana was devastated. Leigh funneled her frustration into detective work behind the scenes. She insisted Alana keep snapshots from Facebook pages (Alana did this, and provided actual transcripts for us to review). Even Alana's brother Tom tried to intervene, to no avail. Here is what one student posted on Facebook in response to Tom's attempts to stop the cyberbullying:

> [Tom] go f**k your sister. We all know she's the camera whore who messes around with upperclassmen. Maybe you should have a talk with her about not letting everyone in her pants for once so people can stop talking about her. You know [School Name] never had this slut problem until she came along.

The girl who posted this missive later disavowed it. But with password-sharing among friends, it's hard to say. Someone at the school posted it.

Finally, Alana's tormentors made a critical mistake. They accused her of "doing it" with the juniors in the back seat of the car while she was home sick with the flu. Additionally, some other students were troubled by what was going on and reported it. Armed with tangible proof, administrators finally expelled the perpetrator from school. About time, don't you think?

ONLINE ANONYMITY

Sad to say, there is more than one way to tarnish someone's reputation online. Smut lists, which rank girls based on sexual experience—and generally include their first and last names—are wreaking havoc in schools nationwide. Posted anonymously, these lists enable cowardly accusers to remain cloaked in anonymity.

One high school in Westchester County, New York, made national news for its smut list, which was initially posted on Facebook and then "sent to students via mass messages on BlackBerry Messenger," according to Fox

News. Before the page was taken down, it reportedly garnered more than seven thousand "likes" in one day. The girls named on the list ranged in age from fourteen to eighteen years old. Said one girl, "If I was on the list I would think it's the end of the world. Nobody wants to be talked about like that."[13]

Anonymity is also wreaking havoc on the social networking site Formspring. Of Formspring, one school administrator told us, "That one blew up on us big-time this year [in 2011]."

Launched in 2009, Formspring is relatively new—in fact, some of the parents and school administrators we talked to had never heard of it. But ask your kids. We bet they know about it. And by the time this book comes out, other sites may very well have cropped up to take its place.

Formspring gained notoriety when one teenage girl in New York, Alexis Pilkington, committed suicide after nasty messages were posted on her Formspring account. Alexis's parents do not believe cyberbullying prompted their daughter to kill herself, but police investigators looked into the link nonetheless. A fifteen-year-old girl in Canada took her life following torment on Formspring (one post told her to kill herself). Her mother believes the cyberbullying was a factor in her daughter's death.[14]

On Formspring, kids can ask questions and post answers anonymously. And are they ever choosing to do it. As of 2011, the "Formspring Facts" section of the social networking site indicated that it had twenty-four million accounts in every country worldwide; three-and-a-half million people visit the site each day. One-third of Formspring's users are reportedly teens ages thirteen to seventeen.[15]

What's the appeal? It's the age-old lure: kids want to get to know other people. And the anonymity promises them unvarnished honesty. Things can get nasty pretty fast, but kids keep going back for more. School counselor Julia Taylor said, "It's a drug. It's like online crack."[16]

A recent *New York Times* article on Formspring's popularity diagnoses the problem pretty effectively: kids can't stop themselves, and *parents—who could stop it—won't*:

There's nothing positive on there, absolutely nothing, but the kids don't seem to be able to stop reading, even if people are saying terrible things about them," said Maggie Dock, a middle school counselor in Kinnelon, NJ. "I asked one girl, 'If someone was throwing rocks at you, what would you do?' She said she'd run, she'd move away. But she won't stop reading what people say about her."

"The comments are all gross and sexual," the mother [a parent of a girl in Westchester County, NY] said. "And yet, of course, this is coming from her friends. I wish I could just erase it, but all of her friends are online, and so much of their social interaction is online that I don't think I could just take away her Internet access. But I do think this whole online social media thing is a huge experiment on our children."[17]

It *is* an experiment. But do you want your middle schooler to be the guinea pig? You *can* take destructive social networking sites away. Yes, we said it, and we advocate it. You need to protect your child from profane and salacious name-calling.

If you don't, who will?

BE IN THE KNOW

We want to tell you what everyone else has been telling us: in the online world, you can't help your child if you don't know what's going on. And from what we hear, there's a lot that kids are keeping from their parents. Internet expert Parry Aftab has compiled some eye-opening statistics on cyberbullying and Internet use among kids. Take a look:

- Only 5 percent of middle schoolers would tell their parents if they were cyberbullied.
- 72 percent of middle schoolers report having more e-mail addresses than their parents know about.
- 83 percent of teens have at least one social networking account.

- 55 percent of seventh and eighth graders polled admitted to having a social networking account.
- 8 percent of ten-year-olds admitted to having a social networking account.
- 70 percent of teens polled said they share their password with their boyfriend or girlfriend or best friend. Sharing your password is the digital generation's equivalent of a "friendship ring."
- 86 percent of elementary school students share their passwords with their friend(s).
- Password theft or misuse accounts for 27 percent of cyberbullying.[18]

Here's what Lori Day, an educational psychologist and former school administrator, has to say to parents about cyberbullying and social media:

> Preteens and young teens simply are not psychologically ready to handle the potential weapon of social media any more than they are ready to handle guns, cars, alcohol, and other items that our society properly withholds from children until they have the maturity to use them in a safe and healthy manner...
>
> A personal anecdote from my days of running a school: Monday mornings sometimes involved the routine of arriving on campus around 8:00 A.M. to find lines outside each of my two office doors. One line in the hallway might contain three or four distraught students. The second line—ready to pounce on me from the front office if allowed access by my administrative assistant—consisted of parents holding stacks of paper and cell phones.
>
> Talk about triage! The crying students had many tales of weekend persecution to tell, and were trying to get ahead of each other in line to see me first. The parents held cell phones with saved text messages and voicemails, and Facebook printouts of dialogue between their child and other children. All wanted to see me *immediately* to "prove" what was going on. . . .

Patron Receipt
Charges

ID   21901024862892

Item   31901051531731
Title From Santa to sexting helping your chil
Call Number 649 1 HUNTER
Due Date: 10/25/2017

Item   31901056469671
Title The art of comic book writing the definit
Call Number 741 51 KNEECE
Due Date: 10/25/2017

Item   31901045321811
Title Muhammad Ali the making of an icon /
Call Number B ALI, M
Due Date: 10/25/2017

Children are *in loco parentis* at school for approximately 35 hours per week; they are the responsibility of their own parents for the remaining 133 hours. Even with the new (and highly flawed) anti-bullying legislation, our society will get nowhere with this problem without parents bearing the primary responsibility for raising their children. As I once told a group of parents, "I can't help you until you help me. Please take Facebook and texting away." I was amazed at how few parents would stand up to their kids and follow through. Sadly, until more do, things could get worse before they get better.[19]

Excellent advice. If your middle schooler is consumed with her cyber-life, step in. You provide the computer, right? That means you can monitor it, or even take it away if your child's use of it is out of control. We promise you—though your child may insist otherwise—he or she will not die if deprived temporarily of computer or Internet access.

Will some kids turn around and set up a social networking account at a friend's house, as we have heard? It's possible. What can you do? Limit Internet use at home, monitor time with friends (and band together with other parents), and do not give a middle schooler a personal laptop. Then you will be making major strides towards combating cyberbullying and promoting healthy Internet use.

THE BULLYING AND CYBERBULLYING SUICIDE LINK

In the cyberbullying realm, the stakes are high. A study evaluating some two thousand middle schoolers showed that kids who were the victims of cyber-bullying were almost *twice* as likely to attempt suicide as kids not involved in cyberbullying. Ironically, even those who perpetrate cyber-abuse are at risk and attempt suicide at rates about one and a half times that of other kids.[20] What about regular (non-cyber) bullying? Suicide attempts are more frequent here, too—for kids on the giving *and* the receiving end.[21]

News reports bear witness to this sad reality, especially for girls. Several girls who have been bullied on the sites Myspace, Facebook, and Formspring have gone on to commit suicide. Cyberbullying can wreak havoc through text messaging as well; in 2010, a North Carolina girl committed suicide days after receiving harassing text messages from male classmates. Research on traditional bullying shows that female bullies and victims are at very high risk of suicide: a Norwegian study of eighth graders found that bullied girl victims were four times as likely to have thoughts of suicide as girls who weren't bullied. And meanness makes girls feel pretty terrible about themselves: girl bullies were eight times more likely to think about suicide than girls who did not bully others.[22]

It's certainly true that some or all bullied kids who have gone on to kill themselves suffered from depression. But depression is widespread among middle schoolers today. So, we as parents must be vigilant about monitoring *any kind* of bullying behavior, both online and off.

CYBERBULLYING, THE LAW, AND PARENTAL RESPONSIBILITY

Most states have laws governing what happens in the cyberbullying realm. The National Conference of State Legislatures divides laws into three areas: those that cover *cyberstalking*, defined as using "the Internet, email or other electronic communications to stalk, and generally refers to a pattern of threatening and malicious behaviors"; *cyberharassment* which, unlike cyberstalking, does not usually involve a "credible threat" and centers more on harassing e-mails or messages, or posts on blogs and Websites; and *cyberbullying*, which refers to "electronic harassment or bullying among minors within a school context."[23]

Now, we know much of cyberbullying does not take place in a school context. It happens outside school hours, via text message, or while kids are online. But some states, according to the National Conference of State Legislatures, have "extended sanctions to include cyberbullying activities that originate off-campus, believing that activities off-campus can have a chilling and disruptive effect on children's learning environment."[24]

What should you do when your child is being bullied online? Contact her school or the bully's parents. Keep evidence. Consider submitting a complaint to the Internet service provider, as abusive posts and language likely violate the site's terms of service.

When should the police get involved? According to the New York State Division of Criminal Justice, you should "contact the police to pursue criminal remedies if cyberbullying involves acts such as: threats of violence; extortion; obscene or harassing phone calls or text messages; harassment, stalking or hate crimes; or child pornography."[25]

A NOTE ABOUT BULLYING POLICIES

We need to say a word about school bullying policies. Many are well-intentioned attempts to protect students, but they do have their problems. Broad, tough, consistently enforced bullying policies are best. Yet bullying has increasingly become a politically charged issue, especially in the realm of students' sexual orientation.

We will say it simply: bullying of gay students is troubling, wrong, and should not be tolerated—ever. No child should have to endure slurs, epithets, or taunts on an ongoing basis at school. This is a basic issue of human kindness. It is a tragedy that so many middle schoolers, gay or straight, are suffering unremitting misery at the hands of classmates.

But the injunction to protect kids from bullying should cover *all* students. As a result, we do not believe policies should enumerate sexual orientation as a "protected" characteristic. As you can see from our examples earlier in the chapter—and from abundant, reliable, and rigorous research—bullying is not relegated just to issues of sexual orientation. But much of the press on this subject is. All children need protection from aggressive bullying.

PARENTAL PUSHBACK

What happens when schools don't do their job to quash bullying? Is there ever a time for parents to push back? You bet there is. We should never condone having children lash out at others without provocation. But children who are bullied repeatedly need to be emboldened to protect themselves. This may be increasingly difficult in a school context that adheres to "zero tolerance" policies on violence. Remember Daniel's stepmom, Tiffany? She had a few insights to share with us about the zero tolerance policy at Daniel's school:

> In the schools, ample provocation is not a factor that's taken into consideration. We have a zero tolerance policy. You can be having the stuffing beaten out of you, and if you hit the kid back, both children are suspended. . . . If one child is horribly bullying another child, there is no recourse for the one being bullied.

Research backs up the fact that zero tolerance policies can backfire. According to a literature review by the American Psychological Association's Zero Tolerance Task Force, there is some concern that "zero tolerance policies may create, enhance, or accelerate negative mental health outcomes for youth by creating increases in student alienation, anxiety, rejection, and breaking of healthy adult bonds."[26]

So, moms and dads, there is a time to push back. We recommend going to the school first and working with the principal. But you may also choose to engage in the time-honored art of grassroots advocacy—reaching out to your local school board or state legislator if you're unhappy with the stance of your school district or state on bullying.

We would remind you of the words of anthropologist Margaret Mead: "Never underestimate the power of a small group of committed people to change the world. In fact, it is the only thing that ever has."

"AN OVAL OF REFUGE"

We want to end with a story of triumph and victory about long track speed skater and Olympic silver medalist Trevor Marsicano:

> Marsicano was a shy seventh grader who was taking medication for depression and was being bullied by classmates. "It was constant

harassment every day," he said. "I guess I was an easy victim."
Marsicano said he was taunted for having a facial rash and extra-long
eyelashes. On the third day of eighth grade, he said, he was jumped
from behind after standing up to a boy who had made some younger
girls cry. Marsicano said no one defended him. "It just got worse and
worse from that point on," he said.

"I had no confidence," Marsicano said. "I was scared of people
for two or three years. I didn't talk to anybody but my family, and
even then, there was not a lot to say. I was overdosing on depression
medication. At the end of eighth grade, I said: I don't want to go back
to school. I don't want to live anymore."[27]

His wise parents pulled him out of school to homeschool him; Marsicano
turned to speed skating. Skating became, as *New York Times* writer Aimee
Berg dubbed it, "an oval of refuge from a cold world."

"I wasn't being belittled or picked on," Marsicano said. "If I was
having a hard time skating, people would try to help. That was the
first time I felt comfortable in a group like that." The sport was also
empowering. "When I skated, I could forget about everything," he
said. "For one moment, I was in control of everything around me. I
started to get my confidence back."[28]

Marsicano also found hope in his faith in God. In 2008, he moved away from
his family to train in Milwaukee, Wisconsin. He says, "I had people telling me
I would not be successful and this path that I had chosen would not work. ...
At the beginning of the year it looked like they were right. However, through
perseverance, a strong will to fight, and my faith in God, I worked my way
through the ranks to become a world champion."[29]

Marsicano's victories have been hard-won. Not only did he endure years
of bullying, but he also sustained a life-threatening injury. In 2004, his leg was
cut to the bone by a competitor's skating blade; Marsicano lost half the blood
in his body. But he kept fighting.[30] Now in addition to his training, Marsicano

travels to schools to speak out against bullying. He is motivated and drawn by his faith in God and by an understanding that life has its good times and its challenges. He says, "I will have to rely on God to pull me through and chase this dream that I and many others have worked hard for. . . . Ecclesiastes 7:14 says, 'When times are good, be happy; but when times are bad, consider: God has made the one as well as the other.'"[31]

Indeed he has. And God will use even those hard times to forge perseverance that will enable us to run (or skate) the race. As moms and dads, though, we must, like Trevor Marsicano's parents, be willing to intervene boldly if we have a child who is suffering.

PARENT TIPS

Monitor moods. Is your child troubled, sad, or consistently depressed? If so, find out what's going on and seek professional help.

Diagnose the problem. Is your child taunted or picked on repeatedly? If so, this is bullying. Take action by going to the school and meeting with the principal.

Take ownership. If this is a friendship fallout or an isolated incident, take ownership of the situation with your child. See if you can work things out with the other parent. This does not warrant school intervention.

Work to change school culture. Encourage school leaders to educate kids about the need to report bullying. Suggest kids sign a bystander's pledge like the one we mentioned in this chapter.

Wait on Facebook or Formspring for middle schoolers. These sites, when used by impulsive middle schoolers at a time when bullying peaks, stack the decks towards cyberbullying.

Mete out consequences. Even if your child is thirteen or older, if he or she is misusing social networking sites, remove privileges.

Chapter Eleven

A WHOLE
LOTTA HURT

"Please don't let mom remember me for the mistakes I've made."
—thirteen-year-old **Hope Whitsell**

This chapter is a walk on the dark side.

Before you close the book or fast forward, let us share what we have learned as we have gotten into the research: most parents have no idea that their sweet girl or darling son is sending nude pictures to a "crush" over their cell phones. Girls have committed suicide after nude photos of themselves, sent to boyfriends, have gone viral. Likewise, most parents cannot imagine that their son or daughter plays the choking game in the privacy of his bedroom or while "hanging out" at a friend's house. And parents are usually unaware that their children are cutting themselves, since kids cut in inconspicuous places. If this is your child, you need to educate yourself about these destructive practices before it is too late. We will tell you how.

Please read on.

Myriad children in this country of plenty live in a world of hurt. Sometimes the hurt comes from broken homes and broken parents. Sometimes it comes from peers. Sometimes it is self-inflicted.

At the end of her seventh grade school year at Beth Shields Middle School in Hillsborough, Florida, Hope Whitsell used a cell phone to send a nude photo of her breasts to a boy she had a crush on—a practice known as *sexting*. Another girl, a "romantic rival," forwarded the photo to classmates and friends; the photo quickly circulated via cell phones at another middle school and high school. Whitsell was suspended for the photo the first week of eighth grade and, when she returned to school, was taunted mercilessly by other students.[1] They called her a "whore" and a "slut" until the taunts became so severe that Hope's friends formed a human shield around her as she changed classes. Hope did not tell her parents about her persecution but instead wrote in her journal, "Tons of people talk about me behind my back, and I hate it because they call me a whore. And I can't be a whore, I'm too inexperienced."[2] A school counselor noticed that Hope was cutting her legs in response to her intense emotional pain and had her sign a "no harm contract." The next night, Hope went to her room and hanged herself. She was thirteen years old.

Her parents found the "no harm contract" crumpled in the trash can after she died; they had no idea she had started to cut herself.

On the last day of her life, September 12, 2009, Hope wrote of her intent in her journal. "I'm done for sure now. I can feel it in my stomach. I'm going to try and strangle myself. I hope it works."[3] Ever girly, she used a pink scarf tied around the canopy of her queen-sized bed to take her life.

Hope is not the only girl to commit suicide because of the fallout from sexting. Jessica Logan, a high school senior at Sycamore High School in Cincinnati, sent a nude picture of herself to her boyfriend during spring break in 2008. He forwarded the photo to others, and soon it had spread throughout seven different high schools. Like Hope Whitsell, Jessica was harassed at school and called "slut, porn queen, and whore."[4] She was no longer invited to parties because of her "reputation." Her friends said her personality changed after this happened—once a sunny extrovert, Jessica now walked with her head down and cried a lot. She was obviously depressed. Soon Jessica began to skip school, but even outside of school strangers texted her, calling her a "whore." Finally, graduation day came and went, but Jessica was not home free. She continued to struggle with social ostracism—with shunning. Then one day that summer, she went to the funeral of a friend who had committed suicide. The same day, Jessica went home, took a shower, brushed her hair, and hanged herself.[5]

THE CELL PHONE AND SEXTING

It's all about the cell phone, the thoughtless impulsivity of youth, and girls who value themselves and their bodies too little. National survey data from the Pew Institute indicate that 4 percent of all twelve- to seventeen-year-olds who own cell phones report sending a sexually suggestive nude or nearly nude photo of themselves to another individual. There was no difference in gender.[6]

All kids have to do to enter the dangerous world of sexting is snap a nude photo with a mobile phone and impulsively hit the "send" key. Teens generally intend for the photos to stay private—ending up on a boyfriend's or girlfriend's phone. But all too often, adolescent curiosity means photos are zapped from one phone to the next at lightning speed. The result? "One in six teens with a cell phone has received a sexually suggestive image or video of someone they know."[7]

Rosalind Wiseman, author of *Queen Bees and Wannabes*, describes the process thus:

Your family is hanging out in the living room on a normal Monday evening. Your son, age ten, is doing his homework on his laptop on the couch while your fourteen-year-old daughter lies in her favorite chair, texting away with her friends, half paying attention to the TV. The Cowboys are playing the Redskins, and your spouse is reading. You look up for a minute and think to yourself, "How awesome that my family can hang out like this. The kids are getting older, but we still spend time together, and everyone's not hiding in their corners of the house." At halftime, you and your daughter banter back and forth about that insane pass Jason Campbell just threw, and she goes to the bathroom before the game comes back on. Little do you know that while she's in there, she flips open her phone, pulls up her shirt, and takes a picture of her boobs. You don't know it, but during the game she's been texting with a guy in the grade above her whom she has a crush on. Their flirtatious texts have escalated and as she hits "send" on the explicit shot captioned "u like?" she feels a little adrenaline rush and hopes he'll ask her to homecoming. . . . She deletes the photo from her phone's memory card, runs the water in the sink for a second, then comes back out and flops down in her chair. She's been gone all of two minutes.[8]

WHY DO IT?

So why do they do it? An article in *Psychology Today* indicates that sexual images are shared to either start up or maintain a relationship with a significant other, and they are often "passed along to friends for their entertainment value, as a joke, or for fun. But the 'fun' is actually sexual harassment and can have tragic consequences."[9]

We have already mentioned that our kids are exposed to salacious sexual content on television and to porn on the Internet that most of us never encountered growing up. What was once adult-only material is now available on television each night before ten. For example, *Glee* has not only normalized homosexuality (and shown males kissing in the school hallways), but one of the main characters, Quinn, has experienced teen pregnancy. Lea Michele, one of the stars of *Glee*, has been criticized for her *second* revealing magazine cover—this time in the March 2011 issue of *Cosmopolitan*.[10] Michele wears a black dress cut almost to the belly button, and the dress covers nipples and little more. One mother of a twelve-year-old son "was confused and offended" by Michele, who plays Glee's good girl, Rachel.[11] Admittedly, *Glee* is not a program for middle schoolers, but it is billed as a popular program about high schoolers and, for this reason, middle schoolers watch it.

With so much overt sexuality in the culture, is it any wonder that some of our girls and boys are all too willing to send nude photos of themselves to crushes?

WILL YOUR CHILD BE PROSECUTED FOR SEXTING?

You need to know that for kids engaged in sexting, the toll isn't just emotional. Those who are caught are often suspended from school. For some, it ends there. But for others, legal charges ensue. Because teen sexting involves the distribution of nude images of a minor, it is considered child pornography and, in most states, is currently illegal.

Kids who engage in sexting may be prosecuted for felonies. When this happens, district attorneys are prosecuting teens using laws generally reserved for the porn industry. Teens are being charged with "disorderly conduct" and "illegal use of a minor in nudity-oriented material," as well as "sexual abuse of children with criminal use of communications facility, or open lewdness—all of which are felonies."[12] Eighteen-year-old Philip Alpert in Florida will be listed as a registered sex offender for the next twenty-five years because he was convicted of sending nude images of his sixteen-year-old girlfriend to family and friends. Even though some states are working to change the laws so that sexting is treated as a misdemeanor rather than a felony,[13] sexting is obviously not something children and teens should ever engage in.

A WORD TO PARENTS

What you as a parent need to realize when you buy your middle schooler a cell phone for safety reasons is that you are providing him or her with a device that could be used for sexting. *And you will probably never know about it.* Even if you tell your child about the possible negative repercussions of sexting, both personal and legal, there is a chance that he or she will pay scant attention to what you say. That's how middle schoolers are. Since the adolescent brain is not fully developed until age twenty-five, it is possible that your child may get carried away in the moment and become reckless.

Jessica Logan forwarded her nude photo to her boyfriend during spring break when other girls were doing the same.[14] You could say, "Well, she was eighteen; she should have known better." But she was probably caught up in the moment with her girlfriends who were also sexting and didn't think about the possibility of negative consequences. Maybe it never occurred to her that her boyfriend, whom she obviously trusted, would shamelessly send the nude picture on.

We'll never know, will we, what thoughts passed through Jessica's brain when she hit the "send" button?

As the stories of Hope Whitsell and Jessica Logan so tragically illustrate, one impulsive act can ruin a life. What began as an attempt to attract a boy-friend's attention resulted in name-calling, deep shame, and utter humiliation. These girls probably believed they could not escape their deep internal pain. They may have felt they had nowhere to turn and no way to escape unremit-ting social censure. Naked on cell phones, they faced their tormentors, both known and unknown, without any psychological defense. It was like going out into the world without skin. The shunning they endured had to be horrific until they lost hope that life would ever get better.

THE CHOKING GAME

Sexting isn't the only risky—and potentially deadly—behavior that may entice early adolescents.

Today some middle schoolers and older teens are engaging in the choking game, which may inadvertently result in death. Other names for the choking game are the space monkey, scarf game, fainting game, flat liner, airplan-ing, and purple dragon. The Centers for Disease Control and Prevention describe the choking game as a "dangerous activity that older children and early adolescents sometimes play to get a brief high."[15] Kids either choke each other or use a noose to choke themselves. Why in the world would they engage in such a painful exercise? Apparently, during the choking process, they experience a brief, euphoric high caused by cerebral hypoxia, or lack of oxygen to the brain.[16] According to the CDC, some eighty-two children and adolescents have died from this activity since 1995. Boys are more likely to die than girls, comprising 87 percent of the deaths. Some 89 percent of the children who died were between eleven and sixteen years old. Nearly all who died played the game alone.[17]

What happens to the brain when kids play the choking game? As kids lose consciousness, brain cells begin to die. Sometimes coma and seizures occur, and within three minutes, memory, balance, and the central nervous system begin to deteriorate, resulting in death.[18] Sadly, choking-game deaths peak at age thirteen.[19]

But this is not what the early adolescent thinks about. Thirteen-year-old Sam Mordecai, whose twin brother Gabriel died playing the choking game alone, also experimented. He said in a news interview, "It's hard to describe how it feels. It's kinda like, just, like somewhere not on earth, but you're just dreaming, kind of. But then it only lasts for a few seconds and when you wake up . . . you don't know where you are or what's going on."[20] His mother says she misses Gabe so much, and she wishes she had known the warning signs. She noticed her son's bloodshot eyes, but didn't connect it to the choking game.

In February 2006, another thirteen-year-old boy played the choking game one evening after he had eaten dinner with his family. An hour after he went to his bedroom to do his homework, his mom went into his room and found him crumpled in a corner with a belt around his neck. His face was blue. His frantic mother performed CPR, but to no avail. An hour later, he was pronounced dead. Days later, his parents learned that he and others had played the choking game weeks before at parties.[21]

Here's another heartbreaking story:

When Mike, age thirteen, tried the choking game, he fell backward onto the pavement, hitting his head with an audible blow. His friends took him to the hospital for observation. Although he had regained consciousness after his fall, by the next morning in the hospital, his condition was noticeably worse. In time, he fell into a coma. His mother said, "For three days we kept our vigil. I prayed for a miracle, but on the morning of the fourth day, I had no choice but to sign the final form giving permission for the life support to be disconnected. Within minutes, his chest heaved and fell for one last time."[22]

Such a tragic loss of young lives. We know that this information is sobering, heavy, and frightening, but probably many of you think your child would never engage in such a deadly game. Unfortunately, the sad truth is, most parents whose children die from this activity have no idea their children are playing the choking game at home or with their friends. Here are some of the signs an informed parent should look for:

- bloodshot eyes
- marks on the neck
- frequent headaches
- ropes, scarves, and belts tied to bedroom furniture or doorknobs, or lying on the floor
- pinpoint bleeding spots under facial skin around eyelids or lining of the eyes
- irritability, hostility, or disorientation after time alone[23]

If you notice signs like these, ask your child if he is playing the choking game. If you suspect this is happening, seek professional help.

THE MIDDLE SCHOOLER WHO CUTS

We now come to an activity that, while not fatal, can seem horrific to parents: cutting. While most of us wish to avoid pain and take painkillers at the slightest hint of an oncoming headache, some young people cut themselves to get relief from intense emotional pain.

One kid who cuts said: "My secret is my blade, it is my obsession, it is my dark secret; when I am empty I bleed, when I am sad I bleed, when I have no hope I bleed."[24]

Clinical psychologist Dr. Charlie Cooper told us that individuals who cut themselves have low self-esteem and are depressed, lonely, and isolated. What purpose does the cutting serve? Dr. Cooper says, "The cutting can so alarm them that they no longer feel the original pain. The original pain often comes about because they have uncomfortable, obsessive thoughts. Their whole system is really disturbed. The cutting focuses their attention rapidly in a different direction." Cooper continues, "Then there are the secondary gains. People get upset about them, so if they're lonely and isolated, the act of cutting calls in all this extra attention."

Cutting apparently releases endorphins and can create a feel-good feeling. According to Amelio D'Onofrio, a clinical professor and director of the Psychologist Services Institute at Fordham University, self-injury has been around for thousands of years, but in the past ten years, we have witnessed "an explosion of young people in emotional pain cutting themselves."[25]

Twenty years ago, Karen Conterio, author of the book *Bodily Harm*, founded a treatment program for self-injurers called SAFE (Self Abuse Finally Ends) Alternatives at Linden Oak Hospital in Naperville, Illinois. Conterio says that while self-injury typically starts at age fourteen, her patients are getting younger, some as young as eleven and twelve. She has also treated thirty-year-olds who started young and for whom cutting became addictive behavior. "People keep doing it for years and years, and don't really know how to quit."[26]

Dr. Cooper agrees that cutting is linked to stress and can become addictive. "It's the way some individuals cope with stress." Why do kids cut? Dr. Cooper says, "They cut when they're heavily stressed and later on they cut when they anticipate stress."

D'Onofrio cites other causes, such as sexual or physical abuse, depression, hatred of one's physical appearance, loss or deprivation of a parent due to divorce, conflicted relationships with family and peers, or high-pressured lifestyles.[27] Kids who harm themselves may also have a psychiatric disorder, such as borderline personality disorder, anxiety disorder, bipolar disorder, schizophrenia, or eating disorder.[28] But many kids who cut themselves are "regular" kids who simply have not learned to cope with life and their emotional reaction to stress. Often they come from repressive families who deny negative emotions, especially sadness. "A lot of families give the message that you don't express sadness," states Conterio.[29]

Dr. Charlie Cooper, who has worked with patients who cut, says cutting is also about the cutter's inability to regulate his emotions when he is upset or distressed. Since the mother helps the baby regulate his emotions in the first year of life, is cutting related to insecure attachment? In other words, did cutters fail to receive comfort from their mothers in infancy and help in regulating their emotions? While Cooper said that cutting could be an attachment issue, he acknowledged that it is not always the case.

Typically, kids cut themselves on their arms, legs, and torso—places that can be covered up and hidden from view. Usually the cuts are small and linear, though a middle schooler we know did carve the word "Love" on her forearm in block letters. If you as a parent notice that your child has cuts that look a bit like cat scratches on her arms or legs, you need to go on hyper-alert. Your child may be cutting as an antidote to intense emotional pain. And if your child insists on wearing long pants and long sleeves in the summer, become suspicious. Ask to see your child in underwear or a bathing suit. Keep a vigilant eye. If you are shocked, control your own emotional response, because the inner world of the cutter is a dark, lonely, and depressing place.

For a moment, let's enter the world of kids who cut. Listen to one cutter:

Amy wrote, "Cutting was my alternative to suicide. It was a comfort; the blood reminded me I was alive."[30]

CUTTING AND THE INTERNET

If kids want to learn about cutting in a graphic way, they have only to go to YouTube and type in "self injury." A study published in the March 2011 issue of *Pediatrics* reveals how curious adolescents are about this behavior. Researchers showed self-injury videos, typing in keywords like "self injury" and "self harm" and found the one hundred most frequently watched videos, which had received a total of 2.3 million hits. These videos contained graphic accounts of cutting and burning, according to Stephen Lewis, PhD, of the University of Guelph in Ontario. Lewis and his colleagues found the videos "worrisome" because they could "normalize the behavior" for kids who are depressed and overly stressed.[31]

In sum, kids cut because they have not yet learned how to cope with deep emotional pain or how to talk about their feelings. If your child is cutting himself, you need to obtain professional help, not only for your child, but also for your family. Your family will need help in finding healthier ways to express human emotions, especially sadness. If your child is growing up in a family where it is taboo to talk about negative feelings, this will increase his loneliness, low self-worth, and depression. Be strong enough to take an honest look at the interactions occurring in your home. Your child needs help; your family does, too.

EMO GIRLS

We first heard about Emo Girls in a focus group of middle school parents. What exactly is an Emo Girl? The term "Emo" was derived from the word "emotional," and refers to girls who feel they are lost, sensitive souls. Emo Girls dress in black, especially tight jeans with T-shirts, studded belts, and sneakers. They dye their hair black and wear it straight, usually with a long fringe brushed to one side. Emos are tied to their music, and to bands which sing songs riddled with references to self-injury and death. One band, My Chemical Romance, had a number one hit on the UK music chart entitled, "Welcome to the Black Parade." The Black Parade refers to the place all Emos believe they will go after death.[32]

As part of an initiation ceremony, Emos often cut their wrists, indicating that self-injury is part of their cult practices. Because of social networking sites, they can chat with other Emo followers all over the world through Facebook, Bebo, and MySpace.[33] Thus, this cult knows no geographic boundaries.

Hannah, an attractive, popular thirteen-year-old girl, gave her parents little to worry about until she started dressing in black, dyed her hair, and started cutting the inside of her wrists. When they questioned Hannah about the cutting, she said that it was part of an initiation ritual for Emo Girls. Three months after she began chatting online with Emo Girls around the globe, she hanged herself. After her death, her parents discovered that she had chatted online about death and the Black Parade, using as her pseudonym "Living Disaster." She even decorated her social networking site on Bebo with a picture of a girl who had bloody wrists.[34]

In a tribute book set up in Hannah's school, one student left this message: "I hope you enjoy your Black Parade."[35]

Whether kids identify with the Emo group or not, parents need to be vigilant. Counselor Linda Reyner says she sees a couple of cutters per year. But they don't always fit a particular profile. She says, "It's not a given that if you're Emo, you're going to cut. Or if you cut, you're an Emo Girl. I've got a cutter right now that you'd never know looking at her that she'd do that. There's not an Emo thing about her."

FINALLY, YOUTH SUICIDE

It was actually the suicide data on young girls that launched this whole book project. In 2007, the CDC released data stating that in 2004 the suicide rate for nine- to fourteen-year-old girls went up 76 percent. As a psychologist, I was shocked and distressed. Why had these young girls chosen to end their lives? And by hanging. In fact, in 2004 hanging or suffocation was the preferred method of suicide, accounting for 71.4 percent of suicides among nine- to fourteen-year-old girls.[36] It seemed inconceivable to me that girls this young should feel so trapped in hopelessness and despair that they would snuff out their lives. Later CDC data have shown that this was a one-year spike and that the suicide rate for this age group has since leveled off; nonetheless, the tragedy stands. These girls killed themselves. Forever. And their families still live with the pain.

> *However, for youth ages ten to twenty-four, suicide remains the third leading cause of death.*[37] *When I spoke to a physician at the Centers for Disease Control and Prevention in Atlanta, I noted that the number of young people who kill themselves is relatively small (approximately 4,400 each year) when compared to the overall youth population. After a moment of silence, he said simply and profoundly, "It is always sad when a young person takes his life."*
>
> *—Brenda*

And so it is. For every parent whose child has either attempted suicide or actually killed himself, the fallout is enormous. And it lasts a lifetime.

LOW SELF-WORTH AND DEPRESSION

Since cutting, sexting, and suicide attempts are obviously signs of low self-worth and depression, these behaviors warrant professional intervention for children and their families. Not only will your child need to change her thinking and behavior, but your family will need to change as well.

Depression is a potentially lethal mental-health problem, and kids who are depressed are trapped in negative thinking about themselves and their world. They feel helpless, hostile, and hopeless. But it is the feeling of pervasive hopelessness that most concerns therapists who work with depressed patients. In fact, any sign of hopelessness in your child should sound a loud and strident alarm. Get help before it is too late.

Think of it this way. We live in a world of stunning light and devastating darkness, of incredible good and evil. And you have been entrusted with your child's life and human soul. Yours is the task of keeping as much of the darkness from invading your home and your child's life as you are able.

While the darkness in our culture is real, so too is the life-giving power of a parent who loves his child. And the light of God is brighter still.

How can you drive the darkness out of your home? You do this by creating a refuge where you, the parents, are in charge. You monitor your children's daily lives, their friendships, all that they are exposed to. You love your kids passionately, and you demonstrate your love by spending time with them regularly. And you pray. You pray for them and with them before you send them out into the world each morning. You pray during the day when they are absent from you. Why? Because powerful, committed prayer banishes the gathering gloom that is on the rise in this country, invading our children's lives.

Nothing sends the darkness packing like the passionate, fervent prayer of a committed parent.

PARENT TIPS

Become a vigilant parent. Make it your job to know what's going on in your child's life, especially in his emotional world. Talk to your child daily. Ask questions about his challenges and any pleasures. Don't assume you know what she is thinking and feeling.

Be in the know. Know what goes on at parties. Make sure parents are present and that they are informed about the choking game.

Talk about sexting. Explain the legal and emotional fallout from sexting to your kids. Talk about the shame and humiliation he or she will feel if a nude photo goes viral.

Discuss sex openly. Talk to your son or daughter about impulsivity, about modesty, and about the moral and proper way to relate to the opposite sex.

Chapter Twelve

IMPARTING FAITH
AND VIRTUE

*"We make men without chests and expect of them
virtue and enterprise.
We laugh at honour and are shocked to find traitors in our midst."*

—**C. S. Lewis**, *The Abolition of Man*

How are American teens faring in the all-important realm of ethics and virtue? Here's the most recent "report card" on the morals of American youth from the Josephson Institute of Ethics, assessing forty-three thousand high schoolers across the country:

- 89 percent of teens agreed that "being a good person is more important than being rich," yet more than 40 percent said they had lied to save money. Almost one-third of boys and one-fourth of girls had stolen from a store in the past year.
- 92 percent agreed with the statement, "I am satisfied with my own ethics and character," yet 80 percent had lied to a parent about something significant, almost 60 percent had cheated on a test, and 34 percent had copied from the Internet for a school assignment.

- 47 percent said they had "been bullied, teased, or taunted in a way that seriously upset" them, yet half had themselves bullied, teased, or taunted someone.
- 79 percent agreed that "when it comes to doing right, I am better than most people I know," but almost 40 percent agreed with the statement, "A person has to lie or cheat sometimes in order to succeed."[1]

MEN WITHOUT CHESTS

These statistics evidence a startling disconnect between American teenagers' personal views and their behavior, don't they? Parental and societal expectations were imprinted on these kids' minds: they knew what they *should* be doing. But their hearts were disengaged. And when the temptations beckoned, as they invariably do, these kids succumbed.

C. S. Lewis, writing in *The Abolition of Man*, extolled the critical importance of the "chest," or the heart, in making men and women of virtue. The heart, Lewis wrote, is what enables the head, or the mind, to rule over the belly, the seat of our feelings. Lewis wrote of the heart's central role: "It may even be said that it is by this middle element that man is man: for by his intellect he is mere spirit and by his appetite mere animal."[2]

It is the heart that makes us truly human.

What happens when we try to teach honor without the heart? We have, said Lewis, a "tragi-comedy" in which "we continue to clamour for those very qualities we are rendering impossible.... We castrate and bid the geldings be fruitful."[3] We make men without chests. Or as the ethics survey illustrates, we rear adolescents who know what to do, but cannot bring themselves to do it.

The Bible cautions us repeatedly to care for our hearts. Indeed, Solomon, the wisest king who ever lived, enjoined us to guard our hearts above all else, "for it is the wellspring of life." All behavior, virtuous or villainous, flows from the heart.

Not only are there spiritual consequences for a misdirected heart, but there are moral and civic ones as well. The scaffolding of society is built on a foundation of goodness, rule keeping, and morality. We falter when citizens disobey laws, cheat on their taxes, and mistreat their fellow man. But more and more in our culture, we are losing touch with *how* to inculcate the virtue and goodness we need. Character education in the schools is fine, even good. But, ultimately, will it mold the heart of a child? No. People do that.

Parents do that.

WHO SACRIFICES?

And how do they do it? Through a lot of parental sacrifice. Although sacrifice has become a dirty word in modern child rearing, it is essential and unavoidable in rearing decent, secure children. Dr. Tim Keller, prolific author and pastor of Redeemer Presbyterian Church in New York City, says that *all love* involves substitutionary sacrifice. What does that mean? "To some degree," says Keller, "you change places" with someone if you love them. "Their weakness," says Keller, "comes upon you in order for your strength to go to them." When we fail to love our children sacrificially, the consequences are long lasting. Says Keller:

> When you get married, you think it changes your life. It doesn't. . . . You're a happy person, you have freedom and independence. You can live your life the way you want. And then you become a parent. And that's all over. Because what comes into your life are these little things—babies, children—and they are utterly dependent on you. . . .
>
> Now there's one thing you could do if you want to, and I've seen some parents do this. You only spend time with your kids when it's convenient for you. You don't let them cramp your style. You don't let them really erode your freedom and independence. You just spend time with them here and there wherever you want to.
>
> And you know what happens? They grow up physically, but in no other way. Because they grow up needy, they grow up emotionally

troubled, they grow up hungry for love because they never got it from you. . . . Because you held on to your freedom and independence, they will never have it. They'll stay emotionally needy, dependent people.

But if you are willing to completely sacrifice your independence and freedom—for about twenty years—so that constantly their needs trump yours, and their interests trump yours, and you're always giving up things you want to do for them—in other words, if you give up your freedom and independence—they will get it. And if you refuse to give it up, they will *never* get it. It's them or you.[4]

YOU ARE THE EXPERT ON YOUR CHILD

Once parents establish a heart connection with a child through sacrifice, they can begin to impart faith. Sadly, those who work with children tell us that parents increasingly are ceding the realm of spirituality and faith to professionals: youth directors, teachers, and the church. These people and the institutions they represent are valuable partners, but they are no substitute for you—your time, your love, your example.

Eric Heiland, the youth director at Hunt Valley Church in Hunt Valley, Maryland, has worked with teens for more than fifteen years. His advice to parents? "Even if they're not experts on middle schoolers, parents are experts on their individual child. Their life experience and what God has done in their own lives is just as critical to their child's spiritual development as anything that anyone learned at a seminary class or from just leading small groups for fifteen years."

AGE OF COMMITMENT

Why is it important that you step up to the plate? Most kids who make a faith commitment to Christianity have done so by the time they hit age eighteen. Research from The Barna Group shows that 43 percent of Americans who become Christians do so by age thirteen; 64 percent have made this decision by the time they are eighteen. Another 13 percent become Christians between the ages of eighteen and twenty-one, while 23 percent do so after they turn twenty-one.[5]

Coming to faith at a younger age has long-lasting consequences. Barna Group research has found that "people who become Christian[s] before their teen years are more likely than those who are converted when older to remain 'absolutely committed' to Christianity."[6] Author and researcher George Barna notes:

> Families, churches and parachurch ministries must recognize that primary window of opportunity for effectively reaching people with the good news of Jesus' death and resurrection is during the preteens years. It is during those years that people develop their frames of reference for the remainder of their lives—especially theologically and morally. Consistently explaining and modeling truth principles for young people is the most critical factor in their spiritual development.[7]

What kind of parent is most likely to raise a "devoted Christian"?

A revolutionary parent, says Barna. What does he mean by this? He says, "Revolutionary parenting, which is based on one's faith in God, makes parenting a life priority. Those who engage in revolutionary parenting define success as intentionally facilitating faith-based transformation in the lives of their children, rather than simply accepting the aging and survival of the child as a satisfactory result."[8]

WALK YOUR TALK

Where to start? We parents must first walk our talk. As English author Oliver Goldsmith wrote, "You can preach a better sermon with your life than with your lips." As you seek to mold and shape your children, you must first look in the mirror.

Life provides ample opportunities for parents to live out their values before an adolescent audience. Death, divorce, job losses, financial hardship, illness—all serve as a boot camp for us to model character to kids. Do we become bitter when others wrong us, or do we process our hurt and forgive? Do we speak up when our restaurant tab is less than it should be, or when the cashier at the grocery store gives us too much change? Our kids know. They're always watching.

If there is a jarring mismatch between what parents say and what they do, the lack of authenticity will permeate kids' character development. Just look at the ethics report card at the beginning of this chapter. Like those students, our kids will say one thing and do another. Conversely, if our children watch us deal with matters of faith and conscience in a way that models integrity and truth, they will be inspired to emulate parental behavior.

MONKEY SEE, MONKEY DO

Jeff, a father of two middle school boys, said he and his wife Beth are aware that they always have an audience. He says:

> I think the thing that we are constantly on guard for is: What example are we setting? Because they're going to see. They can hear us talk, but they're more likely to imitate our actions.
>
> . . . [Beth's] father was an alcoholic, her mother is a . . . hmm . . . little abrasive at times [laughs]. That's probably an understatement! And I was raised in a family that on the surface was a fine family in the community, but there were problems. . . . They would be one way in public, but then they'd just be tearing people apart and putting people down behind closed doors. That's just wrong. And it has spilled over, and it has actually manifested itself now in my brother's and my sister's lives. But you can trace it all back to—where did they learn how not to be forgiving toward others? Where did they learn that you look after your own interests and not the interests of others? They learned it by watching my mother and father.

He's absolutely right. Kids learn by watching us—how we treat other people or whether we value and nurture our faith. Dan, a father of four children and stepchildren, who is remarried to Eliza, says he knows his kids pick up on whether he prioritizes his own faith. Dan states:

> The absolute most important, most fundamental [thing] is for them to see how we behave and to see us model that. They're seeing us talk about things. They're seeing us with our Bibles open. They're seeing me lead a small group on Tuesday nights. . . . That's what I remember from my own parents growing up: their taking us to church, seeing my dad's Bible on the kitchen table and knowing that's where he did his devotions, praying at meals—we do all that stuff. That is a central part of our life, and I want the kids to see that. That's the stuff that's going to stick later in life.

It is going to stick. And the warm heart ties that bind us to our kids are the glue. We've said a lot in other chapters about the importance of a strong parent-child attachment. This holds true when it comes to inculcating virtue and imparting faith. As one wise parent told us, "You can't influence a child you don't have a connection with." Research backs up this contention. Dr. John Gottman, author and prolific researcher in the area of marriage and family, says, "Compliance, obedience and responsibility come from a sense of love and connectedness children feel with their families. In this way, emotional interactions among family members become the foundation for instilling values and raising moral people."[9]

MODELING FAITH

For the parent of faith, the injunction to teach our children about God's law comes from Moses' words to the Israelites in the book of Deuteronomy. Listen to this Old Testament prophet:

> Love the Lord your God with all your heart and with all your soul and with all your strength. These commandments that I give you today are to be upon your hearts. Impress them on your children.

Talk about them when you sit at home and when you walk along the road, when you lie down and when you get up. Tie them as symbols on your hands and bind them on your foreheads. Write them on the doorframes of your houses and on your gates.

How do we impress God's commands on our children? We talk about our faith in God wherever we are—at home, away from home, in the car, at bedtime, in the morning, and in the evening. We talk and pray daily.

When the girls were young, my husband Don and I read Bible stories at the breakfast table and chapters from classic children's literature at night. We felt it was so important to expose the girls to the enduring Word of God in the morning before we all separated for the day. Those twenty or so minutes grounded me for the day, especially when Don prayed aloud from the head of the table. I hoped it grounded the girls as well. Then came middle school, and one day Kristen interrupted our nighttime reading session. "Stop," she said. "I can read to myself."

And so our evening read-aloud family sessions ceased, but we continued reading from the Bible each morning. Years later, when Holly enrolled at Columbia University in New York City as a freshman, she wound up studying the Bible during a class on the Western Civilization Canon. She found she knew much more about the Bible than most other students in her class.

Now the girls are long gone. Yet Don and I still sit at our table, two white heads reading aloud from the Bible. Having this time together, to read and to pray, is the most intimate thing we do.

—Brenda

THE POWER OF STORIES

Not only do we teach our children about God and faith by reading the Bible, but we teach them about character and virtue through the power of stories and literature. Dr. Bill Bennett, author of the best-selling compendium of moral fables and literature, *The Book of Virtues*, writes:

> Moral education—the training of heart and mind toward the good—involves many things. It involves rules and precepts—the *dos* and *don'ts* of life with others—as well as explicit instruction, exhortation, and training. Moral education *must* provide training in good habits. . . . Along with precept, habit, and example, there is also the need for what we might call moral literacy.[10]

Moral literacy, then, encompasses the writings, in both poetry and prose, which have shaped and molded character for generations. Dr. Bennett's compilation includes stories of courage—Julius Caesar crossing the Rubicon—as well as virtue embodied in poetic verse, such as a poem by Longfellow about friendship.

Stories provide a springboard from which parents can teach about the ethical decisions of life. As children hear the lessons of faith and virtue, lived out by characters they come to love in the pages of a book, these stories take root in their hearts and minds.

Jenny, a mother of two middle school girls and two older teenage boys, says she seeks to "build on classic literature" in her moral instruction, especially with her daughters. She and her sixth and eighth grade daughters, Cathy and Amanda, read aloud at night, perusing books such as *The Secret Garden* and *Little Women*, and celebrate the positive character attributes of their much-loved heroines.

As they read, Jenny asks her girls what they love about their favorite literary characters. "I'll never forget," she says, when "my older daughter said, 'I love the chapter in *Little Women* when Meg gets married. When I get married, I want to go back and read that very chapter about Marmi's wisdom.'" Jenny adds, "There's so much wisdom in literature that is caught" as children read aloud with their parents.

> *We have used the book* Sticky Situations *as a springboard for moral discussion around the dinner table. As we plow through chicken and potatoes, we evaluate the range of moral dilemmas our kids might experience at school or in life, all couched in the context of a short passage of Scripture that we look up in the Bible and read aloud. Once they have assessed the hypothetical "sticky situation," Austin and Katie then choose among a variety of resolutions. We weigh in with our own thoughts about morality or interpretations of Scripture.*
>
> *We don't always agree. Lively discussions and disagreements often characterize our evenings. That's fine with us. We believe these conversations offer Austin and Katie a chance to talk through with us some of the difficult decisions they might face in everyday life, evaluated through the lens of faith. How should they confront temptations to cheat? To bully? To sell out for popularity? We try to address these pressures in the context of a supportive, but faith- and character-based, conversation.*
>
> —*Kristen*

MAKE IT SAFE TO TELL THE TRUTH

As children get older, the issues they confront are more serious. How will we respond when they come to us with distressing news of their failures? Even more importantly, will they come to us at all with their confessions, or will they keep things bottled up inside, knowing we could never handle the truth? In his work with adolescents over almost three decades, Rob Crocker, a Southeastern Young Life area director, has learned that life can get messy.

Parents need to be OK with that and should be more concerned about their child's well-being and long-term character development than about outside appearances. He says, "We need to set up an environment in our homes where a child can be honest. It's not always going to look great. We can't always have an 'I told you so' kind of attitude."

During these early adolescent years, parents also find that they and their children benefit from the support of other adults who offer kids a place of safety and acceptance. Youth director Eric Heiland and his leaders foster an environment where kids feel safe to tell the truth about what they're really doing, even if the news isn't so good. He says, "You can't share something with us about how far you've gotten away from God that's going to make us feel you're unapproachable." He adds, "We're creating a safe environment for you to share what you're really dealing with in life. And then we speak into it based on our own faith."

FALLIBILITY AND FORGIVENESS

How should we respond when kids make mistakes and tell us their truth? Once children are disciplined and face the natural consequences of what they have done, parents need to move quickly to assure the child that forgiveness has been granted and to restore that child to a place of love and acceptance. Amy says she and her husband have prayed with their children almost every time they have been disciplined, or "whenever there was an issue where repentance needed to take place." The time following discipline can be one when children also confess their misdeeds to God and are assured that he forgives them, too.

But confession and forgiveness cut both ways. Amy, a mother of four, says, "The whole idea of repentance and making sure the slate is clean on both sides—admitting when you make a mistake as a parent and asking for forgiveness"—is critical in maintaining healthy parent-child relationships. Dan and Eliza told us they ask their kids for forgiveness when they slip up themselves—even when it's difficult to do. Dan says that when Eliza speaks sharply to the kids, she asks for forgiveness. Dan is honest and says he has a harder time "'fessing up. I'm less apt to do that." He laughs, "I don't like admitting my own mistakes. It pierces the illusion that I'm perfect!"

THE SINGLE PARENT

We've talked a lot in this chapter about two-parent families. What about those of you who are flying solo? Your role in imparting faith and virtue in your child is indisputably important. Some of you are your child's only parental touchstone.

Yet others can come alongside you and stand in the gap, helping your child feel loved in practical and tangible ways. Rob Crocker, who had an absentee father, says he learned a lot about life from a young man who mentored him. He says, "My Young Life leader taught me how to change the oil in my car. I learned how to shave from him. It wasn't because he taught me. I just watched him because my dad wasn't around. My parents were divorced, and I didn't have anybody else there showing me."

When evidenced during impressionable adolescence, that message of love can have lasting consequences. Dr. Howard Hendricks, a professor at Dallas Theological Seminary, was raised in a rough neighborhood in north Philadelphia, in a home short on love and attention. He writes:

> With the kind of start I had in life, I'm sure I could have soon died and gone to hell and nobody would have particularly cared. I was born into a broken home, my parents having separated before I was born. The only time I ever saw them together was eighteen years later when I was called to testify in a divorce court.[11]

But Walt, a man from Hendricks's church who possessed only a sixth-grade education, reached out to him and changed his life forever. Writes Dr. Hendricks:

> Walt picked up a total of thirteen boys in that community [of north Philadelphia] for his Sunday school class, of whom nine were from broken homes. Eleven of the thirteen are now in full-time vocational Christian work.

Actually, I can't tell you much of what Walt said to us, but I can tell you everything about him . . . because he loved me for Christ's sake. He loved me more than my parents did.

He used to take us hiking, and I'll never forget those times. I'm sure we made his bad heart worse, but he'd run all over those woods with us because he cared.

He was not the most scintillating person in the world, but he was for real. I knew it, and so did everyone else in that class.[12]

A DAD WHO SERVES

Even as a single parent, you can have a powerful impact on your kids just by how you live and serve. Doug Young, a divorced father to seventeen-year-old Maggie and twelve-year-old Anna, is working actively with his girls to ensure that they have a heart for others through missions and service. Maggie has been to Belize three times to build a school and teach kids at vacation Bible school; In the summer of 2010, she and her dad went to Kentucky for a week and worked on construction projects with the Appalachian Service Project.

Soon Doug and Maggie will travel to Puerto Rico for a mission trip; younger daughter Anna is headed out on her first mission trip. Doug, who says he believes in giving back, lives out a commitment to service in his own life. He and a team of men from his church prepare breakfast for residents at a rescue mission every other month. He has been to New Orleans to help rebuild the house of a Hurricane Katrina victim and has traveled to Guatemala for missions.

What does he believe happens to his girls as they serve? He says:

I think it gets them out of their bubble of middle-class society that we have and how much we take for granted. It gets them to see that there are people, right in our own cities—you don't have to go to Kentucky or Puerto Rico or Guatemala or Belize to experience that. It gives them a broader picture of the vast needs that are out there and that really, what we should be doing is giving back as much as we can.

REVOLUTIONARY PARENTS

We want to share the experience of a family who exemplifies all of what we've tried to say. John and Lisa Nagle, whom you've met before, think a lot about imparting faith to their girls, Laura, age thirteen, and Julia, age eleven. Says Lisa, "It's good to be intentional with our kids. The world is."

Weekdays at the Nagle house begin with Bible and prayer time. Lisa says, "We have a family worship and devotion time every morning, Monday through Friday, right before they go to school. Laura plays the piano, and we read a devotion. Then we pray about it." Ten minutes later, the girls dash out the door to their waiting carpool. John, a professor in the law school at Notre Dame University in South Bend, Indiana, has taken his family to live in far-flung locations such as China, Hong Kong, and London, so he can pursue research and fellowships. But wherever the Nagles are, their family spiritual life remains a constant.

So, too, does their heart for service. Enabled in part by John's work as a professor, the Nagles have taken their girls on mission trips around the world. Lisa says, "We've been to Cameroon, Ghana, Thailand, China, Cambodia, and Vietnam on family mission trips abroad."

Like Doug Young, Lisa says her girls learn through mission and service to care for others. Listen to Lisa's account of one mission trip:

> I took Laura on a mission trip to Cameroon in January [last year], and we were in a jeep traveling up the really bumpy roads from Yaoundé up north to Bamenda. And it was just really neat to talk with our partner there, a local leader. He thanked God the whole way along—that we arrived at our destination, even when things didn't go the way he wanted it to—the car broke down several times, and our place where we were going to stay that night wasn't expecting us as we thought. I would have gotten really uptight if I were on my own, but living it with him, that's a part of life. He was praising God for the good stuff and still praising him when it didn't go well.

The impact on the Nagle girls has been profound. Laura wrote about her experience in Cameroon for her eighth grade graduation. Lisa says, "She was really blown away by the vibrancy of the church. She saw miracles, healings, the power of prayer, the reliance on the word of God."

To invoke George Barna, the Nagles are revolutionary parents. They think long-term and talk about purpose and calling for their girls' lives. As her girls serve and see the global church, Lisa is convinced their hearts will change. She says, "I want their hearts to be broken for what breaks God's heart—so looking at not just the spiritual needs of people from different countries, but also the health issues, safety issues, clean water, environment, education issues." She says she already hears it in their prayers.

Their hearts are engaged.

THE LARSONS' STORY

So there you have it: modeling, Bible reading, moral education, and service. But it is all rooted and grounded in parental love and sacrifice. We want to leave you with a story of a couple whose capacity for parental love and personal sacrifice have been tested severely.

In the fall of 2009, Scott and Jen Larson were enjoying a family walk near their home in Saint John, New Brunswick, Canada. But something didn't seem right. Says Jen of her middle son, six-year-old Isaac, "He had to stop and sit down. And I said, 'Isaac, come. Come on.' And suddenly I thought, 'What if something is really wrong with him?' I remember that moment and thinking, no, no, no, it couldn't be. But then he started to lose weight." Isaac also developed blue feet—what his mother describes as "little old man feet."

Doctors' visits led to a trip to the emergency room; lab tests revealed low platelets. Soon after, Isaac developed a high fever, and doctors thought he had meningitis. Then they told Jen, "OK, there's something going on with the shape of his blood cells, so we're going to send you to a children's hospital." Along with Isaac, Scott and Jen rode the four or five hours to Halifax, Nova Scotia, in an ambulance.

They were sent straight to oncology.

That's when Scott and Jen first realized the doctors were looking for cancer. She says, "I wasn't too surprised, but I had the feeling, 'My nightmares are coming true.'" After a bone marrow test, the Larsons were told to go home: Isaac had a virus and not leukemia. They were elated.

Unfortunately, Isaac's condition worsened. On Christmas Day, he was doubled over in pain. Meanwhile, Isaac's test results were wending their way around the world. A San Francisco physician finally revealed the truth: Isaac had juvenile myelomonocytic leukemia, or JMML, a rare form of leukemia. Jen and Scott were afraid—as Jen says, JMML is "even worse than regular leukemia"—but they were also relieved to finally have a diagnosis and treatment plan. With JMML, chemotherapy alone provides no cure. The only hope is a bone marrow transplant.

Since they found no match within their family, a global search for a donor began. After finding a living donor, doctors scheduled Isaac for a bone marrow transplant in June in Toronto. Several weeks before the procedure, his bone marrow was eradicated with intense chemotherapies. One doctor described the treatment thus, "You take them to the edge of life."

These were terrifying days. Jen said that Isaac was on a lot of morphine, had chest pain, and at one point doctors thought he was going into cardiac arrest. He became nonresponsive, his pupils were dilated, and they called the emergency response team. Jen said, "There were a couple of times I thought I was losing him."

The transplant day came. Isaac and his parents spent the weeks immediately following the transplant in a tiny, sterile room, reading and doing magic tricks. After a month, he was transferred back to a children's hospital in Halifax. Because of complications, Jen, who had left her job at a law practice in February 2010 to care for Isaac, would end up taking a full year away from work. The family separation was especially painful, as she and Isaac saw Scott and the other boys only on weekends.

Says Jen, "Sometimes I wonder, how did I get through this past year? I think it may have been just a matter of one foot in front of the other—and holding Isaac. And just appreciating every minute with him."

They knew God was for them. Scott says:

> God's plans for us aren't known to us and are unfathomable to us. When we don't know what's going on and we don't understand why it's happening, we can always be assured that God has a plan. . . . And so I thought whatever happens here, somehow God is going to end up using it for good. I don't know if I was just in denial, but I thought everything would turn out all right in the end.
>
> It always has.
>
> No matter how sick Isaac got, I kept thinking, it's going to get better. I was still very sad for Isaac being sick, but at the same time, I knew it wasn't permanent. . . . It's unfortunate that Isaac had to experience it. It just seems so unfair. But God ultimately is fair, not in the fact that sickness happens, but in the grace that he gives us. . . . I really felt God's presence with us—that he would take care of us. So, for me, that was a very reassuring and calming feeling. I didn't know how he was going to take care of us. But I felt that assurance.

Now approaching the one-year anniversary of his bone marrow transplant, how is Isaac? His cancer is gone, and he's no longer a "skinny mini," says his dad. He still has his challenges. According to Jen, "He's a seven-year-old in a ninety-year-old body." But in the fall, Isaac will start third grade, right on track with his peers.

This couple illustrates sacrificial love beautifully. Remember what Dr. Tim Keller said? "It's them or you."

PARENT TIPS

Reclaim your spiritual role. You, even more than the church, are the most powerful spiritual influence on your child. Share your life experiences and evidences of God's faithfulness to you with your children.

Read the Bible regularly. Expose kids to God's Word at home, at church, and through youth ministries, such as WyldLife, Young Life's national ministry to middle schoolers.

Look for opportunities to teach. Whenever possible, speak to kids about their lives and the problems they encounter through the lens of faith and God's Word.

Pray with your children daily. Nighttime, when kids are most vulnerable and open, is a great time to pray with children about their concerns, confessions, and anything that is bothering them.

Share stories of virtue. Whether written or retold verbally by parents, stories instruct and teach children about what virtues and character traits we value and hold dear.

Let them experience real-life consequences. Teach kids to make it right with others when they make mistakes. Do not spare your child from the real-world consequences of his or her actions.

Forgive quickly. When kids act out or misbehave, they need to be assured of our forgiveness once they have been disciplined.

Say you're sorry. Be willing to admit your mistakes. Your kids know anyway when you've messed up.

Be careful when kids confess. Watch your reactions closely. If you're combustible and overreact when kids mess up, they will learn that you can't handle the truth. Don't make them wall off their hearts. Make truth-telling safe.

Chapter Thirteen

REBUILDING
FAMILY WALLS

"I feel like there's a shifting sense of authority.
I don't think kids look at their teachers and adults with the
same type of respect and fear factor that we did when we were
growing up. . . . Every individual is an equal."

—Jami Burns, middle school gifted specialist

"Become the change you want to see."

—Gandhi

It was my first day teaching English at Clarence High School in Clarence,
New York. I walked into the classroom feeling afraid and intimidated as,
minutes later, the students filed into my class and slouched into their seats.
Hey, some of them were taller and bigger than I was, and they probably
knew I was a rookie teacher fresh out of college. What did I know about
establishing authority, maintaining order, and instructing them in the
wonders of literature? Probably few of them cared anyway. When I heard

a radio playing softly from the back of the room, I knew I was in trouble. Gotta deal with that quickly! I scanned the back rows and spotted a girl with a smirk on her face. "Would you please turn off the radio?" I asked firmly. Silence. Grateful for her compliance, I spoke crisply to the class, telling them who I was and what I expected from them as students. While one of the students passed out an assignment sheet, I walked over to my desk, opened the drawer, and shored up my confidence by reading the words a friend and veteran teacher had spoken to me the day before. "Read this," she had said, "whenever you're afraid." The magical words? "They are the students; you are the teacher."

Emboldened, I straightened up and faced the class, launching into an introduction to Greek mythology.

—Brenda

As we come to the end of our time together, we would like to speak about the state of parenting today—as we have heard it described by the professionals who work with your children. Our purpose is not to be judgmental, but to make you aware of how some psychologists, teachers, social workers, and school counselors see you, the parent. In psychology, it is widely known that each of us has a "blind spot." That is, there are things that others know about us that we don't. With your permission, we'd like to share what others have said about parental blind spots, and then propose ways to move from blindness to greater awareness.

What we have heard repeatedly is that parents have lost their power and authority in their children's lives, as well as in the culture. No longer captain and first mate of the family ship, some parents today do not hold their children accountable for their actions or allow them to experience the consequences of their irresponsible behavior. We have been told over and over again that parents are simply too distracted, tired, or busy to be consistent in discipline.

Moreover, no longer is there a clear divide between parent and child. The divide has been erased by a great parental need to be a friend and buddy rather than an authority figure in the lives of children. In fact, we have heard the word "buddy" more times than we can count! Why "buddy" rather than "parents"? Because many parents are absent long hours each day from their children, they don't want to have conflict in the brief time all are together. Said one social worker in a middle school in Northern Virginia, "Lots of parents work; they come home and want their kids to like them. So parents don't say, 'No, you can't have that cell phone.' They're afraid to set limits."

In addition to turning their children into buddies, parents have relinquished whole areas of their children's lives to other adults, the way a nation cedes its territories to other countries. Youth director Zac Collins pushes back, saying, "Every year, I tell my parents in our meeting at the beginning of the year, 'If your kid turns out great, it's not because of me, and if he turns out awful, it's not because of me either. We gotta remember that. I'm here to support you, not to take your place.'"

Schools, which have fed students breakfast and lunch for years and provided after-school care for working parents, now must care for the kids' emotional and psychological development as well. About parents, one school administrator said, "They want us to be the nurse, they want us to be the doctor, they want us to be the psychologist, they want us to mother their children. But they want us to do it on their terms."

OUTSOURCING CHILD REARING

Modern parents can outsource just about everything. It starts in infancy. You can hire a night nurse for your baby so you can enjoy uninterrupted sleep postpartum. Then once your child becomes a toddler, you can outsource potty training. Bike riding? No problem. No task is too small. Shoe tying? Locally, the children's shoe department at Nordstrom has offered shoe-tying classes for kids. The store clerk told us one mother had signed her daughter up for the class but failed to hear back from the store. She called the shoe department, angrily stating that now she would be forced to return her daughter's lace-up shoes. Why? She had no time to teach the child herself.

This modern outsourcing of child rearing is the by-product of major cultural shifts that have put teachers, youth leaders, coaches, and psychotherapists in charge of large chunks of children's lives. The shifts include the escalating divorce rate in the late sixties, the sexual revolution, the women's movement, and the exodus of millions of mothers into the workforce beginning in the seventies. The net result? Millions of kids spend scant hours with either parent on a daily basis.

SO WHAT'S A PARENT TO DO?

Given this reality, what's a parent to do? Reclaim the territory you have ceded to professionals. Stop outsourcing the important roles of parenthood to others. You, mom and dad, need to make sure you are the spiritual directors, the moral teachers, the protectors, and the nurturers in your child's life. And you can only do this if you are emotionally and physically accessible to your children for hours each day. We have said repeatedly in this book that you cannot rear good children in absentia.

Unfortunately, middle school is the time when many parents start to disengage from their children. School counselor Linda Reyner says that parents feel that once their children are out of elementary school, they become more self-sufficient and do not need as much parental time. And the kids themselves want parents to back away.

Reyner adds, "That's when a lot of mothers will reenter the workforce." If moms have stayed home, they often go to work about this time, thinking most of their job is done. Whether both parents work outside the home or not, they still need to make plenty of time for connecting with their children. Reyner believes, just as we do, that these middle school years are pivotal. She thinks those first few minutes when you see your child at the end of the day are critical for reconnecting and allowing a child to unload the day's joys and trials. She says, "If you're not ready to hear it in fifteen minutes, it's gone."

BE A PARENT, NOT A BUDDY

In a classic rewind of the 2007 Mother's Day show on *Oprah*, Maria Shriver interviewed both Vanessa Williams and her mother. After Vanessa explained that she, a rebellious middle schooler and teen, didn't begin to understand her mother until she married and became a mother herself, Maria asked Vanessa's mother if she and her daughter were friends. The mother's quiet but firm response? "I'm her mother; she has her friends."[1]

As one psychotherapist said about the mother-daughter relationship, "You will always be big to her little." The same is true for all parents and children.

If you don't have warm, supportive friendships yourself, you need to work on this so that you can model friendship with peers for your children. Then you will be happier and less needy. And if you don't have girlfriends—or, if you're a dad, male buddies—then look at your own heart and ask yourself why not. Often it's because we were not emotionally close to the same-sex parent and simply didn't learn to be comfortable with our own kind. If that is true for you, we would encourage you to find a psychologist and work through your difficult parental relationship(s). Trust us, if you do, you will have a healthier relationship with your son or daughter, and deeper—and appropriate—intimacy with your children. But remember: concentrate on your child's needs; don't use him or her to meet yours. Role reversal never works.

HOW'S THE STATE OF YOUR MARRIAGE?

As part of this examination of your own heart, you may need to look at the state of your marriage. Sometimes in an unhappy marriage, a parent will turn to a child to meet emotional needs. Don't do it. Even though a miserable marriage is one of the loneliest places on earth, it is not fair to supplant a spouse with a child. Everybody loses, and dangerous things, like sexual abuse, can happen. No, work on your marriage and rediscover the fun, excitement, and love of the early years. What did you love to do when you were dating? What gave you joy? One couple, lost in the throes of child rearing, has begun to schedule time to go horseback riding twice a month, leaving the kids with a sitter. As every marital therapist knows, it's much better to take care of a marriage in the moment than to let the years go by and the anger, resentment, and loneliness build. Just as your child needs you to do a heart-check daily, so too does your husband or wife need you to ask: How are you *really?* And then look into your spouse's eyes and listen with all of your being. Just listen.

What if you are a single parent and have no spouse to share your life with? Then you have a greater need for emotional and perhaps even financial support from friends and family. If you have a friend or a mother you can talk to on a daily basis, maybe late at night, then you will be a better parent to your children. None of us should parent alone without the friendly help and wisdom of others. We all have to build our own village to rear emotionally healthy children. And if we can't get the help we need from our biological family, then in the spirit of Charles Dickens' *Nicholas Nickleby,* we are free to create our own new family from the people we choose to have in our lives.

JUST SAY NO

Teachers tell us that parents are so driven by guilt that they often don't say no. Teacher Jaime Knox says, "I talked to a parent whose child was failing—failing all of his classes across the board. And the parent said, 'I don't know what to do.'"

> And I said, "What does he do when he comes home?"
>
> "Well, he has a cell phone, and he gets on the computer, or he's playing Xbox," replied the parent.
>
> "OK, well, maybe he should be doing his homework."
>
> "I know. We tried that for a week and we just felt so bad."
>
> I'm like, *"Come on!"*

You must be able to say no as a parent and make it stick. If you can't say no, then your yes is meaningless. The ability to say no and mean it no matter how loud or manipulative a child becomes is a brave act. It is what part of parenting is all about. If you can't say no, and God surely can, then go into your own soul, and ask yourself, "What's this all about?" And if you find that guilt keeps you from saying no, by all means deal with your guilt. Don't ignore it or suppress it. Guilt can be a God-given warning system, admonishing us to change our behavior. If you are doing a good job as a parent, you will not have crippling guilt. You will be raising decent, likable kids who can keep their behavior in check.

Of course, you must have a clear and articulated set of priorities. Otherwise, playing video games is on par with succeeding in school. If all of this sounds daunting, then you need a plan—a parenting plan. And if you don't have one, we're here to help you create one.

DR. J: THE MAN WITH THE PLAN

Dr. Matthew Johnson, a six-foot-nine former collegiate basketball player who goes by the moniker Dr. J, is a clinical psychologist who has trained sixty thousand professionals and several thousand parents. He speaks widely in the United States, Canada, and Europe, and says that the problem with most families today is that parents are clueless about how to raise their kids and are "flying by the seat of their pants. They have no game plan for training children to function in life." Dr. Johnson says that his parenting program, *Positive Parenting with a Plan*, is a family systems program in which parents are required to change along with the kids.

He told us, "Most programs do not require mom and dad to change; instead, they allow mom and dad to get away with murder." His program requires parents to model the kind of behavior they want from their kids. Parents get consequences just like the kids if they don't follow family rules and get their chores done. Dr. Johnson states firmly that if only the kids have to change and nothing is required of the parents, "you're not going to get anything out of the kid."

His parenting program is so successful that it is being used in schools, churches, seminaries, and in-patient psychiatric facilities and is now mandated by the Los Angeles Family Superior Court System for divorcing couples. It is also being implemented with an 85 percent success rate in the juvenile offenders program in the state of Georgia. Yes, even the parents of juvenile offenders are required to get involved.

What are some of his key ideas? Dr. Johnson says that the *real world is ordered and structured.* But many families are ruled by chaos and disorder. The missing link? Effective discipline and family rules. He contends that the primary role of the parent is to be a disciplinarian first, followed by being a caring adult as close second. He says that the root word of *disciplinarian* is "disciple," which means "to teach, guide, instruct, direct, and correct."

Dr. Johnson believes that the primary role of parents is "to paint the lines on the road of life and teach their children 'these are the lines, the lines are your friends, stay between the lines.' In addition, parents are the guardrails on the road of life, and they communicate clearly, 'I'm not going to let you go off on the dangerous curves.'" He also believes in a hierarchical model within the family and is opposed to what he dubs "King Arthur's round table" for family decision making, in which everyone has an equal voice. In his book, *Positive Parenting with a Plan,* he states that "authority flows downward within families—not upward." He believes that children must learn to respect authority in parents, teachers, police, clergy, and others.[2]

A REVERENT FEAR OF AUTHORITY

Dr. Johnson has sympathy for families who are struggling to discipline their children. He told us that, decades ago:

> We passed laws to protect children from being abused. Then we told parents what they *couldn't* do, but we never told them what they *could* do. We created a shark eating frenzy when we took away the most important parental intervention—*a reverent fear of authority.* And we gave nothing back. Consequently, today many kids have no reverent fear of authority in the home or at school. Kids will go up to their principal in school and say, "These are my hallways. You are not going to tell me what to do, or my parents will sue." And the

principal knows that the school board will not back her up to keep order and structure in her classrooms and her hallways. Today the sharks have multiplied in our homes, our schools, and our streets.

Dr. Johnson states that his parenting program instills "a reverent fear of authority" in children without using any corporal punishment. So how does he advise parents to get their kids to respect authority?

A great believer in family rules, this clinical psychologist says, "There's not a behavior or attitude that you can't target with the rules. There's not a place you can go on the planet that doesn't have policies, rules, treaties, and contracts written down, except for the most important institution on the planet, the family. In the family, any rules that exist are floating around inside mom and dad's heads." He continues, "My parenting program pulls these rules out of parents' heads, and they write them down on paper. And no rule can go on that list unless both parents are in agreement."

Dr. Johnson is quick to say that if parents *can* agree on the rules, then the child will comply and "not get away with anything." What about divorced parents? In *Positive Parenting with a Plan*, he says that many divorced couples use his system of family rules successfully in two homes.[3]

Dr. Johnson states that the book of Deuteronomy tells us to write down God's rules (to love him with all our heart, soul, and strength) on the door frames of our houses and on the gates, and to bind them to our wrists and foreheads. "If it was important enough for God to write down the Ten Commandments, why are we not writing down family rules in our homes?" he asks. Indeed.

The beauty of writing down family rules? According to Dr. Johnson, parents are no longer in charge of whether their children get grounded. The children become responsible through the choices they make. He adds, "If children break a rule or do not do daily and weekly chores that have been assigned, then they choose to ground themselves."[4] What happens next? The child draws from fifty Good Habit Cards—the number of cards he must draw is based on the infraction—and then he can either go to his room (no electronics allowed) or do his Good Habit Cards immediately. But he still has to do the chores listed on the Good Habit cards no matter how long he chooses to stay in his room. Parents are held to the same standard: if they don't do their designated daily and weekly chores, they too must draw some Good Habit Cards.[5] These include chores, such as scrubbing the bathroom tub and tile or cleaning out the refrigerator.

Kids love this! They love to see mom and dad held to the same standard they are. Dr. Johnson says his parenting plan works, and he is taking it around the world with great success because God's principles and truth never return void.

CREATING A FAMILY IDENTITY

As you work to rebuild the walls of your family, don't forget to add the sweet stuff to family life. One family we know chose Sunday as family day. After church, they rotated choosing the afternoon activity, from touch football to visiting a museum to playing board games to singing together as a family. And their voices blend beautifully. The Sunday family rule? Each member had a turn and no complaining was allowed. Over the years, they built a strong family identity. Even as adults, they gather together several times a year.

Long after your middle schooler is grown and gone, he will need a strong family to come home to. Always. For Christmas and Thanksgiving. For a wedding. After a baby is born.

To celebrate the highs and lows of life.

He will carry the imprint of your family with him, inside his head and heart, as long as he is alive. And you will want him to come home. Sad, indeed, are those parents who failed to build strong ties and seldom see their children. The elder President Bush, after he had left office, was interviewed by a journalist who asked him: "What was your life's greatest accomplishment?" This former pilot, ambassador, and president replied, "That my children still want to come home."

"MY FAMILY IS EVERYTHING"

We decided to end this chapter with an interview with a young man who, once a middle schooler himself, is the second child of a woman we feel is an Awesome Mother. You have met Nilda Melendez before. When we spoke with Nilda, a straightforward, hands-on mother, she mentioned that her son, Francisco Javier, had written an essay for entrance to the Naval Academy about his family, stating that his mom "ran a tight ship." We thought that was clever: ship at home, ship at sea. Those admissions officers at the Naval Academy must have thought so, too: Francisco was admitted to the Academy and is now a senior. He will be serving in the Marines for five years after graduation.

A friendly, open guy, Francisco agreed to talk to us and answer a few questions.

How do you feel about the way you were raised?

I loved the way I was raised. I learned not just respect for my parents but respect for my elders as a whole. And now when I see and hear little kids yelling and screaming at their parents, I think my younger brothers and sisters aren't like that. Because of the way I was raised, though I never said "ma'am" and "sir" at home, now I find myself saying, "Yes, ma'am," and "Yes, sir," to my elders. What does my family mean to me? *My family means everything to me.* I know that if I make a dumb mistake, they're going to let me know it was a dumb thing to do, but they'll support me. Now three of us are older and are married or in school. But when we get together, if even one person is missing, the family doesn't feel as solid as when we're all together.

Most of my friends have been raised just like me. I look for people with similar backgrounds to be friends with. Most of us at the academy are from strong, intact families with military backgrounds.

Do you have good communication with your parents, even now?

When I get upset or when I need someone to talk to, I always call my parents. My mother stressed communication when I was growing up. My mom was going to get a doctorate in marine biology but felt that she wouldn't be around to raise us like she wanted to. With both parents gone or both failing to communicate, that can leave a kid feeling, "No one cares about me," or "I can do whatever I want." Mom has always stressed communication with all of us.

Are you close to your dad?

Growing up, I used to get upset when my dad would get mad at me, and it took me awhile to realize it has made me who I am today. He always had the best intentions. When I was younger and he got mad at me, I didn't understand. We got closer in late middle school and high school; later, I realized his parenting has gotten me where I am today. My mom would come in and tell me, "He loves you, he cares about you, he wants the best for you." When I didn't understand something, my mom would come in and help me understand. My dad is still tough on me—on all the kids, but we are very close today.

Did your mom run a tight ship?

My mom is a no-nonsense person. Respect is large in our family. She started when we were young. We grew up knowing she wasn't going to mess around. Throwing a little fit did not get you what you wanted. She never made a scene, but she always let us know if we were out of line. If we started acting up in church, she'd give a little pinch on the arm and tell us we were going to "catch it" when we got home. We always listened to her. We had discipline, but we had a lot of love. If you have discipline but no love, I guess that could even be considered abuse.

Last year, I had to make a major career decision; my mom refrained from giving advice and telling me how she felt, even though she didn't agree with my decision. When I asked her about this, she said, "It's your life; I love you, but I don't want to make you do something you don't want to do or make you *not* do something because of how I feel." She cared enough to let me make my own decision without trying to influence me one way or another. She knows I would do anything for her. She's the one I go to for comfort. She's a great mom. She's a saint—to deal with us. We're all crazy and obnoxious and rowdy. She has the most patience and strength of anyone I've ever seen.

What did your family give you?

I have a pretty strong faith in God, and I thank my parents for that. I can make it in any environment because of what they taught me. They taught me how to care for myself and help others. *They've given me everything I have and am.* And I see them doing the same things for my younger brothers and sisters. I have a lot of pride in my family. Everybody I know loves my family. When I come home for the weekend, all my friends from Annapolis try to come with me. My parents are always cool with it. They have always opened our home to other people.

FINAL THOUGHTS

This young man was not allowed to watch TV during the week when he was growing up and was always encouraged to play outside. Family time, dinners together with scintillating conversation about one's day and the state of the world—these were in abundance. And this future soldier, who will soon help protect our country, says he feels sorry for kids who don't play outside, who never climb trees, who don't know the "joy of the bruised knee."

We want to celebrate the Melendez family, and the millions of others like them, who have built strong, sturdy walls around their families for shelter and protection—who know what part of the culture to allow into the home and what part to keep out. And if you need to rebuild your family walls, have faith. Hold your framing hammer in one hand and your sword in the other. Expect opposition. But then, like ancient Nehemiah and the Israelites, prepare to celebrate what you and God have done together.

And the good that you do in your family will endure for generations to come.

Notes

Chapter One

1. Lindsay M. Howden and Julie A. Meyer, "Age and Sex Composition: 2010," US Census Bureau, May 2011, 4, http://www.census.gov/prod/cent2010/briefs/c2010br-03.pdf.

2. Vicky J. Rideout, Ulla G. Foehr, and Donald F. Roberts, *Generation M²: Media in the Lives of 8- to 18-Year-Olds*, Henry J. Kaiser Foundation, January 20, 2010, 2, www.kff.org/entmedia/mh012010pkg.cfm.

3. Ibid.

4. Vicky J. Rideout, Webcast release of *Generation M²: Media in the Lives of 8- to 18-Year-Olds*, January 20, 2010, http://event.netbriefings.com/event/kff/Archives/20jan10media/index.html.

Chapter Two

1. Louise Bates Ames, Frances L. Ilg, and Sidney M. Baker, *Your Ten- to-Fourteen-Year Old* (New York: Delacorte Press, 1988), 145.

2. Ibid.

3. Laurence Steinberg, *Adolescence,* 9th ed. (New York: McGraw-Hill, 2011), 5.

4. Ibid.

5. Ibid.

6. Laurence Steinberg, *You and Your Adolescent* (New York: Simon Schuster, 2011), 13.

7. Ibid.

8. "Adolescent Development," Medline Plus, Web article, last modified January 17, 2011, www.nlm.nih.gov/medlineplus/ency/article/002003.htm.

9. Ibid.

10. Ibid.

11. Ibid.

12. Ames, Ilg, and Baker, *Your Ten- to-Fourteen-Year Old*, 77.

13. Ibid., 66–67.

14. Ibid., 63.

15. Ibid., 77.

16. Ibid., 96.

17. Ibid., 100–101.

18. Ibid., 112.

19. Ibid., 126.

20. Ibid., 167–168.

21. "Identity Status Theory (Marcia)," Web article, accessed March 10, 2011, http://www.learning-theories.com/identity-status-theory-marcia.html.

22. "Identity Development—Aspects of Identity," Web article, accessed March 10, 2011, http://social.jrank.org/pages/322/Identity-Development.html.

23. Ibid.

24. David P. Ausubel, *Theories and Problems of Adolescent Development*, 3rd ed. (New York: Writers Club Press, 2002), 152–155.

25. Ibid., 155.

26. David Walsh, *Why Do They Act That Way?* (New York: Free Press, 2004), 17.

27. Ibid., 37.

28. Ibid., 60.

29. Ibid., 65.

30. Susan Hinebauch, "Nurturing the Emerging Independent Adolescent," *Independent School* 61 no. 4 (Summer 2002). www.nais.org/publications/ismagazinearticle.cfm?Itemnumber=144294&sn.ItemNumber=145956.

31. Ibid.

32. Steinberg, *You and Your Adolescent*, 15.

33. Lon Solomon, "Mothering with No Regrets," Mother's Day sermon at McLean Bible Church, May 9, 2010.

Chapter Three

1. Charlene Giannetti and Margaret Sagarese, "Cliques and Fitting In: Help Your Middle Schooler Identify the Social Hierarchy," *Family Education*, accessed February 9, 2011, http://life.familyeducation.com/peer-pressure/self-esteem/36541.html?page=2.

2. Ibid.

3. Ibid.

4. Rosalind Wiseman, *Queen Bees and Wannabes* (New York: Three Rivers Press, 2002, updated 2009), 79.

5. Ibid., 87.

6. Ibid., 90.

7. Ibid., 96.

8. Ibid., 98.

9. Michael Thompson and Catherine O'Neill Grace with Lawrence J. Cohen, *Best Friends, Worst Enemies: Understanding the Social Lives of Children* (New York: Ballantine Books, 2001), 164.

10. Ibid., 165, 164.

11. Wiseman, *Queen Bees,* 276.

12. Quoted in Sadie Dingfelder, "Whispers as Weapons," *Monitor on Psychology* 37, no. 4 (April 2006): 62. www.apa.org/monitor/apr06/whispers.aspx.

13. Ibid.

14. Wiseman, *Queen Bees,* 189.

15. Dingfelder, "Whispers as Weapons."

16. Quoted in Sadie Dingfelder, "Whispers as Weapons."

17. Ibid.

18. Charlene C. Giannetti and Margaret Sagarese, *Cliques: 8 Steps to Help Your Child Survive the Social Jungle* (New York: Broadway Books, 2001), 190–191.

19. Kathryn R. Wentzel, Carolyn McNamara Barry, and Kathryn Caldwell, "Friendships in Middle School: Influences on Motivation and School Adjustment," *Journal of Educational Psychology* 96, no. 2 (June 2004): 195–203.

20. Ibid.

21. Quoted in Melissa Dittman, "Friendships Ease Middle School Adjustment," *Monitor on Psychology* 35, no. 7 (July 2004): 18. www.apa.org/monitor/julaug04/friendships.aspx.

22. Lawrence J. Cohen, "Is Your Child a Loner or Alone?" Parenthood.com, Web article, accessed March 5, 2011, www.parenthood.com/article-topics/is_your_child_a_loner_or_alone.html/full-view.

23. Ibid.

24. "When Your Child's a Loner," Education.com, Web article, accessed March 5, 2011, www.education.com/magazine/article/When_Your_Childs_Loner.

25. Cohen, "Is Your Child a Loner or Alone?"

26. "When Your Child's a Loner," Education.com.

27. Giannetti and Sagarese, *Cliques: 8 Steps*, 28.

Chapter Four

1. "Mattie Stepanek," Humanmedia.org., radio broadcast, accessed March 11, 2011, www.humanmedia.org/catalog/program.php?products_id=89.

2. President Jimmy Carter, "Eulogy for Mattie Stepanek," presented June 28, 2004, www.cartercenter.org/news/documents/doc1791.html.

3. Ibid.

4. Ibid.

5. Anne-Marie Dorning, "Teens Who Burn Boy May Be Tried As Adults," ABC News, October 14, 2009, http://abcnews.go.com/Health/US/burned-boys-attackers-adults/story?id=8829393, accessed March 12, 2011.

6. Daniel Goleman, *Working with Emotional Intelligence* (New York: Bantam Books, 2000), 135.

7. Ibid.

8. Interview with Dr. Tanya Beran, professor at the medical school of the University of Calgary, Canada, March 7, 2011.

9. William Damon, *Social and Personality Development* (New York: W. W. Norton & Company, 1983), 129–30.

10. Ibid., 130.

11. Ibid.

12. Dr. Tanya Beran, interview.

13. Alan Sroufe and Everett Waters, "Attachment as an Organizational Construct," *Child Development*, 48 (1977): 1186.

14. Jeremy Holmes, *John Bowlby and Attachment Theory* (New York: Routledge, 1993), 3.

15. John Bowlby, *Attachment and Loss*, vol. 1, *Attached*, 2nd ed. (New York: Basic Books, 1982), 177.

16. Ibid., xiii.

17. Sigmund Freud, *Outline of Psychoanalysis*, SE23 (London: Hogarth Press, 1940), 188.

18. Robert Karen, *Becoming Attached* (New York: Warner Books, 1994), 151.

19. Ibid., 159.

20. Ibid.

21. Ibid., 160.

22. Ibid.

23. Ibid., 199.

24. Graham Music, *Nurturing Natures* (New York: Psychology Press, 2011), 55.

25. Winnie Hu, "Gossip Girls and Boys Get Lessons in Empathy," *New York Times*, April 4, 2009, www.nytimes.com/2009/04/05/education/05empathy.html.

26. Ibid.

27. Maia Szalavitz, "How Not to Raise a Bully: The Early Roots of Empathy," *Time*, April 17, 2010, www.time.com/time/health/article/0,8599,1982190,00.html.

28. Karen, *Becoming Attached*, 198.

29. Ibid., 199.

30. J. Elicker, M. Englund, and L. Sroufe, "Predicting Peer Competence and Peer Relationships in Childhood from Early Parent-Child Relationships," in *Family-Peer Relationships: Modes of Linkage*, ed. R. Parke and G. Ladd (Hillsdale, NJ: Erlbaum, 1992).

31. Karen, *Becoming Attached*, 200.

32. Amanda Nickerson, Danielle Mele, and Dana Princiotta, "Attachment and Empathy as Predictors of Roles as Defenders or Outsiders in Bullying Interactions," *Journal of School Psychology* 46, no. 6 (December 2008): 687–703.

33. Megan Eliot and Dewey Cornell, "The Effect of Parental Attachment on Bullying in Middle School," Virginia Youth Violence Project (2006), http://youthviolence.edschool.virginia.edu/pdf/2006-APA-the-effect-of-parental-attachment-on-bullying-in-middle-school.pdf.

34. Laura M. Walden and Tanya N. Beran, "Attachment Quality and Bullying Behavior in School-Aged Youth," *Canadian Journal of School Psychology* 25, no. 1 (March 2010): 5–18. http://cjs.sagepub.com/content/25/1/5.abstract.

35. WXYZ news, Detroit, Michigan, "A Woman Is Calling Her Teenage Neighbor an Angel for Saving Her," radio broadcast, February 24, 2011, www.wxyz.com/dpp/news/region/detroit/a-woman-is-calling-her-teenage-neighbor-an-angel-for-saving-her.

36. Jeni Stepanek, interview by Oprah Winfrey, radio station on Sirius XM, March 10, 2011, from Oprah's classic programs, 2004.

Chapter Five

1. Claudia Wallis, "The Myth About Homework," *Time*, August 29, 2006, www.time.com/time/magazine/article/0,9171,1376208,00.html.

2. Duke Today, "Duke Study: Homework Helps Students Succeed in School, As Long as There Isn't Too Much," press release, March 7, 2006, www.dukenews.duke.edu/2006/03/homework.html.

3. Ibid.

4. Angela L. Duckworth and Martin E. P. Seligman, "Self-Discipline Outdoes IQ in Predicting Academic Performance of Adolescents," *Psychological Science* 16, no. 12 (2005): 941.

5. Ibid., 944.

6. Carolyn Click, "Teacher tips: Exhilarating, challenging middle school years," *The State*, August 11, 2010.

7. National Mathematics Advisory Panel, *Foundations for Success: The Final Report of the National Mathematics Advisory Panel* (Washington, DC: US Department of Education, 2008), xx.

8. Ibid.

9. Ibid., 9.

10. Ibid., xiii.

11. Ibid.

12. National Endowment for the Arts, *To Read or Not to Read: A Question of National Consequence* (Washington, DC: Office of Research & Analysis, 2007), 8.

13. Ibid., 15, 17.

14. Ibid., 16.

15. National Center for Education Statistics, "Grade 8 National Results: Reading," The Nation's Report Card, accessed January 28, 2011, http://nationsreportcard.gov/reading_2009/nat_g8.asp?subtab_id=Tab_1&tab_id=tab2#tabsContainer.

16. Center on Education Policy, *State Test Score Trends Through 2007-08, Part 5: Are There Differences in Achievement Between Boys and Girls?* (Washington, DC: Center on Education Policy, March 2010), 1.

17. Nicholas D. Kristof, "The Boys Have Fallen Behind," *New York Times*, March 27, 2010, www.nytimes.com/2010/03/28/opinion/28kristof.html.

18. Southern Regional Educational Board, *Making Middle Grades Work: An Enhanced Design to Prepare All Middle Grades Students for Success in High School* (Atlanta, GA: SREB, 2006), http://publications.sreb.org/2006/06V15-R08_MMGW_Brochure.pdf.

19. Quoted in Rachel Muir, "The Pressure to Achieve," *George Washington Today*, January 10, 2011.

20. Vicki Abeles, interview by Katie Couric, CBS News video, March 1, 2011, www.cbsnews.com/video/watch/?id=7358158n.

21. "Harrow School," winstonchurchill.org, Web article, accessed March 14, 2011, www.winstonchurchill.org/learn/biography/the-child/harrow.

22. Howard Gardner, *Intelligence Reframed: Multiple Intelligences for the 21st Century* (New York: Basic Books, 1999), 41–43.

23. "Howard Gardner's Multiple Intelligence Theory," PBS.org, accessed May 12, 2011, www.pbs.org/wnet/gperf/education/ed_mi_overview.html.

24. Gardner, *Intelligence Reframed*, 41.

25. Ibid., 42.

26. Ibid., 4.

27. Ruth Curran Neild, Robert Balfanz, and Lisa Herzog, "An Early Warning System," *Educational Leadership* 65, no. 2 (October 2007): 30.

28. Ibid., 29.

29. Ibid., 31.

30. Dr. Art Lindsley, "C. S. Lewis: His Life and Works," published on the C. S. Lewis Institute Website, September 11, 2006, www.cslewisinstitute.org/cslewis/index.htm.http://www.cslewisinstitute.org/node/28

Chapter Six

1. Richard A. Swenson, *Margin* (Colorado Springs, CO: Navigator Press), 13.

2. Ibid., 50–51.

3. Sharon Hwang, "Excessive Fatigue and Our Crazy Busy Culture," SelfGrowth.com, Web article, accessed February 26, 2011, www.selfgrowth.com/articles/Excessive_Fatigue_and_Our_Crazy_Busy_Culture.html.

4. Ibid.

5. Ibid.

6. American Psychological Association (APA), "APA Survey Raises Concern about Health Impact of Stress on Children and Families," press release, November 9, 2010, www.apa.org/news/press/releases/2010/11/stress-in-america.aspx.

7. Rob Stein, "Stress in America," *Washington Post*, Health, November 9, 2010, http://voices.washingtonpost.com/checkup/2010/11/stress_in_america.html.

8. American Psychological Association, "APA Survey."

9. Ibid.

10. John Gottman, "Raising an Emotionally Intelligent Child," Gottman.com, video, July 9, 2009, www.gottman.com/48995/parenting.html.

11. Robert E. Wubbolding, *Using Reality Therapy* (New York: Harper & Row, 1988), 50.

12. Ibid., 51.

13. Swenson, *Margin*, 78.

14. Ibid.

Chapter Seven

1. Vicky J. Rideout, Ulla G. Foehr, and Donald F. Roberts, *Generation M2: Media in the Lives of 8- to 18-Year-Olds*, Henry J. Kaiser Family Foundation, January 20, 2010, 2-3, www.kff.org/entmedia/mh012010pkg.cfm.

2. Ibid., 5.

3. Webcast release of *Generation M2: Media in the Lives of 8- to 18-Year-Olds*, January 20, 2010, http://event.netbriefings.com/event/kff/Archives/20jan10media/index.html.

4. Rideout, Foehr, and Roberts, *Generation M2*, 2.

5. Ibid., 36.

6. Ibid., 2.

7. Christina M. Kelly, "Lights out, phones on: Many teens text all night long," MSNBC.com, November 1, 2010, www.msnbc.msn.com/id/39917869/ns/health-kids_and_parenting.

8. Rideout, Foehr, and Roberts, *Generation M2*, 10.

9. Steven J. Blumberg and Julian V. Luke, "Wireless Substitution: Early Release of Estimates From the National Health Interview Survey, July–December 2008," Division of Health Interview Statistics, National Center for Health Statistics, Centers for Disease Control, May 6, 2009.

10. Pew Internet and American Life Project, *Teens and Mobile Phones* (Washington, DC: Pew Research Center, April 20, 2010), 5.

11. Aliyah Shahid, "'Night-texting' taking its toll on N.J. teens," *New Jersey Star-Ledger*, September 28, 2009, www.nj.com/news/local/index.ssf/2009/09/night-texting_taking_its_toll.html.

12. Ibid.

13. Pew Internet, *Teens and Mobile Phones*, 2.

14. Rideout, Foehr, and Roberts, *Generation M2*, 18.

15. "JFK Doctors Warn Teens About Health Risks of Overnight Hypertexting," John F. Kennedy Medical Center, December 8, 2010, www.jfkmc.org/about-jfk/media-center/in-the-news/303-jfk-doctors-warn-teens-about-health-risks-of-over night-hypertexting.

16. Ibid.

17. Ibid.

18. Quoted in Aliyah Shahid, "'Night-texting' taking its toll on N.J. teens."

19. Rosalind Wiseman, *Queen Bees and Wannabes* (New York: Three Rivers Press, 2002, updated 2009), 25.

20. Stefanie Olsen, "When to Buy Your Child a Cellphone," *New York Times*, June 9, 2010, www.nytimes.com/2010/06/10/technology/personaltech/10basics.html.

21. Byron Acohido, "Sex Predators Stalk Social Media," *USA Today*, March 1, 2011.

22. Sharon Vaknin, "How to Disable Mobile Geotagging," CNET News, video, March 9, 2011, http://cnettv.cnet.com/disable-mobile-geotagging/9742-1_53-50101455.html.

23. Russ Ptacek, "Smartphone picture uploads can reveal the location of your children's home, school, and play areas," NBC Action News, November 9, 2010, www.nbcactionnews.com/dpp/news/local_news/investigations/smartphone-picture-uploads-can-reveal-the-location-of-your-children's-home,-school,-and-play-areas.

24. Ibid.

25. Chris Cox, "Making it Easier to Share With Who You Want," The Facebook Blog, August 23, 2011, https://blog.facebook.com/blog.php?post=10150251867797131, accessed September 20, 2011.

26. "What Is Foursquare?" *The Week*, March 15, 2010, http://theweek.com/article/index/200751/what-is-foursquare.

27. Anne Collier, "Foursquare and other geolocation apps: For young adults, not kids," ConnectSafely.org, accessed May 21, 2011, www.connectsafely.org/Safety-Advice-Articles/foursquare-a-other-geolocation-apps-for-young-adults-not-kids.html.

28. Maria Cheng, "Cellphones 'possibly carcinogenic,' report suggests," MSNBC.com, May 31, 2011, www.msnbc.msn.com/id/43225917/ns/health-cancer.

29. Mary Brophy Marcus, "Study: Cellphone Use Affects Brain," *USA Today*, February 23, 2011.

30. Ibid.

31. Devra Davis, "Fine Print Warnings," Disconnectbook.com, accessed March 14, 2011, www.disconnectbook.com/cell-phone/fine-print-warnings.

32. Devra Davis, *Disconnect* (New York: Dutton, 2010), 73, 82.

33. Denis Aydin, et al, "Mobile Phone Use and Brain Tumors in Children and Adolescents: A Multicenter Case-Control Study," *Journal of the National Cancer Institute* 103, Issue 16 (August 17, 2011).

34. Ibid., 6, 9.

35. Ibid., 3.

36. "Environmental Health Trust Questions New Study Claiming No Cell Phone-Brain Cancer Link Among Children and Adolescents," press release, Environmental Health Trust, Jackson, WY, July 27, 2011, at http://www.environmentalhealthtrust.org/content/press-release-environmental-health-trust-questions-new-study-claiming-no-cell-phone-brain-ca, accessed September 21, 2011.

37. Davis, *Disconnect*, 212.

38. Ibid., 213.

39. Ibid., 245–246.

40. Pew Internet & American Life Project, "Teens, Video Games and Civics," PewResearch.org, September 16, 2008, http://pewresearch.org/pubs/953/.

41. Nick Bilton, "Call of Duty Smashes Five-Day Sales Records," *New York Times*, November 18, 2010.

42. David Walsh, *Why Do They Act That Way?* (New York: Free Press, 2004), 165–166.

43. American Academy of Pediatrics Policy, "Policy Statement: Media Violence," *Pediatrics* 124, no. 5 (November 2009), published online November 1, 2009, http://aappolicy.aappublications.org/cgi/content/full/pediatrics;124/5/1495.

44. Ibid.

45. Michael Rich, "Response to controversy over violent video game answer," *Ask the Mediatrician*, blog, January 14, 2010, http://cmch.typepad.com/mediatrician/2010/01/response-to-controversy-over-violent-video-game-answer.html.

46. Douglas Gentile, et al., "Pathological Video Game Use Among Youths: A Two-Year Longitudinal Study," *Pediatrics* 127, no. 2 (February 2011).

47. Ibid.

48. Ibid.

49. David Walsh, *Why Do They Act That Way?*, 165, 166.

Chapter Eight

1. "Statistics," Facebook Press Room, Website, accessed September 23, 2011, www.facebook.com/press/info.php?statistics.

2. "That Facebook friend might be 10 years old, and other troubling news," *Consumer Reports*, June 2011, www.consumerreports.org/cro/magazine-archive/2011/june/electronics-computers/state-of-the-net/facebook-concerns/index.htm.

3. Common Sense Media, "Is Social Networking Changing Childhood? A National Poll," August 10, 2009, www.commonsensemedia.org/teen-social-media.

4. Ibid.

5. David Kirkpatrick, *The Facebook Effect* (New York: Simon Schuster, 2010), 92.

6. Trinity School of Durham and Chapel Hill, "Student-Parent Handbook, TK-12, 2010-2011."

7. Jen Maxfield, "Middle school principal says 'no' to Facebook," WABC–TV, Ridgewood, New Jersey, May 11, 2010, http://abclocal.go.com/wabc/story?section=news/local&id=7412436.

8. Rosa Golijan, "Michelle Obama says young kids don't need Facebook, but who does?" Technolog, MSNBC.com, February 9, 2011, http://technolog.msnbc.msn.com/_news/2011/02/09/6017345-michelle-obama-says-young-kids-dont-need-facebook-but-who-does.

9. "Obama Advises Caution in Use of Facebook," YouTube video, uploaded by Associated Press, September 8, 2009, www.youtube.com/watch?v=si1gNXqH7iw.

10. "Online Safety for Middle and High School," New York State Internet Crimes Against Children Task Force, September 2, 2010, 14.

11. Athima Chansanchai, "Secret Service interrogates 13-year-old over Facebook post," MSNBC.com, May 18, 2011, http://digitallife.today.com/_news/2011/05/18/6667233-secret-service-interrogates-13-year-old-over-facebook-post.

12. Facebook, "Profile: When I share something, how do I choose who can see it?" Facebook.com, https://www.facebook.com/help/?faq=120939471321735, accessed September 23, 2011.

13. "The Kids are Alright* Improvement Needed," TRUSTe, national survey, October, 2010, http://www.truste.com/pdf/Truste_SNS_shortdeck.pdf, 5, 10.

14. Facebook Safety Center, "Playing it Safe," Facebook.com, https://www.facebook.com/safety/groups/teens/, accessed September 23, 2011.

15. "How to Protect your Teen on Social Networks: Privacy Tips for Parents," TRUSTe, http://www.truste.com/pdf/TRUSTe_ParentTeenPrivacyTips.pdf, 2, accessed September 23, 2011.

16. Ibid.

17. Electronic Privacy Information Center, "In re Google Buzz," epic.org, accessed May 21, 2011, http://epic.org/privacy/ftc/googlebuzz/.

18. Jessica Guynn, "Google Buzz poses a major privacy risk for kids, analyst (and parent) says," Technology blog, *Los Angeles Times*, February 22, 2010, http://latimesblogs.latimes.com/technology/2010/02/google-buzz-privacy-kids.html.

19. "Children's Online Privacy Protection Act," coppa.org, accessed May 20, 2011, www.coppa.org/comply.htm.

20. Ibid.

21. Joshua Rhett Miller, "Debate Looms Over Teens' Privacy Rights on the Web," FoxNews.com, July 7, 2010, www.foxnews.com/scitech/2010/07/07/proposal-include-teens-childrens-online-privacy-act-hurt-free-speech-privacy.

22. "That Facebook friend," *Consumer Reports*.

23. Parry Aftab, "The Three Steps to Internet Safety," aftab.com, Website, accessed May 30, 2011, http://aftab.com/index.php?page=internet-safety-1-2-3.

24. New York State, "Online Safety."

25. David Walsh, *Why Do They Act That Way?* (New York: Free Press, 2004), 173.

26. William Powers, *Hamlet's BlackBerry* (New York: Harper Collins, 2010), 178.

27. Vicky J. Rideout, Ulla G. Foehr, and Donald F. Roberts, *Generation M2: Media in the Lives of 8- to 18-Year-Olds*, Henry J. Kaiser Family Foundation, January 20, 2010, p. 1, www.kff.org/entmedia/mh012010pkg.cfm.

28. Rosalind Wiseman, *Queen Bees and Wannabes* (New York: Three Rivers Press, 2009), 32.

Chapter Nine

1. American Psychological Association, "Sexualization of Girls," executive summary Web page, apa.org, February 19, 2007, www.apa.org/pi/women/programs/girls/report.aspx.

2. Ibid.

3. Ibid.

4. Ibid.

5. Dannah Gresh, "The Modesty Project," http://www.secretkeepergirl.com/bod_squad_petition.aspx, accessed September 18, 2011.

6. Ibid.

7. Ibid.

8. Christine J. DeRosa, et al., "Sexual Intercourse and Oral Sex among Middle School Students: Prevalence and Correlates," *Perspectives on Sexual and Reproductive Health* 42, no. 3 (September 2010). http://onlinelibrary.wiley.com/doi/10.1363/4219710/full.

9. "Youth Risk Behavior Surveillance United States, 2009," Morbidity and Mortality Weekly Report, Centers for Disease Control and Prevention, *Surveillance Summaries* 59, no. SS-5 (June 4, 2010). www.cdc.gov/mmwr/pdf/ss/ss5905.pdf.

10. University of Texas Health Science Center at Houston, "Middle School Youth as Young as 12 Engaging in Risky Sexual Activity," *ScienceDaily*, news Website, April 10, 2009, www.sciencedaily.com/releases/2009/04/090408145354.htm.

11. Ibid.

12. "Oxnard Middle School Rocked by Teen Sex Scandal," *HuffPost Los Angeles*, news video, May 12, 2010, www.huffingtonpost.com/2010/05/12/oxnard-middle-school-rock_n_573192.html.

13. Leonard Sax, *Girls on the Edge* (New York: Basic Books, 2010), 18.

14. Claire Shipman and Cole Kazdin, "Teens: Oral Sex and Casual Prostitution No Biggie," *Good Morning America*, May 28, 2009, http://abcnews.go.com/GMA/Parenting/story?id=7693121&page=1.

15. Ibid.

16. Ibid.

17. Bernadine Healy, "Clueless on STDs, Throat Cancer, and Oral Sex," *U.S. News & World Report*, February 19, 2008, http://health.usnews.com/ health-news/family-health/sexual-and-reproductive-health/ articles/2008/02/19/clueless-on-stds-throat-cancer-and-oral-sex.

18. Ibid.

19. Ibid.

20. Caitlin Flanagan, "Are You There God? It's Me, Monica," *Atlantic Monthly*, January/February 2006, www.theatlantic.com/magazine/archive/2006/01/ are-you-there-god-it-apos-s-me-monica/4511.

21. Leonard Sax, *Girls on the Edge*, 25.

22. Rebecca Dube, "Kathie Lee on 'Skins': 'I Get Mad at Parents Who Don't Tell Their Kids the Truth,'" msnbc.com, TODAY Moms blog, video interview, January 26, 2011, http://moms.today.com/_news/2011/01/26/5925115-kathie- lee-on-skins-i-get-mad-at-parents-who-dont-tell-their-kids-the-truth.

23. Christina Huffington, "Yale Students File Title IX Complaint Against University," *Yale Herald*, March 31, 2011, http://yaleherald.com/topstory/ breaking-news-yale-students-file-title-ix-suit-against-school.

24. Sharon Jayson, "Study: Young People Shun Sex," *USA Today*, March 4, 2011.

25. Sharon Jayson, "Is Dating Dead?" *USA Today*, March 31, 2011.

26. "National Survey of American Attitudes on Substance Abuse XV: Teens and Parents," The National Center on Addiction and Substance Abuse at Columbia University, research report, August 2010, http://www.casacolumbia.org/ upload/2010/report.pdf.

27 Beth Furtwangler, "Danger Years for Starting to Drink as Young as Fourth Grade," *USA Today*, November 5, 2011, www.usatoday.com/news/health/2007- 11-05-kids-drinking_N.htm.

28. Ibid.

29. Ibid.

30. Linda Carroll, "Letting Teen Drink Under Parent's Watch Backfires," msnbc.com, April 29, 2011, www.msnbc.msn.com/id/42807670/ns/ health-childrens_health/t/letting-teen-drink-under-parents-watch-backfires/.

31. "National Survey of American Attitudes on Substance Abuse XV: Teens and Parents."

32. "The Importance of Family Dinners IV," The National Center on
Addiction and Substance Abuse at Columbia University, press release,
September 2007, http://www.casacolumbia.org/templates/
pressreleases.aspx?articleid=5028zoneid=65

33. Rebecca Dube, "Kathie Lee."

Chapter Ten

1. "Bullying," Facts for Families no. 80, American Academy of Child and
Adolescent Psychiatry, March 2011, www.aacap.org/cs/root/facts_for_families/
bullying.

2. "Characteristics of Children Who Are Bullied," MSN.com, Healthwise,
accessed April 12, 2011, http://health.msn.com/kids-health/
articlepage.aspx?cp-documentid=100079437.

3. Rachel Rettner, "Bullies on Bullying: Why We Do It," LiveScience, Web article,
August 26, 2010, www.livescience.com/11163-bullies-bullying.html.

4. Ibid.

5. "Bullying Prevention Is Crime Prevention," Fight Crime: Invest in Kids,
report, written 2003, posted online July 22, 2009, www.fightcrime.org/state/
usa/reports/bullying-prevention-crime-prevention-2003.

6. "Bullying," National Crime Prevention Council, Web page, accessed May 14,
2011, www.ncpc.org/topics/bullying.

7. Barbara Coloroso, *The Bully, the Bullied, and the Bystander* (New York:
HarperCollins, 2003), xvi.

8. Michele Borba, "Mobilizing Student Bystanders to Stop Bullying," Reality
Check blog, February 23, 2011, www.micheleborba.com/blog/2011/02/23/
mobilizing-bystanders-to-stop-bullying-6-teachable-skills-to-stop-a-bully.

9. John McDonald, "What Is Bullying?" bullysolutions.com, Web article, April
12, 2010, http://bullysolutions.com/index.php/what-is-bullying.

10. Sameer Hinduja, and Justin W. Patchin, "Cyberbullying Identification,
Prevention, and Response," Cyberbullying Research Center, summary fact
sheet, 2010, www.cyberbullying.us/Cyberbullying_Identification_Prevention_
Response_Fact_Sheet.pdf.

11. "Teens and Cyberbullying," National Crime Prevention Council, executive
summary, February 28, 2007, www.ncpc.org/resources/files/pdf/bullying/
Teens%20and%20Cyberbullying%20Research%20Study.pdf.

12. Parry Aftab, "Statistics and a Snapshot of Cyberbullying Trends," aftab.com, Web article, accessed April 15, 2011, http://aftab.com/index.php?page=cyberbullying-statistics.

13. Andrea Day, "Outrage Over High School 'Smut List,'" MyFoxNY.com, March 17, 2011, www.myfoxny.com/dpp/news/outrage-over-high-school-smut-list-20110317.

14. Nirvi Shah, "Anonymous Bullying on Social Network Seeps Into Schools," *Education Week*, March 30, 2011.

15. Ibid.

16. Quoted in Nirvi Shah, "Anonymous Bullying."

17. Tamar Lewin, "Teenage Insults, Scrawled on Web, Not on Walls," *New York Times*, May 5, 2010, www.nytimes.com/2010/05/06/us/06formspring.html.

18. Parry Aftab, "Statistics and a Snapshot."

19. Lori Day, "Kids, Social Media Use, and Cyberbullying: The Role of Parents," Web article, accessed September 12, 2011, http://www.funderstanding.com/v2/gurus/kids-social-media-use-and-cyberbullying-the-role-of-parents/.

20. Sameer Hinduja and Justin W. Patchin, "Bullying, Cyberbullying and Suicide," *Archives of Suicide Research* 14, no. 3 (2010), 206–221.

21. Ibid.

22. Ibid.

23. "State Cyberstalking, Cyberharassment and Cyberbullying Laws," National Conference of State Legislatures, January 26, 2011, www.ncsl.org/default.aspx?tabid=13495.

24. Ibid.

25. New York State Division of Criminal Justice Services, "Dealing with Cyberbullying," Web page, accessed September 16, 2011, http://www.criminaljustice.state.ny.us/missing/i_safety/cyberbullying.htm.

26. American Psychological Association Zero Tolerance Task Force, "Are Zero Tolerance Policies Effective in the Schools?" *American Psychologist* 63, no. 9 (December 2008): 856.

27. Aimee Berg, "An Oval of Refuge from a Cold World," *New York Times*, May 17, 2009.

28. Ibid.

29. "Trevor Marsicano," Beyond the Ultimate, Web article, accessed April 18, 2011, www.beyondtheultimate.org/athletes/Trevor-Marsicano.aspx.

30. Ibid.

31. Ibid.

Chapter Eleven

1. Elizabeth Meyer, "Sexting and Suicide," *Psychology Today*, December 16, 2009, www.psychologytoday.com/blog/gender-and-schooling/200912/sexting&suicide?page=2.

2. Andrew Meacham, "Sexting-Related Bullying Cited in Hillsborough Teen's Suicide," *St. Petersburg Times*, November 29, 2009, www.tampabay.com/news/humaninterest/article1054895.ece.

3. Ibid.

4. Cindy Krantz, "Nude Photo Led to Suicide," cincinnati.com, news article, March 22, 2009, http://news.cincinnati.com/article/20090322/NEWS01/903220312/Nude-photo-led-suicide.

5. Ibid.

6. Amanda Lenhart, "Teens and Sexting: Major Findings," Pew Research Institute's Internet Project Survey, December 15, 2009, www.pewinternet.org/Reports/2009/teens-and-sexting.aspx.

7. Ibid.

8. Rosalind Wiseman, *Queen Bees and Wannabes* (New York: Three Rivers Press, 2009), 39.

9. Elizabeth Meyer, "Sexting and Suicide."

10. Cover, *Cosmopolitan*, March 2011, www.cosmopolitan.com/celebrity/exclusive/lea-michele-cosmo?click=main_sr.

11. Mandi Bierly, "Lea Michele 'Cosmo' Cover Controversy: Much Ado about Nothing?" *Entertainment Weekly*, February 7, 2011, http://popwatch.ew.com/2011/02/07/lea-michele-cosmo-cover.

12. Amanda Lenhart, "Teens and Sexting."

13. Ibid.

14. Cindy Krantz, "Nude Photo Led to Suicide."

15. "The Choking Game: CDC's Findings on a Risky Youth Behavior," Centers for Disease Control and Prevention, research update, January 19, 2009, www.cdc. gov/ncipc/duip/research/choking_game.htm.

16. Centers for Disease Control and Prevention, "Unintentional Strangulation Deaths from 'The Choking Game' Among Youths Aged 6–19 Years—United States, 1995–2007" *Morbidity and Mortality Weekly Report* 57 no. 6 (February 15, 2008):141–144. www.cdc.gov/mmwr/preview/mmwrhtml/mm5706a1.htm.

17. "The Choking Game," CDC.

18. Ibid.

19. CDC, "Unintentional Strangulation Deaths."

20. "Kids' Deadly Choking Game," CBS News, video, July 28, 2005, www. cbsnews.com/video/watch/?id=712438n.

21. Ibid.

22. "Choking Game—Wake Up!" YouTube, video, June 13, 2010, www.youtube. com/watch?v=cWgEaBVVuRI.

23. "The Choking Game," CDC.

24. Jennifer Goodwin, "Teens Posting Cutting Videos on YouTube," *Bloomberg Business Week*, http://www.businessweek.com/lifestyle/content/ healthday/650107.html, accessed September 16, 2011.

25. Liza Frenette, "What can you do to help students who cut themselves?" *New York Teacher*, April 4, 2007, www.nysut.org/newyorkteacher_7219.htm.

26. Jeanie Lerche Davis, "Cutting and Self-Harm: Warning Signs and Treatment," WebMD, Web article, accessed February 11, 2011, www.webmd. com/mental-health/features/cutting-self-harm-signs-treatment.

27. Liza Frenette, "What can you do?"

28. Ibid.

29. Jeanie Lerche Davis, "Cutting and Self-Harm."

30. "Cutting—Self-injury from the Teen's Perspective," http://egi.org/cutting1. htm, accessed September 16, 2011.

31. Todd Neale, "Self-Injury Videos Popular with Teens," MedPage Today, Web article, February 21, 2011, www.medpagetoday.com/Pediatrics/ GeneralPediatrics/24975.

32. Tom Rawstorne, "Why No Child is Safe From the Sinister Cult of Emo," Daily Mail, Mail Online, May 16, 2008, www.dailymail.co.uk/femail/article-566481/Why-child-safe-sinister-cult-emo.html.

33. Ibid.

34. Ibid.

35. Ibid.

36. Centers for Disease Control and Prevention, "Suicide Trends Among Youths and Young Adults Aged 10–24 years—United States, 1990-2004." *Morbidity and Mortality Weekly Report* 56 no. 35 (September 7, 2007): 905–908.

37. Ibid.

Chapter Twelve

1. "The Ethics of American Youth: 2010," Josephson Institute, Center for Youth Ethics, survey report, February 10, 2011, http://charactercounts.org/programs/reportcard/2010/installment02_report-card_honesty-integrity.html.

2. C. S. Lewis, *The Abolition of Man* (New York: HarperCollins, 1944), 24–25.

3. Ibid., 26.

4. Timothy Keller, "He Died for Our Sins," Island Evangelical Community Church, podcast, Hong Kong, China, May 24, 2009.

5. "Evangelism Is Most Effective Among Kids," The Barna Group, Web article, October 11, 2004, www.barna.org/barna-update/article/5-barna-update/196-evangelism-is-most-effective-among-kids.

6. Ibid.

7. Ibid.

8. "Research Shows Parenting Approach Determines Whether Children Become Devoted Christians," The Barna Group, Web article, April 9, 2007, www.barna.org/barna-update/article/15-familykids/106-research-shows-parenting-approach-determines-whether-children-become-devoted-christians?q=salvation.

9. John Gottman, "Books, Lectures, and Tools," Gottman Relationship Institute, Web page, accessed February 23, 2011, www.gottman.com/51166/Books-and-Lectures.html.

10. William J. Bennett, *The Book of Virtues* (New York: Simon and Schuster, 1993), 11.

11. Howard Hendricks, *Teaching to Change Lives* (Colorado Springs: Multnomah Books, 1987), 13.

12. Ibid., 14.

Chapter Thirteen

1. Vanessa Williams and Helen Williams, interview by Maria Shriver, radio station on Sirius XM, May 3, 2011, from Oprah's classic programs, 2007.

2. Matthew A. Johnson, *Positive Parenting with a Plan* (Peoria, AZ: Intermedia Publishing Group, 2009), 20.

3. Ibid., 90.

4. Ibid., 94.

5. Ibid., 96–97.